The Muzzle-Loading Rifle . . . . . Then and Now

by

Walter M. Cline

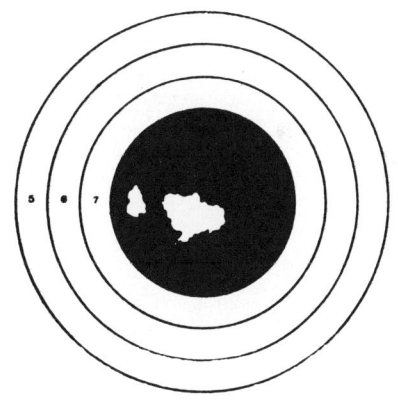

Published by
Wolfe Publishing Company
6471 Airpark Drive, Prescott, Arizona 86301
1993

Originally Published by
STANDARD PRINTING AND PUBLISHING COMPANY
HUNTINGTON, WEST VIRGINIA
1942

Edited by
HERMAN P. DEAN

Copyright © 1993
National Muzzle Loading Rifle Association

Manufactured in the United States of America
Reprinted June 1981, September 1993
Library of Congress Catalogue Card Number 81-82251

ISBN 1-879356-34-1

WOLFE PUBLISHING COMPANY
6471 Airpark Drive
Prescott, Arizona 86301

PUBLISHER'S NOTE:

Just as Walter M. Cline had about completed his manuscript for this book, the order came to "Cease Firing," and he passed from among us at the hand of one of the old rifles he loved so much.

Both Walter and Mrs. Cline (who has so faithfully carried the torch since Mr. Cline's passing) were insistent that this book should portray and glorify the Muzzle-Loading Rifle of other days and that personal references and photographs of the Author and his Family be eliminated, as far as possible. However, the publishers of this volume hold a somewhat different opinion, for we believe that the book would not be complete and satisfying to the friends of the Author without these intimate personal sidelights. Therefore, we have drawn generously from his copious files of personal experience.

Though he is now a participant on the Range Eternal, yet he left us a priceless heritage in the manuscript and photographs which he had so painstakingly accumulated over the years.

THE PUBLISHER

SPONSOR'S GREETING:

We appreciate the privilege which is ours to sponsor and endorse this volume, "The Muzzle-Loading Rifle—Then and Now," written by one of the most enthusiastic and beloved men in our group. Walter M. Cline contributed generously of his time and effort to the cause of the Muzzle-Loading fraternity at large, and by so doing he established an imperishable memorial for himself in the hearts of our membership and our friends throughout the entire Country.

THE NATIONAL MUZZLE-LOADING
RIFLE ASSOCIATION

FOR MORE INFORMATION, PLEASE WRITE TO:

NATIONAL MUZZLE LOADING RIFLE ASSOCIATION
P.O. Box 67
Friendship, Indiana 47021

DEDICATION

To Sergeant Alvin York

Match shooting provided unerring marksmen for the defense of America in pioneer border warfare and in each war fought by the United States. Alvin York's outstanding service in the First World War was due in part to the accurate marksmanship which has been developed in the shooting matches which have been held in the small mountain settlements of Tennessee, Kentucky, Virginia and North Carolina, as they have been held each Saturday at his home in Pall Mall, Tennessee, from pioneer days up to the present time. In these settlements have lived fearless marksmen skilled in "deadly shooting," superior to that of any other soldiers.

The author included York and his rifle in his chapter on "Frontier Riflemen in American History." (See Chapter 13) He is not here today to know of Sergeant York's rallying to the defense of his country in another war; nor to agree with and applaud his conviction that no rifle training in marksmanship equals that of match shooting; but it appears to me as appropriate that this volume, with its record of Raven Rock matches and the roster of Tennessee match shooters, with whom he shot for two-thirds of his life, be dedicated to the world-famous match shooter, Alvin York. I believe it would be Walter Cline's wish, and therefore I so dedicate his book.

LUCY HALEY CLINE

ACKNOWLEDGMENTS

This book contains only bits from the extensive knowledge of the muzzle-loading rifle accumulated by the Author, Walter Matson Cline. He became interested in this type of gun because of the great part it played in the early history of our Country. He studied the muzzle-loader in all of its aspects; he tried it in all its powers; he became its master. While the outline of material as prepared by Mr. Cline for his book was not followed as minutely as he would have done had he lived to finish his manuscript, yet his original outline as set forth in the table of contents has been faithfully followed in all relevant respects. The text, of course, was all written by Mr. Cline himself, except where it is noted otherwise. He had expected to add many other facts from his wealth of knowledge and experience in his plan to give the World a complete book on the subject so dear to his heart. His untimely passing prevented the complete fulfillment of this task.

It has been my endeavor, in publishing this book, to save this valuable material in the hope that others might glean some information and inspiration for further research and knowledge concerning the muzzle-loading guns and their makers, both for the enrichment of their own enjoyment and also for the welfare of future generations. I am greatly indebted to many friends and associates of Mr. Cline for invaluable assistance in the preparation of his manuscript for publication. I am taking this opportunity to thank everyone who has contributed in any way to this work and I would especially acknowledge the cooperation received from the following:

Miss Daisy Barrett, of Chattanooga, Tennessee, who faithfully served as Mr. Cline's secretary for many years; American Rifleman Magazine, Washington, D. C., for the use of article in that publication by Mr. Cline, Chapters 1-4, and other cooperation; E. M. Farris, Secretary of the National Muzzle-Loading Rifle Association, Portsmouth, Ohio; Herman P. Dean, President-Treasurer, Standard Printing & Publishing Company, Huntington, West Virginia; Boss Johnston, President of the National Muzzle-Loading Rifle Association, and all present and past officers of that Organization; E. Y. Chapin, Walter C. Johnson, Claude E. Fuller, C. J. Kellem, Carlin Shackleford, Captain Philip P. Quayle, Bull Ramsey, L. G. (Daddy) Moore, Henry Howard, J. T. Holley, Chester B. Pratt, Dr. Thomas B. Hall, William Large, Walter Grote, Walter Heightshoe, L. C. FitzGerald, Al Marciante, M. S. Risley, Willis E. Wooster, Harold D. Smith; Glen S. Echols, Margaret Haley Duncan, Mrs. Tye Holcombe, and the following mountain men with whom the author shot in so many matches: Jack Morgan, Byrd Fann, Gilbert Angel, Arthur Kelley, Jim Barker Kelley, Paul Freeman, Jenkins of Soddy, Daddy Kress, Mysinger of Soddy, Frank Ferguerson, Arthur Hale, Hugh Mansfield, Bob Freeman, John Wheeler, G. W. Allen, Rube Swafford, John Clifton, R. D. Holt, Byrd Freeman, John Horn, Meredith Wolfe and Enoch Hardin, and to every other person who has in any way contributed to the success of this publication.

—Lucy Haley Cline

INTRODUCTION

Inheriting the love of the long rifle and the great outdoors from ancestors who had a part in the early beginning of our country, I began many years ago to accumulate and preserve data on the handmade rifle. Being fortunate enough to know and associate with many famous gunsmiths who had learned their trade in the flintlock days, I have been able to secure much reliable information and many excellent specimens of the long rifle. I have taken part in many of the old-time matches and have known intimately many noted marksmen. For many years I have hunted with the mountaineers of the Southern highlands. Brought up with a rifle in their hands just as the pioneers of old, they acquired that deadly skill that can be attained in no other way except by daily use of a weapon. Tradition has handed down to us some of the remarkable shots made in the early days of the muzzle-loading flintlock rifle. They seem like fairy tales to those who know little of the accuracy of these early rifles. But the long rifle of the pioneer was an instrument of precision and served its purpose well.

It is not my intention to attempt to write a history of the rifle and its development through the ages since its discovery, as that part has been well covered by competent writers. We know that the long-barreled accurate shooting early American rifle made its appearance sometime about 1730 in Pennsylvania and that it was the product of the immigrant gunsmiths. Just who developed this accurate shooting rifle has not been recorded. Its manufacture spread rapidly as the pioneer conquered the wilderness and the savage.

In the following pages, it shall be my purpose to record facts concerning the development of the rifle, its use in War and hunting and matches, and something about the men themselves who have made, and the men who have used these hallowed old arms of the Southern highlands.

WALTER M. CLINE

FOREWARD

As the National Muzzle Loading Rifle Association moves near the completion of its first fifty years, we find ourselves at the center of an activity expanding so rapidly that its size is almost beyond comprehension. With this growth has come the development of many areas of specialized interest. This specialized interest has fostered both technical and historical research designed to help us better understand the muzzle loading firearm and the life style of which it was a part.

By reprinting this book we are making available to this and future generations of muzzle loading enthusiasts a first person look at "the way it was." The people of the Southern Highlands had retained gunmaking, hunting, and shooting skills which had long disappeared in most parts of the country. Walter M. Cline sought out, became friends with, and recorded the activities of these people, who in the 1920s and 30s were still utilizing the muzzle loading firearm in the tradition of their forefathers.

In addition to recording the activities of the Southern Highlanders, this text contains comments from both Mr. Cline and E. M. "Red" Farris describing those events leading to the organization of the NMLRA and its early years. Because they were both a part of that movement, their words are not just "history," but also express the feelings of that group who nearly fifty years ago felt the need to preserve this part of our heritage.

The Cline family must be given much credit for its contribution to the NMLRA. Mr. Cline was the fifth person to sign his name to the original membership list. In addition, he served the Association as its second President, from 1934 to 1939. Following his death, the family donated generously toward the purchase of the first acreage for the National Range—fittingly named in memory of Mr. Cline.

In preparation for this reprint, it was my privilege to visit with Walter M. Cline, Jr. He, along with his sister, Sara Cline Caldwell, very generously gave their permission to reprint their father's work.

On behalf of the National Muzzle Loading Rifle Association, its members, and others who will enjoy this book, I offer them both a sincere "Thank You."

As each of us persues our own area of muzzle loading interest, hopefully we will not lose sight of the heritage upon which our sport is based. We cannot hold on to the past, but we can let it influence the future. We hope that this book—its words and pictures—will reinforce the traditional values which are the core of our interest in muzzle loading firearms.

OWEN S. COLLINS
President
National Muzzle Loading Rifle Association
May 1981

CONTENTS

Chapter		Page
1	The Muzzle-Loader is Born	9
2	Making the Barrels	13
3	Shootin' at Raven Rock	17
4	Development of the Rifle	23
5	The Rifle in the American Revolution	33
6	Arms and Ammunition in the U. S. Civil War	38
7	My Gun Collection	50
8	Modern Vs. Old-time Methods	53
9	Proving Accuracy by Tests	62
10	Hunting in the Great Smokies	69
11	Mountain Smiths and their Craftsmanship	77
12	Building Two Rifles from a Junk Pile	95
13	Frontier Riflemen in American History	99
14	Match Shooting Today in Tennessee	112
15	The Revival of the Matches	118
	The Appendix	132

ILLUSTRATIONS

	Plate Number
Walter M. Cline	1
Lucy Haley Cline	2
A Story of Three Bears	3
Horace Warner Rifle and Accessories	4
H. H. Rowell, California Gunsmith	5
W. S. Blankenship, Hot Springs, North Carolina	5
Bud Sackett Plays Dan'l Boone	5
Norman S. Brockway in 1931	5
A Grim Visaged Frontiersman	6
Harry Pope, the Muzzle-Loading Wizard	6
Les FitzGerald, Pontiac, Michigan, in Pioneer Garb	6
Deer Killed with the Muzzle-Loader	6
An Early Machine for Rifling Barrels	7
Homemade Tools Used by Early Smiths	7
One of the Author's Favorite Flintlocks	8
An Early Rifling Bench in Operation	8
Welding Technique in a Rifle Barrel	8
A Head Block Guides the Rifle Saws	8
The Author Firing a Beloved Flintlock	9
Meredith Wolfe, Gunsmith, at his Bench	9
Barrels Forged on a "Buffalo Head"	9
Famous Painting "Shooting for the Beef"	10
Rube Swafford	11
A Sale Creek Shooter	11
Mysinger of Soddy	11
R. D. Holt, Pikeville	11
Arthur Kelly	11
Jenkins of Soddy	11
Rifle Left by Revolutionary Ancestor	12
Col. Sam Houston, Southern Leader	12
Cline at the Age of Five	12
The Author with his Two Children	12
His Home in the Mountains of Sunny Tennessee	13
A Pair of Engraved Colt Percussions	14
Powderhorn and Pouches for the Rifle	14
Sonora Rifle Club Target in 1879	15
Medals Won at Muzzle-Loading Matches	16
A Group of Tennessee Match Shooters	17
Some Southern Shops Were Merely Sheds	18
Forty-shot Group by George Ferris of Utica	19
A Group of Three Early Powderhorns	20
A Notable Gallery of Schuetzen Shooters	21 to 27
Variety in Design Adds to Their Interest	28
"Daddy" Moore, Picturesque Bear Hunter	29
Patience Required in Welding a Barrel	29
William Greene, Confederate Sharpshooter	30

	Plate Number
"Daddy" Kress, Gunsmith and Shooter	30
Norman A. Brockway, Maker of Renown	30
John Selfridge, Tennessee Gunsmith	30
A Group of Early Pennsylvania "Kentuckys"	31
Four Rare Rifles Still Used Today	32
A Mountain Man and His Gun	33
Henry Howard of Chattanooga	33
William Walker Has Killed More Than One Hundred Bears	33
National Rifle Club, Vernon, Vermont, 1886	34
Modern Shooters With Ancient Weapons	34
On His Range in Piney Nook	35
Four Important Smithing Tools	35
John S. Sumner, Newton, Massachusetts, 1879	36
A Wild Pig of the Smokies	36
Hound Used by the Author	36
Powder and Bullets Were Sometimes Carried in Gourds	36
The Famous Whitmore and Trophy it Won	37
On His Way to the Matches	38
E. M. Farris, Secretary, N. M. L. R. A.	38
Enoch Hardin, Tennessee Gunsmith	38
Measuring a Close Match	38
Woman Shooter at a Muzzle-Loading Match	39
Tennessee Block House, Still Standing	39
Calling Turkeys With a Simple Leaf	39
Molding Bullets on the Chase	39
Sergeant Alvin York in World War I	40
Boss Johnston, President, N. M. L. R. A.	40
Charles J. Kellem, Joliet, Illinois	40
Bad Weather Doesn't Stop Shooters	40
John Shell, Leslie County, Kentucky	41
Frontiersman in Characteristic Pose	41
Davy Crockett, Hero of the Alamo	41
Two Bullets that Met Head-on	41
Loading the Brockway With Paper Patch	42
Accessories and Composite Bullet of the Brockway	42
Boring a Rifle	43
Rifling a Barrel	43
Getting Ready for the Shoot	43
On the Firing Line	43
Prone Position — Mountain Style	43
A Token of Many Matches	44
The End of a Perfect Day	44
Three Mountain Musketeers	44
Some Favorite Shooters from the Author's Collection	45
Miscellaneous Group of Interesting Arms	46
A Rifle Owned by Simon Kenton and Three Others	47
Four Rifles, Old in Years but Fine in Condition	48
A Quartet of Interesting Old "Shooting Irons"	49
Alvin York Shoots in a 1942 Match	50

Chapter I.

THE MUZZLE-LOADER IS BORN

THERE is a growing interest in the rifle of bygone days, so interwoven has it been in the lives of our people and the destiny of our country. We glory in the deeds of our border riflemen of '76, of the Kentucky and Tennessee backwoodsmen under Andrew Jackson at New Orleans, and of Crockett and his companions at the Alamo. Tradition and early records by reliable authorities have handed down to us accounts of some of the remarkable shots made in the days of the muzzle-loading flintlock rifle. They seem like fairy tales to those who know little of the accuracy of these early rifles, but the long rifle of the pioneer was an instrument of precision and served its purpose well.

What we know of the first rifled arms has come down to us from a dim past. Captain Beaufoy, one of the best early writers on the rifle, says that the knowledge of the grooved barrel and the effect of spiral motion was known in Russia and the more northern parts of Europe long before its use by the more advanced nations of Central and Southern Europe. It is quite probable that the theory of spiral motion was known at a very early date. Arrow points beveled so as to produce a rotary motion have been found in considerable numbers, showing that the aborigines were familiar with this principle.

With the discovery and use of gunpowder as a propellant for the missile or ball from the first firearms, began the search for accuracy. Just when the lead ball was first used is not known, but no doubt it came into use with the handgun. Yet it was several hundred years before the effect of gunpowder on the lead ball was discovered. All efforts of the early makers and users of the first rifled arms were to force the ball into the grooves before the arm was fired. Bullets of groove diameter were used and were forced down the barrel with an iron ramrod and mallet.

The greased wad and patch were used very early and are mentioned by a Spanish writer, Alonzo Martinez de Espinar, in 1644, who says: "It is necessary to have felt wad cut with a punch, which

The Muzzle-Loading Rifle—Then and Now

must be exactly fitted to the mouth of the barrel. This must be pitched with Greek pitch, wax, and tallow. All this should be dissolved and the wads thrown into it, and after they have absorbed the pitch they must be allowed to cool and then they remain very hard and greasy; these are very important for rifled Arquebuses, because with them the balls go in more easily, for they have to fit very closely in the barrel, having to be driven to the bottom by blows of the ramrod." Robbins, in his tracts on gunnery, makes mention of the Swiss using the greased patch; but the ball still remained a very tight fit in the bore and had to be forced into the grooves in loading—the very thing that is not productive of accuracy with a round ball. This difficulty of loading caused the barrel of the rifle of Central Europe to be short.

The discovery that a ball of bore diameter used with greased patch could be loaded without difficulty and better accuracy secured, must have been made before there was any change in the design of the rifle. To have attempted to use the same method of loading the long-barrel flintlock rifle as that used in loading the rifle of Central Europe would have rendered the former useless.

The use of the greased patch, together with a ball of bore diameter, allowed the gunsmith to experiment with different lengths of barrels. As the musket and fowling piece of this period had long barrels, it followed that the rifle should have a long barrel. It was not the conditions in this country—America—that caused this radical change in the rifle, but that age-old quest for accuracy. With the development of the long-barreled flintlock rifle by the pioneer gunsmiths of Pennsylvania, and its appearance at about the beginning of the great influx of Germans and Scotch-Irish into America, there was available an accurate shooting rifle that made possible the advance of these home-seeking people beyond the then established frontiers.

The manufacture of the rifle spread rapidly as the pioneer conquered the wilderness and the savage. From Pennsylvania, its birthplace, down the valley of Virginia into the Carolinas, and on westward across the mountains into Tennessee, this rifle followed the rapidly-advancing frontier. Tried and tested in hundreds of

The Muzzle-Loader is Born

desperate conflicts in the hands of the American pioneer, its use became almost universal. It was not devised by any board of ordnance, but was the product of a race of practical men developed over a period of many years and with the improvements which were contributed by each generation of skilled workmen; and it became a weapon of wonderful precision at distances within its range.

During the decade preceding the Civil War, and the period of transition of the muzzle-loading to the breech-loading rifle, the muzzle-loading rifle attained its highest development. Every town and city had one or more gunsmiths, and rifle-making spread the length and breadth of the land. The shooting match became the greatest of all American sports. Here the excellence of each riflemaker was put to a test, by which his reputation was made. In many places where these matches were held every Saturday, for years, the writer has seen the stumps of large trees which had been shot down by having had the targets placed against them.

There were three types of the muzzle-loading rifle which were in use during the late percussion period: the hunting rifle with its different lengths of barrel, an all-purpose rifle, in general use; the long, heavy, soft-metal-barreled match rifle; and that weapon of precision, the American target rifle, with false muzzle, swages, bullet-starter, and other accessories.

In the manufacture of the hunting-rifle the accepted weight was that which a man could conveniently carry—running, usually, from 7 to 12 pounds, with an occasional one weighing as much as 14 pounds. The proportion of the weight of the gun to that of the ball was about 500 to 1, this being approximately the heaviest ball this rifle would throw without excessive recoil. The names of many of the early gunsmiths who became noted for the excellence of their arms, together with specimens of their work, have been preserved, but among the present generation there are many skeptics who doubt the accuracy of the muzzle-loading rifle. There are few persons living today who have had the opportunity of handling in actual use, either in hunting or target work, a perfect specimen of the long rifle made by a master workman, and who also possess the skill in loading these arms that is acquired only by long practice.

The Muzzle-Loading Rifle—Then and Now

Fenimore Cooper's hero, Hawkeye, in *"The Last of the Mohicans,"* advising Uncas in regard to loading his rifle, tells him that he is "wasteful of his powder," and that "a kicking rifle never carries a true bullet"; that "of all weapons the long, soft-metal-barreled rifle is the most dangerous in skilled hands, though it wants a strong arm, a quick eye, and great judgment in charging to put forth all its beauties." While Cooper's characters are fictitious, and he may have over-rated the skill of Hawkeye a bit, these words, penned many years ago, show a knowledge of the rifle that could have been acquired only by use and close association.

Handed down from generation to generation, each new discovery and improvement was thus preserved; and the rules and methods for regulating the amount of powder, the thickness of the patch, the proper size of the ball for the bore, and the pressure required to seat the ball down on the powder, are the same today as they were over a hundred years ago. All gunsmiths used the same methods, with slight variations, in the fabrication of their arms.

Chapter II.

MAKING THE BARRELS

BARRELS were welded from a flat bar of iron. Lap-welding was used by most workmen. The edges of the bar were flattened out, then turned and welded over an iron rod. Only an inch or so of length was welded at one time, then the rod was knocked out and another inch welded, and so on, until the entire barrel was welded. Half a day was usually required to weld a barrel 48 inches long. The short bit and the long bit were used in boring the barrel. The short bit was made by welding a short bar of squared steel to the end of a long round iron rod, for a shank. The square end was then heated, twisted, and tempered. This did the cutting. This bit would follow the hole in the barrel left by the rod in welding. A short point left straight, not twisted, at the end of the bit prevented the latter from leading off, so that the barrel could be bored from both ends, and the two bored holes meet on line in the middle.

The long bit was next used. This was made by welding to the side of a small squared bar of iron a thin piece of steel. This welding was done by the aid of borax as a flux, to make the steel stick to the soft piece of iron. This bit was now welded to the end of a rod of sufficient length so that all cutting could be done from one end of the barrel. The steel portion was now tempered, and then straightened. The steel, backed by the soft iron, was laid on the anvil and tapped with a hammer. It required considerable skill in tempering to get just the right degree of hardness so that the steel would not crack in straightening. The two edges of the steel which were to be the two cutting edges, were ground sharp; and on the back of the bar, opposite to the steel, was fastened a strip of hickory wood, rounded to conform to the bore. This strip of hickory prevented any iron cuttings from scratching the barrel; and by placing small shims of paper between the wood and the iron, as many cuts could be made as were necessary. All cutting with the long bit was made from the breech to the muzzle, the slight wearing away of the wood as the bit traveled through the barrel in successive cuttings giving a taper, or very slightly choke, bore.

The barrel was now straightened. A silk thread was stretched through the bore, and was kept taut by a hickory bow. By looking through the barrel toward the light, the crooked places could be detected by the shadow that the silk thread cast on the polished sur face of the bore. This crooked place was marked on the outside of the barrel by moistening the fingers with saliva and then touching the place opposite the shadow. The barrel was then placed on the anvil and tapped with a hammer. This was repeated, if necessary, until no shadow showed in the bore, the work progressing from the middle toward the ends of the barrel. Meredith Wolf, one of the early gunsmiths of Tennessee, told the writer that in his fifty years of experience he had seen only one barrel that did not need straightening.

The barrel was now ready for rifling. The rifling machine consisted of a cylinder of wood, sometimes as much as 4 inches in diameter—the larger the better, as this tended to reduce lost motion when working through a small bore in the barrel. This cylinder of wood had spiral grooves cut in the outer surface, to the number of six, seven, eight, or whatever number of grooves the workman decided to cut in a barrel, or the order called for. There were extra cylinders, each having a certain number and pitch of grooves. One gunsmith had eight extra cylinders, each one different, and all interchangeable in a framework of wood. An "index" fastened in the bench, had fingers fitting into the spiral grooves in the wooden cylinder, and revolved the cylinder when the latter, held in its frame, was pushed back and forth along the top of the bench. This cylinder carried an iron rod at one end, and at the other end of this rod a piece of hickory wood was fastened which carried the cutting tool, or saw, this piece of hickory being cylindrical in shape, and a close sliding fit in the bore. These saws were made in different shapes, some having teeth inclined in only one direction, others with teeth inclined both ways and cutting with both movements of the rod, back and forth through the bore. Still others had straight teeth that scraped the metal rather than cut it. The finished result was dependent upon the skill of the workman.

Making the Barrels

After the saw was set in the hickory "rifling head," the latter was passed through the barrel, the first cut being a very heavy one. The saw was worked back and forth until it would not cut any more. The cylinder was then turned so that its next groove engaged the fingers of the index, and the next groove was cut in the barrel; and so on until all grooves were cut to the same depth. The saw was then raised and a thin shim of paper placed under it, and the above process repeated. So slight was the cut taken at each operation that for each groove the saw was passed through the bore as many as forty times for each time it was raised. With a 7-groove barrel, that would mean 280 strokes for each time the saw was raised. This was repeated from ten to fifteen times for each groove, depending upon the size of the ball to be used, making 2,800 or more times the saw was passed through the barrel to complete the job. A barrel rifled by this process needed no smoothing out with emery, and a few shots would remove the wire edge from the lands. No more perfect job can be done today with the finest machinery than the barrels rifled by the master gunsmiths of the muzzle-loading days.

The outside of the barrel was then filed, ground, or left just as it was welded—some customers preferred it that way—after which it was breeched, stocked, sighted, and tested. The gunsmith made his own tools for the work.

That these old rifles were accurate beyond the belief of present-day riflemen is borne out by targets preserved by the writer from the old-time shooting matches, and by the performance of the rifles in the mountains of Tennessee on black bear, deer, wildcat, and various species of small game. The writer has used these rifles with regular loads, and has also used them double-charged and double-patched. He has killed game as dead at 100 yards as could have been done with a high-power rifle. The long-barrel Kentucky, with its half-ounce soft-lead ball, driven with a full charge of powder, was all that could be desired, and a second shot was seldom required. The longest shot I ever saw was made by William Walker on a black bear, with his rifle that he called "Death." The distance as measured was 290 yards. The bear was crossing a deep hollow on a log, and was hit in the left fore-shoulder and so disabled that it was easily overtaken and killed.

The Muzzle-Loading Rifle—Then and Now

Very few shots were thrown away by men who used the muzzle-loading rifle. It was accurate, economical of ammunition, and deadly. Recent measurements of the velocity of the muzzle-loading rifle have shown that with a powder charge of only two-fifths the weight of the bullet, using FFFg granulation of powder, a velocity of over 1,700 feet per second was attained. This test was made by the late Dr. Philip P. Quayle, of the Peters Cartridge Co., with a rifle made by B. W. Amsden, of Saratoga Springs, N. Y. This rifle has a 28-inch barrel and is in perfect condition. By double-charging and double-patching, as was often done in hunting big game, the velocity went over 2,000 feet per second.

A remark was made by one of my mountaineer friends, as a party of us sat around the camp fire one night while on a hunting trip in the Cumberland Mountains, when the conversation turned to the old days, when we all used muzzle-loading rifles. This man, a true mountaineer, said that he "wished there had never been any other gun made except the muzzle-loading rifle, because in that case we would always have had plenty of game."

The match rifles differed from the hunting rifles in length of barrel, weight, and caliber, very few being less than .40 caliber. The barrel lengths ran from 48 inches to 60 inches, with some few even longer. The barrels were made of the softest iron, and were always welded. Very few of the best makers of match rifles would put their names on the barrels unless they had welded them themselves. After the barrel was welded, it was annealed and made as soft as possible. One very successful maker used a process that had been handed down in the family for four generations. He would place the barrel on a level piece of ground prepared especially for it, then pile a long heap of dry chestnut wood over it, and then set fire to the wood and leave it until all the wood had been consumed and the barrel had slowly cooled. I have in my possession two rifles that were annealed by this process, and one may shave them with a pocket knife and not dull the blade—in fact, the sides of the octagons were shaved true with a draw-knife made by the smith himself. These barrels would not shoot slick like a steel barrel, and were much in demand. There is no doubt that these heavy match rifles were the most accurate round-ball rifles ever made.

CHAPTER III.

SHOOTIN' AT RAVEN ROCK

SEVERAL weeks ago I received a post card which read as follows:

"Hello Boys!

>A big shooting match at the
>Raven Rock next Saturday, for
>Two fat sheep. Come! Tell all
>The boys and let's have a big match.
>
>Yours for luck,
>
>GILBERT ANGEL."

Here, in one of the most picturesque spots in America, is still held the old-time shooting match, in which the long, heavy, soft-metal-barreled match rifles are still used. Rifles that would delight the eye of "Deerslayer!"

Raven Rock is a high cliff where for years the ravens had nested and reared their young, until, with advancing civilization and the building of highways into this mountain fastness, they had passed on, no one knows where, leaving only their name in memory of the days when the air about the place was black with these somber-winged birds. The mountain trail which gained the summit through a cleft in the rocks has been replaced by a fine highway to the summit of the Cumberlands, and on westward across the broad plateau.

No more wonderful panorama is seen than that viewed from the Raven Rock. Southward stretches the Sequatchie Valley for more than 70 miles. Midway of the valley runs the Alvin York Highway, named for Sergeant York, who had learned to handle a rifle in the Cumberlands long before his country called him overseas to become the nation's hero. He is one of the mountain men whose deadly skill with the rifle was acquired through daily use of the weapon in the hills around his home.

The Muzzle-Loading Rifle—Then and Now

As our car topped the mountain on the way to the match, the sharp reports of rifles were heard, and the air was pungent with the smell of black powder. The big match was on, and we were invited to take part. One dollar was the entry fee.

There were several muzzle-loading rifles in our party; one especially, "Long Tom," the property of the writer, and a famous match rifle made by Enoch Hardin, a noted maker of match rifles in his day. This rifle has a 56-inch barrel, is .40 caliber, and the grooves are seven in number, with a twist of one half turn in the length of the barrel. It weighs 20 pounds, and is a typical 60-yard mountain match rifle. This rifle was rescued from an old outbuilding, where it had been placed by its owner after his last match, many years before. This man had cleaned it well, and then poured it full of melted beef tallow, which had preserved it from the ravages of time. "Now Old Tom only needs a man behind it," as one of the mountain men good naturedly remarked to me, "to make it shoot plumb center."

The shooting range is situated in a little cove surrounded by higher ground. Sixty yards, with a rest, or 40 yards offhand, is the distance. A big fire of logs was burning when we arrived, as the air was crisp and invigorating. Some of the men were burning their boards in the fire to make a black surface for their targets. A charred board is an intense black, and the aiming point, or bull's-eye, of white cardboard shows up clear and sharp on the black surface. Some were moulding bullets; others cleaning their rifles. Men had come from all sections of the mountains, ridges, and valleys. Some had come on foot, others on horseback, and some even in motor cars, now that highways have been built into the mountains.

These mountain men love the rifle, and will go miles to take part in a shooting match. Each man pays his entry fee of $1 which entitles him to 5 shots. He then takes his board, which has been blackened in the fire, fastens on it his bull's-eye of white cardboard, writes his name on it, and gives it to the man who marks the targets. He is allowed two practice shots, as they are called. He calls for his board by calling out his name to the marker. It is set up for him, and he shoots his two sighting or practice shots. He then makes his

Shootin' at Raven Rock

"cross," which consists of two knife cuts in the black board, crossing each other. If his two practice shots cut into each other, or are very close together, he will move his bull's-eye to a new place on the board, and make the cross through the two bullet holes, or between them if they are not together. He is then ready to shoot for "meat," and has 5 shots for counters—one shot for each choice: two fore quarters, two hind quarters, and the hide and tallow. If his first shot is close enough to the center of the cross to cut all four lines, which would be called a "four-point center," or if only close enough to pull wood from the center, he is instructed by the marker to move his cross. This is done in order that it may be possible to measure each shot, for, if 2 shots should break into the cross, it would be impossible to measure each shot. The marksman then makes a new cross on his board, moving his bull's-eye or aiming point also. He is allowed to inspect his target after each shot, and can move the cross at any time. The match progresses with much good-natured bantering, and many small bets are made as to whether or not a certain marksman will shoot to within a certain distance of his cross. Each man shoots in turn, calling for his board to be set up.

Much of the fine accuracy of these old-time rifles depends upon the skill in loading. The shot pouch, powderhorn, and charger are very necessary parts of the equipment. The powderhorn is worn next to the body, so that the temperature of the powder may remain as uniform as possible, as it has been found that the temperature affects the strength of the powder. A difference of an inch or so in center of impact has been noticed when shooting a muzzle-loading rifle on a cold, and on a warm, day.

Bullets are carefully moulded, and so marked in the mould that they can always be loaded in the same position, neck down. The powder is carefully measured in the charger, great care being taken that the amount is the same each time. The charger is poured rounding full from the horn, and then leveled off. This is a very accurate way of measuring. Some few have the copper powder flask with the measuring nozzle. One man gives his flask five taps against his leg to settle the powder in the charger, and claims it is as accurate as if each charge were weighed.

The Muzzle-Loading Rifle—Then and Now

There are different methods for determining the proper amount of powder for use with a certain size of bullet. One method is to use the amount of powder that it takes to just cover a bullet when laid in the palm of the hand and the powder carefully poured over it. After this quantity of powder has been determined, a charger is made to hold just this amount. Another rule is to use a certain number of moulds full of powder, using the mould in which the bullet was cast. Large balls call for three moulds full; small ones, four moulds full, etc., a charger being made in each case to hold the exact amount of powder required.

The patching is usually of drilling, of a certain thickness for each individual rifle. This is wet with saliva, laid on the muzzle of the rifle, and the bullet seated with a starter, the latter being so formed that it aways seats the bullet and patch to the same depth in the bore. The edges of the patching are then gathered together in the left hand and cut off close to the muzzle with a knife, the edge of which is beveled so as not to injure the end of the barrel. This makes a circular patch with the bullet seated exactly in the center, and the patch is always the same size. A bullet loaded off center of the patch will shoot wild. The rifles are not fired rapidly, but are allowed to cool between shots, so that the temperature of the barrel is as nearly the same for each shot as possible.

Open sights only are used. The front sight is of the wide blade type, the rear sight having a rectangular slot in which the front sight is accurately centered. The top of the front sight is so held as to show an equal strip of white at the top and at each side of the bull's-eye. This sight was invented by Enoch Hardin about forty-five years ago, who told the writer that he had laid awake at night trying to figure out how to beat a competitor that was getting the better of him in the matches. Both front and rear sights are shaded by a piece of sheet iron so bent as to slip on over the barrel. This makes the sights stand out clearly and also eliminates the problem of changing lights on them. Wherever the location permits, the targets are placed to the south of the shooter, so that they will be shaded, and all shooting be done toward the light. There were many noted marksmen at this match on Raven Rock. There was Gilbert Angel, who

Shootin' at Raven Rock

shot a 24-pound gun called the "Jake Keedy Gun," and who cut center three times in succession. There was Uncle Byrd Freeman, who rode up from the valley, bringing his pet rifle, "Old Beck," which had a 58-inch barrel, bearing the outside hammer marks and all, just as it had been welded by the maker, but with the inside as true as could be made. Uncle Byrd shot a fine match, all shots being cut together; but he cut the cross only once. Then there were Bert Fann and Rudolph Holt, from Waldens Ridge—both fine shots. Holt could never get a barrel long enough to suit him, so he welded two barrels together, end to end, bored and reamed out this long barrel, and rifled it; and now he has a fine shooting rifle with a 60-inch barrel. The only trouble he says he has with it is that, as he is nearsighted, it takes him so long to see the front sight that it is always dark before he gets his 5 shots fired. I have never seen a *short-barrel rifle win a match;* and while these may be just as accurate as the long barrels, they have no place in one of these old-time matches. All the shooting is done from a rest, either from a prone position, resting the muzzle on a log and the elbows on the ground, or from a shooting bench, which permits the shooter to be seated, and affords an elbow and muzzle rest.

There were 25 contestants in that match and it was almost dark before the shooting was finished. Then came the measuring to determine the winners. This is a very particular job, and was especially so in this match, as the shooting had been very close and a number of crosses had been cut. Dividers are used for measuring. Each man that has a close shot furnishes a half bullet of the size his rifle uses, on the cut face of which the center has been marked. This half bullet is placed in the bullet hole in the board, and the cross lines extended across the bullet. Then the measurement is taken from the center of the bullet to the center of the cross lines. The bullet that has its center nearest to the center of the cross wins first place; and so on until the best 5 shots have been measured. Fortune favored the writer in this instance, his second shot cutting a dead 4-point center, winning first place, though his fourth shot, only a little more than an eighth of an inch off, did not get anything. This will give some idea of the fine accuracy of these old-time match rifles, and the closeness of the contest.

The Muzzle-Loading Rifle—Then and Now

There was a sixth prize in this match, which consisted of the lead cut out of the tree against which the targets had been placed. And here is where a little superstition enters in, for all firmly believe that the lead shot in a match, if moulded into bullets and shot in another match, will never win anything. This lead is all right to use in hunting, but never in another match! During a match everything is taken good naturedly, and no finer group of sportsmen ever gathered together than men who take part in these old shooting matches.

CHAPTER IV.

DEVELOPMENT OF THE RIFLE

THE American target rifle, as developed in the late percussion period, had the greatest accuracy and power of any muzzle-loading rifle, and it is doubtful if its accuracy at medium ranges has ever been surpassed. The earliest specimen in the line of development of this rifle that has come to the notice of the writer is a fine piece by Tryon, of Philadelphia. It is of the late flintlock period, and must have been made after 1811, as that was the year Tryon established his rifle works in Philadelphia. This rifle has a cast-steel barrel 34 inches in length, caliber .40, and has narrow grooves which make a three-quarter turn in the length of the barrel. The end of the barrel is turned round and fitted with a brass starter of the piston type. That it used the sharp-pointed ball is indicated by the end of the starter-rod, which is reamed out to fit a ball of that type. The rifle has a fine rainproof lock by Parker, stock of curly maple, with a drop of 5 inches. The weight is 14 pounds. This is quite a departure from the long heavy-barreled flintlock match rifle, and is the only specimen known to the writer.

An example of the next step in the line of development is a rifle marked "Edward Wesson, Northboro, Mass.," and dated 1826. The number 225 is stamped on the barrel. The barrel has a length of 37 inches, and is marked "Cast Steel." It has six grooves .015 inch in depth, and the rifling makes a three-quarter turn in the length of the barrel. The lands are twice the width of the grooves; the caliber is .44. This rifle uses the sharp-pointed picket ball with slightly rounded base. Moulds, swage, and charger are a part of the equipment; and the charger has a loading-funnel attached. The muzzle of this rifle also is turned and fitted with a brass starter, the same as the Tryon rifle. Its weight is 16 pounds. So great was the improvement in accuracy of this type of rifle and ball that a powerful incentive was given the gunmakers to continue its development. Experiments were conducted with every conceivable shape and design of ball, with different pitches of rifling, varying widths and depths of grooving, different lengths and weights of barrels, as well as powder charges, to develop greater accuracy and range.

The next step in the improvement of the rifle was the false muzzle, said to have been invented by Calos Clark, of Windsor, Vt., in 1836. The earliest rifle with this attachment known to the writer is one by Frank Wesson, of Hartford, Conn., and which has the name "Clark" stamped on the false muzzle. The invention must have spread rapidly, as this rifle was made in 1837 and is numbered 433. The false muzzle is made after the barrel is bored and ready for rifling. Four small holes are drilled in the muzzle end of the barrel as near the outside edge as possible. A piece is then cut off the barrel of the same length as the outside diameter of the barrel. Four steel pins are now fitted in the holes in the piece that was cut off, and this piece is clamped to the barrel, the pins fitting in the holes in the barrel which were drilled before the piece was cut off, and which were drilled deep enough to go on through the length that was to be cut off, and into the barrel proper. The grooves are now cut in both barrel and false muzzle, thus making the grooves in the latter correspond exactly with those in the barrel. The bore of the false muzzle is now beveled, or countersunk, to permit the loading of the bullet and patch by the aid of the starter, so that the patch is not cut and the bullet is accurately centered in the bore of the rifle each time it is loaded, with the axis of the bullet coinciding exactly with the axis of the bore. The false muzzle is then removed before the rifle is fired.

The use of an elongated bullet—that is, a bullet in which the length is greater than the diameter—had been tried many years before. Lautman, writing in 1729, recommended the eliptical ball, and the Englishman Robbins in 1742 recommended a ball of this type. But the difficulty of loading at that early date prevented its use to any extent, and it was soon discarded. It remained for the ingenuity of the American gunsmiths to develop a rifle and a method of loading it with this type of bullet so as to attain the greatest accuracy and range of any muzzle-loading rifle. In this they reverted in a way to the methods employed in Central Europe. The bullet was forced into the grooving in loading, and this still holds true

PLATE 3

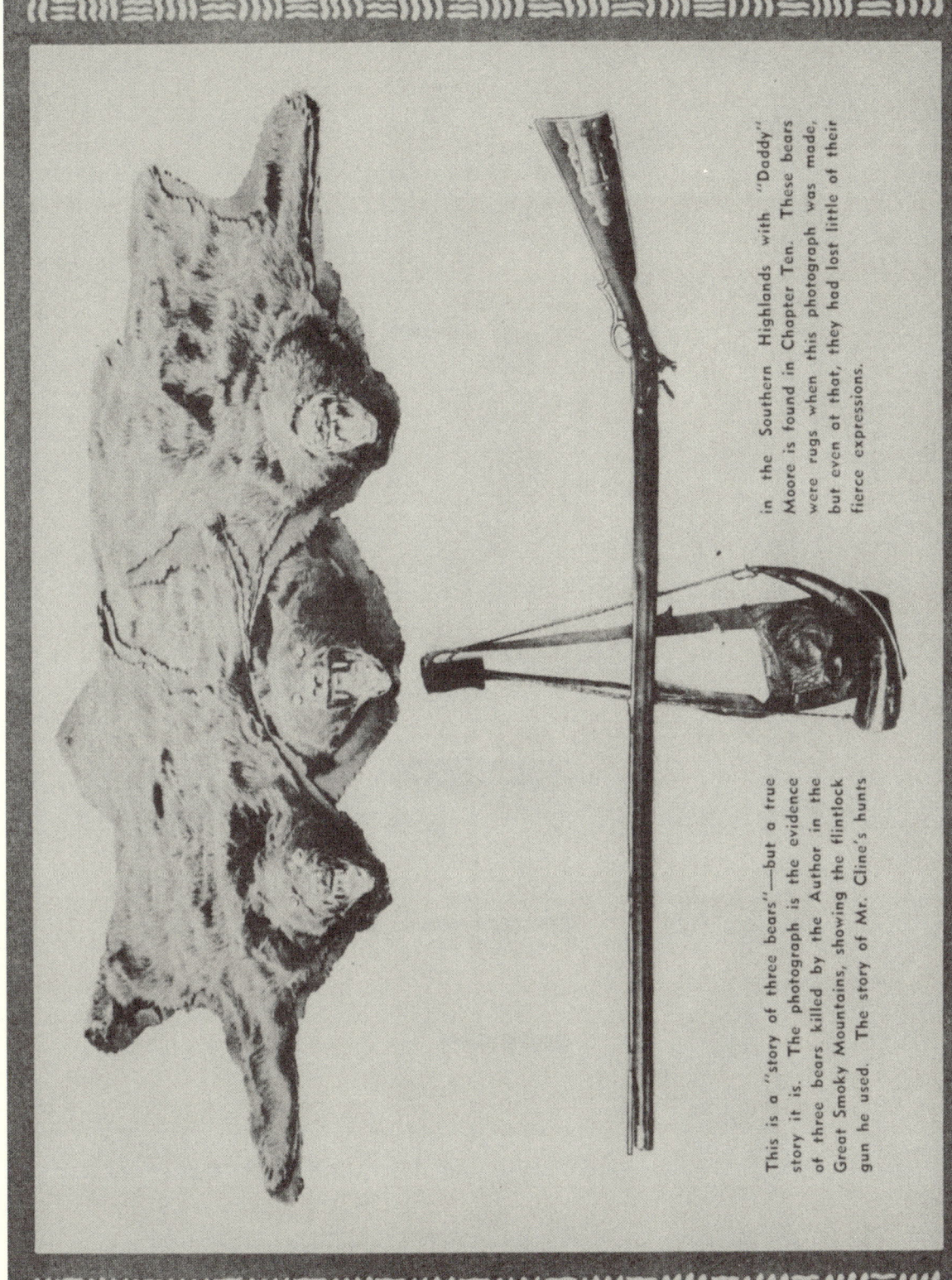

This is a "story of three bears"—but a true story it is. The photograph is the evidence of three bears killed by the Author in the Great Smoky Mountains, showing the flintlock gun he used. The story of Mr. Cline's hunts in the Southern Highlands with "Daddy" Moore is found in Chapter Ten. These bears were rugs when this photograph was made, but even at that, they had lost little of their fierce expressions.

PLATE 4

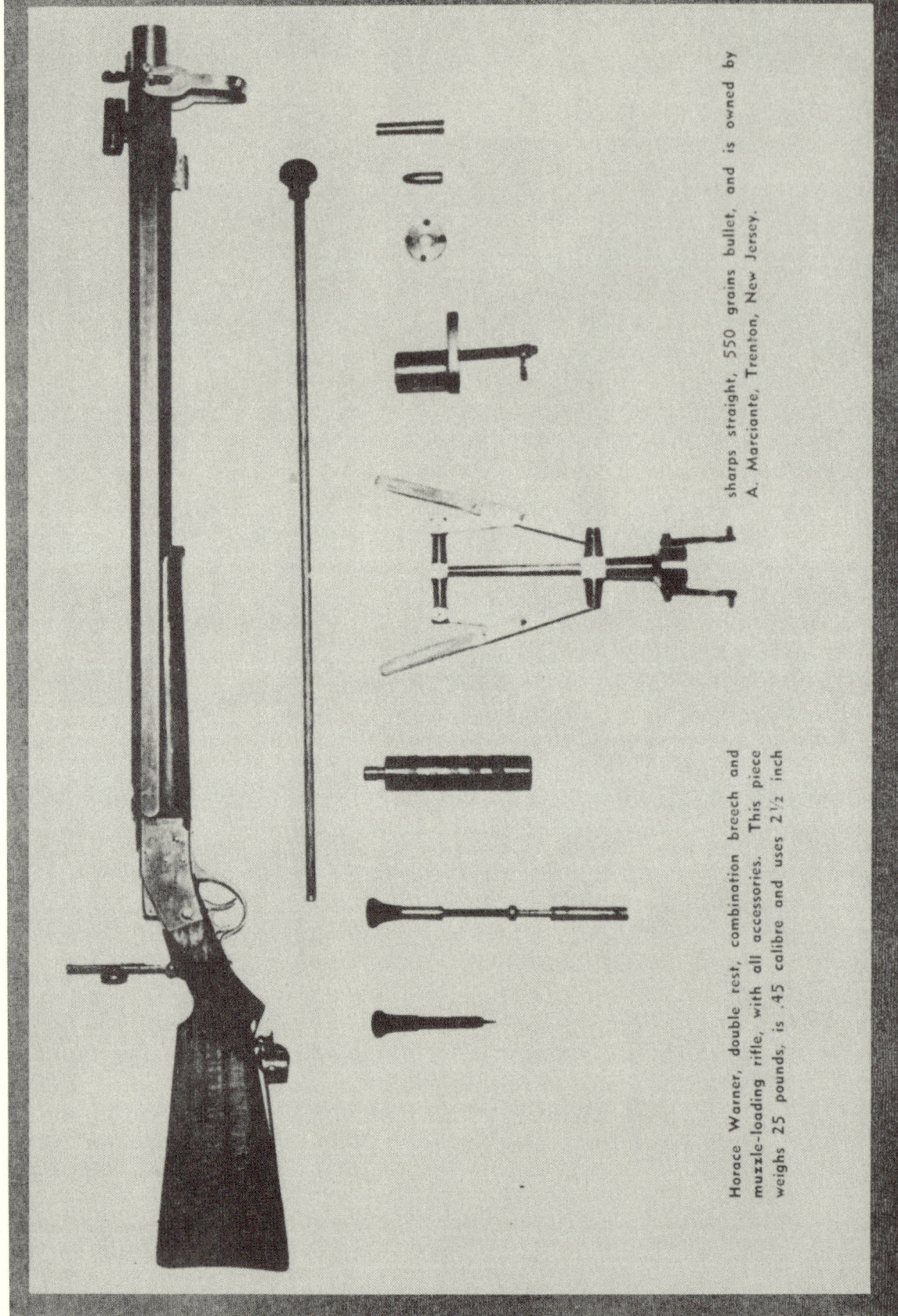

Horace Warner, double rest, combination breech and muzzle-loading rifle, with all accessories. This piece weighs 25 pounds, is .45 calibre and uses 2½ inch sharps straight, 550 grains bullet, and is owned by A. Marciante, Trenton, New Jersey.

PLATE 5

H. H. Rowell,
gunsmith of Sonora, California, 1876,
before and after.

W. S. Blankenship,
mountain smith, Hot Springs, North Carolina

Budd Sackett,
Anaheim, California shooter, takes
the role of Dan'l Boone.

Norman S. Brockway
with woodchuck he shot in 1931.

Plate 6

Determination was written deeply into the very countenance of our frontier rifleman.

Harry Pope, gunsmith, is known to every muzzle-loading enthusiast throughout the Country.

Les FitzGerald, Pontiac, Michigan, dresses and hunts as did our pioneers.

The deer on the right was shot by FitzGerald with the flintlock gun shown in the picture. The story of this hunt will be found in the appendix.

PLATE 7

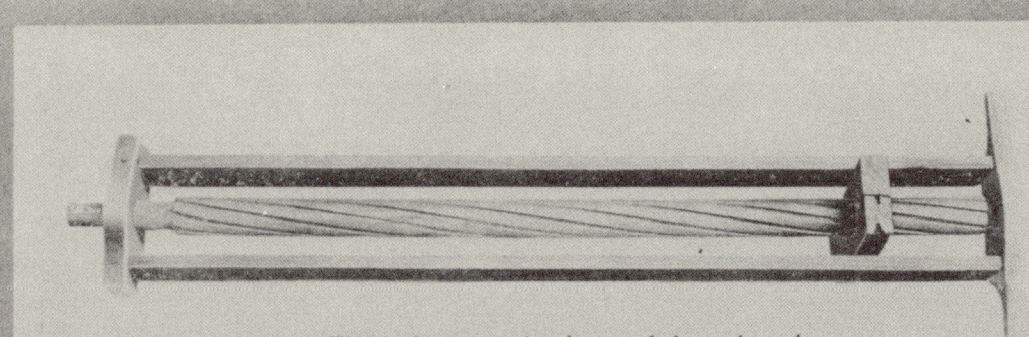

This is the conventional type of the early tool used for rifling barrels.

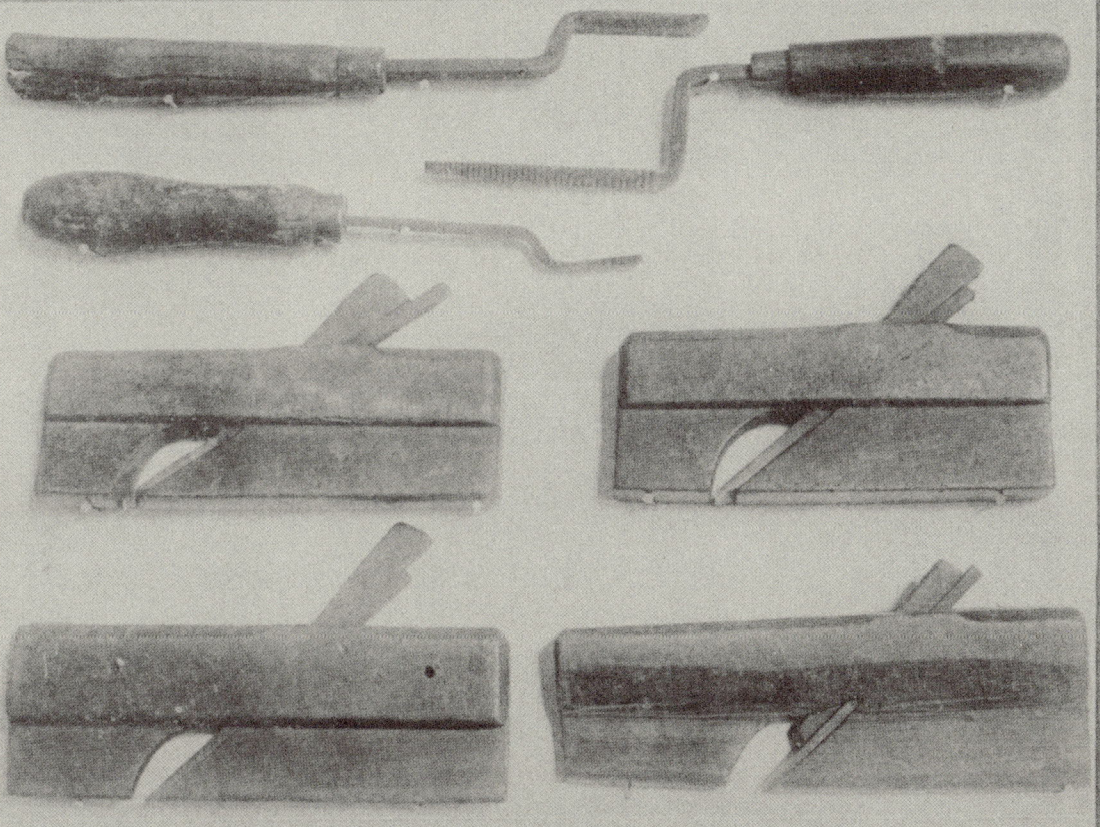

Homemade tools used for making the stocks of muzzle-loading rifles. These tools, as well as the rifles themselves, were made in their entirety by the ingenious smith. The group here illustrated includes three checkering tools and four block planes.

PLATE 8

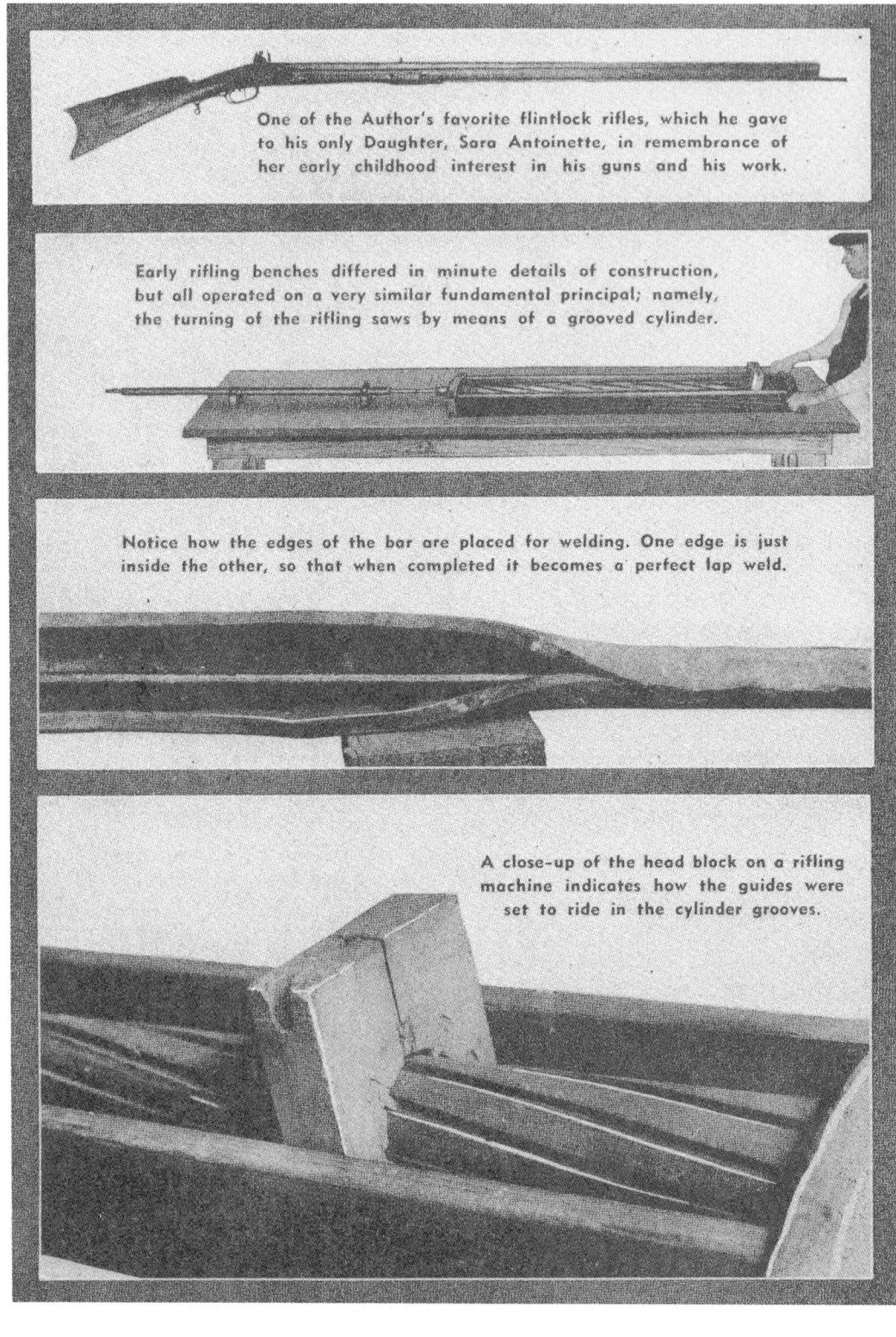

One of the Author's favorite flintlock rifles, which he gave to his only Daughter, Sara Antoinette, in remembrance of her early childhood interest in his guns and his work.

Early rifling benches differed in minute details of construction, but all operated on a very similar fundamental principal; namely, the turning of the rifling saws by means of a grooved cylinder.

Notice how the edges of the bar are placed for welding. One edge is just inside the other, so that when completed it becomes a perfect lap weld.

A close-up of the head block on a rifling machine indicates how the guides were set to ride in the cylinder grooves.

PLATE 9

Meredith Wolfe, gunsmith, at his bench.

The Author firing a beloved flintlock.

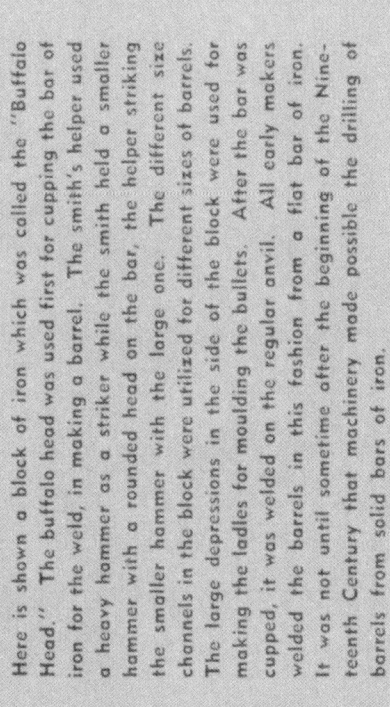

Here is shown a block of iron which was called the "Buffalo Head." The buffalo head was used first for cupping the bar of iron for the weld, in making a barrel. The smith's helper used a heavy hammer as a striker while the smith held a smaller hammer with a rounded head on the bar, the helper striking the smaller hammer with the large one. The different size channels in the block were utilized for different sizes of barrels. The large depressions in the side of the block were used for making the ladles for moulding the bullets. After the bar was cupped, it was welded on the regular anvil. All early makers welded the barrels in this fashion from a flat bar of iron. It was not until sometime after the beginning of the Nineteenth Century that machinery made possible the drilling of barrels from solid bars of iron.

PLATE 10

Reproduction of the famous painting, "Shooting for the Beef," painted by George Caleb Bingham and used by courtesy of the Mabel Brady Garvan Collection, in the gallery of fine arts, Yale University. This masterpiece faithfully depicts an early American shooting match.

Development of the Rifle

with all rifled arms. The bullet must be made to take the grooves and be perfectly centered in the bore, either in loading or upon being fired.

The so-called gain, or gaining, twist was next developed in the target rifle. Chapman gives Edward Wesson the credit for first employing this system of rifling. In 1855 the Fishers, of Virginia, were advertising the gain twist in rifles of their own make. It is doubtful whether it can be credited to any one man, as it had been tried many years before. The object of the gain-twist method of grooving was to permit the use of heavy charges of powder without the danger of the bullet stripping, or being driven across the lands. J. W. Stillman, writing in the *Atlantic Monthly* in 1859, says that the American gunsmith has solved the problem by adopting the gaining twist, in which the grooves start from the breech nearly parallel to the axis of the bore, and gradually increase in rate of twist, until at the muzzle they have a much sharper pitch. In this way the rotation of the bullet is begun very gently, with less tendency for the surface metal of the soft bullet to be stripped off in the grooves. The gaining twist is the greatest improvement since grooving was successfully applied. To reject it is to reject something indispensable to the best performance of the rifle.

The barrels of all these rifles were "freed"; that is, in the final boring of the barrel a slightly deeper cut was taken from the breech up to within 1½ or 2 inches of the muzzle. The idea was to reduce friction and permit easy loading, the plunger of the bullet starter carrying the bullet through the tighter muzzle section, and on into the looser, "freed" portion of the barrel below.

It was soon found that the sharp-pointed picket bullet with its straight lines was not the best form, for if loaded slightly off center each revolution would throw the point into a wider circle, and the bullet would become more erratic than a round ball. Therefore the point of the cone was gradually brought to more of a curve, and the so-called "sugar-loaf" bullet was the result. Very fine accuracy was developed with this new bullet, and Stillman records two targets shot by rifles made by Morgan James, of Utica, N. Y. The first target was shot by a rifle of 60-gauge, 25 shots being fired, the average deviation being 1¼ inches; the second was shot by a rifle of 90-gauge, the average being 8-10 of an inch, both at a distance of 220 yards. Stillman also states that in the northern part of the State of New York the practice at shooting matches was at turkeys at 100 rods (550 yards); and that a good marksman was expected to hit one turkey on an average of every three shots.

By 1860 a new bullet had been designed that far surpassed the sharp-pointed sugar-loaf bullet in accuracy, and had been universally adopted in various calibers and lengths to suit each individual pitch of rifling. One of the most accurate bullets of this new type as designed for a certain rifle measures .420 in diameter at the base, 200 at the point, is .735 in length, and weighs 225 grains. The rifle that used this ball would be considered a 60-gauge, as measured by the round-ball method, as round balls of this size would run sixty to the pound. Another bullet is .500 in diameter at the base, .250 at the point, is .950 in length, and weighs 1 ounce and 48 grains.

By this time the length of barrels had been reduced to almost a standard, although opinions were various on this subject. Experiments had developed the fact that a barrel of 26 inches was the best for the strongest shooting, and for the best accuracy one of 34 inches, while for a combination of both, a barrel of 30 inches was considered the best length.

Telescope sights were in use, and extended the full length of the barrel; many of them were interchangeable with the peep and covered bead front sights. A telescope sight brought out by Daniel Wood, of Rochester, N. Y., in 1861, especially designed for the American sharpshooter, had a range-finding and elevation device consisting of eight horizontal cross hairs parallel to each other and at certain definite distances apart. These cross hairs were intended to indicate the fall of the ball for different ranges, and were so spaced as to exactly correspond with it. When used as a range-finding device, the height of an object as measured between the cross hairs indicated the range. The telescope was also used in correcting shots on the target. If the first shot was low, the rifle was held immovable with the cross hairs on the center of the bull's-eye. The elevating screw

Development of the Rifle

was then turned up until the cross hairs centered the bullet hole. In this way the correct elevation was secured; and if the calculation had been correct the next shot should strike the bull's-eye. If the distance were so great that the bullet hole could not be seen, something easily seen was placed over the bullet hole, and the adjustments made. Try this some time when sighting in a rifle, and see how much ammunition you will save.

The following data will give some idea as to how accurately range and wind variation had to be judged to make good scores when using these rifles. A test was made of a certain rifle, the barrel of which weighed 8 pounds and was 29 inches in length. A conical ball was used weighing 65 to the pound, with a charge of 2½ inches of Hazard's No. 1F powder. At 110 yards the drop of the bullet was 3 inches; at 220 yards, 30 inches; and at 440 yards, 18 feet! All this will vary, of course, with different rifles, charges of powder, weight of bullets, etc.

Back in those days flags were used on the range, set every 40 yards between firing point and target. These were made of red cotton cloth about 6 feet long, and of cylindrical shape, 3 or 4 inches in diameter. They were kept spread by the use of wire rings sewed inside. These flags tapered slightly, and had a slit in one side in which a weight could be placed in case of a heavy wind. They were fastened to the edge of a strip of tin, 3 x 10 inches, on one end of which were brazed lugs to slip over a rod fastened to the top of a pole. The strip of tin acted like a weather vane and was free to turn in any direction. The idea was by the aid of these flags to select an average wind velocity, and fire when the flags showed an even wind over the entire range.

That the old-time riflemen could dope wind is evidenced by that famous match in 1886 between Warner and Perry, at Warren, Ohio. The match was a 50-shot affair for $500 a side; distance, 220 yards. Though it was a very windy day, Warner won the match, placed his 50 shots in a group measuring 42 inches; and Perry's group was just over 50 inches. There was always great rivalry between Warner and Perry, Warner always claiming that Perry copied him. There are other similar achievements recorded for both. It is recorded by

The Muzzle-Loading Rifle—Then and Now

Barber that at a meeting of a rifle club in Ohio just before the beginning of the Civil War, 30 men put 10 shots each inside of a 10-inch circle at 300 yards. It is also recorded that at a distance of three-quarters of a mile a number of shots have been placed in a flour barrel, without a miss.

With the breaking out of the Civil War many sharpshooting regiments and companies were organized in the Federal Army. These were composed of picked men from various States—men of known ability as marksmen. In Berdan's two regiments of sharpshooters no one was permitted to join who could not place 10 shots in a target, measuring 50 inches or under, at a distance of 200 yards —an average of 5 inches to the shot. It is recorded that one of these men, by the name of Townsend, fired a 5-shot group at 200 yards that measured $3\frac{1}{2}$ inches. Two companies of this regiment furnished their own rifles, which were the heavy target rifles with false muzzles, and telescope and peep sights.

Then there were the Andrew Sharpshooters from Massachusetts —a company of picked men named for Governor Andrew of that State. Each man provided his own rifle. A description of these rifles published in a history entitled, "Massachusetts in the War," says that they were very heavy, and were considered to be the most efficient rifles known. They weighed from 20 to 70 pounds, and were necessarily fired from a rest. They were made by various gunsmiths in different parts of the country to suit each individual. They were muzzle-loading, shooting a conical ball with a patch, and propelled by a heavy charge of powder. An expert in their use could load, aim, and fire about once in 2 minutes. It is also recorded that at Yorktown many of the Confederate batteries were silenced by the sharpshooters using these heavy rifles. One incident is related in which some of the Federals, working in the trenches, were annoyed by a Confederate sharpshooter who had posted himself in a tree 800 yards distant, from which point he could make their position an uncomfortable one, while it was impossible for them at that distance to distinguish him with the naked eye among the branches of the tree. Two of Andrew's sharpshooters were put in the trench, a telescope sight held on the man in the tree, and the first shot brought him down.

Development of the Rifle

In the Western Federal Army, General Fremont organized a regiment of picked men selected from many different States, and known as "Birge's Western Sharpshooters." They were first armed with the American target rifle obtained from the sporting-goods stores of St. Louis. These rifles varied in caliber, and each man carried a mould to fit his rifle.

Reports of the officers of both the Confederate and Federal armies contain the information that the fire of the sharpshooters was very accurate. After the war these muzzle-loading target rifles were still preferred for fine target work to the breech-loading rifle that was fast coming into use.

One of the last developments was the two-strip paper patch and the adaptation of the Berdan primer to be used with the muzzle-loading rifle. The false muzzle was altered to handle the composite bullet with the two-strip paper patch. This composite or combination bullet was made in two parts. The point was of an alloy, and much harder than the base. These two parts were swaged together so as not to twist apart when fired. The bullet was lengthened, requiring heavier charges of powder; the recoil was heavy, and machine rests were devised for use in firing the rifles in target work. A cross head was attached under the barrel near the muzzle, having a V-notch into which fitted a piece of metal attached to the shooting bench. The rear portion of the rest permitted the sliding of the rifle in recoil, and had fine screw adjustments for both windage and elevation. To fire, the rifleman seated himself to the left of the rifle, with his right hand against the butt and the first finger of the left hand on the trigger. When the rifle was fired the right hand took the recoil as the gun came back on the bench. The rifle was then loaded again, and returned to the original position.

After the Berdan primer came out, some of these rifles, to keep pace with the new development, were adapted to use it. Instead of the regular tube, or nipple, there was used a small tube of steel, the upper end being formed the same as the head of a brass cartridge shell, and receiving the primer. A cap was made, with a plunger, to screw down on the cylindrical portion. The hammer, striking the plunger, fired the primer, which communicated with the charge

The Muzzle-Loading Rifle—Then and Now

in the barrel through a small hole. This arrangement prevented any escape of the powder gases.

The false muzzle for loading the two-strip patch was formed in the same way as the false muzzle already in use, except that the center was bored out to a depth of three-quarters of the length of the bullet, and about three-quarters of an inch in diameter, this latter size depending upon the caliber of the bullet. The above dimensions are for a ball of .50 caliber and a length of 1½ inches. In this hole in the false muzzle another muzzle was placed that protruded an eighth of an inch beyond the original false muzzle. The bore at the outer end of this extra false muzzle was filed square, gradually tapering down to the other end. Two channels were cut across the outer end of this piece, at right angles to each other, and to a depth that brought their bottoms flush with the end of the original outer false muzzle. Two pieces of bond paper, slightly oiled, were laid across each other in these two channels, and the bullet pressed into the square opening of the inner false muzzle, the channels guiding the paper strips, which made a perfect fold around the bullet. The starter was then used as usual to seat the bullet and center it in the bore.

A rifle of the above type is in the possession of the writer, and was made by Brockway, of Bellows Falls, Vt. It weighs 20 pounds, has a 30-inch barrel, including the false muzzle, which is constructed to use the two-strip paper patch; a full equipment of accessories; swages for two different sizes of bullets; moulds for the points and base of the composite bullet, and also for the solid ball, and a charger that indicates the amount of powder for the charge, which is 4 inches in the bore of the rifle. One swage forms a bullet that measures .520 at the base, .245 at the point, is 1½ inches in length, and weighs 700 grains. The other swage forms a bullet that measures .515 at the base, .240 at the point, is 1 9-16 inches in length, and weighs 680 grains. There are eight narrow lands in the rifling, which make 1¾ turns in the length of the barrel. The rifle is in perfect condition, and is as accurate as the day it was made. Ignition is by use of the Berdan primer. This rifle is equipped with a full-length telescope sight. A machine rest is also part of the equipment.

Development of the Rifle

To those who are not familiar with the capabilities of these old rifles, the results of the following test of one may be of interest: Recently, at the invitation of the late Dr. Philip P. Quayle, of the Peters Cartridge Co., the writer made a trip to Kings Mills, Ohio, where the Peters plant is located, taking with him one of the finest target rifles in his collection, as Dr. Quayle had expressed a desire to measure the velocity of one of these old arms. The rifle tested was one of the finest, if not the finest specimen in existence, and was made by N. J. Whitmore, of Pottsdam, N. Y. It is in splendid, new condition, inside and out. Length of barrel, 31¾ inches over all, including false muzzle and patent breech. The grooves are cut on a gaining twist, beginning with one turn in 6 feet and ending with one turn in 3 feet 4 inches; bore diameter, .432; depth of grooves, .008; width of grooves, .103; widths of lands, .69; weight of rifle, 16½ pounds. The bullets are of the flat-pointed picket type, with slightly rounded base, measuring .440 at the base, .740 in length, and weighing 225 grains. These bullets were formed of pure lead, hammered and then swaged, after which they were carefully weighed and only those used which were within 0.5 of a grain of the standard weight. Experiments were conducted in the laboratory with various powder charges, in which the velocity was carefully measured, and a charge of 64.7 grains of King's Semi-Smokeless, FFG granulation, was selected giving a mean muzzle velocity of 1,638 feet per second. This rifle has a full-length telescope sight of about 12-power, adjustable for elevation by a finely cut screw, and a single set trigger. The starter will fit on the muzzle in only one position, insuring that each bullet will be centered exactly the same in the bore as every other one. Much depends upon the proper powder charge; and the method used in the laboratory for predetermining this, together with the accuracy of the forecast of its behavior before the rifle had fired a shot, seem incredible.

The rifle was taken to the range in its case, and there assembled. The bore was carefully wiped out, and one of the weighed charges of powder was poured into the muzzle, using a small wooden funnel that is part of the equipment. A felt wad 3-16 of an inch in thickness was seated on the powder. The bullet was then centered in a circular patch wet with saliva, placed in a depression in the muzzle provided for this purpose, the bullet-starter set in place, and the bullet forced into the bore, the bullet being seated down on the powder with a flat-ended ramrod. This flat-ended ramrod is used so that there will be no change in the axis of the bullet as fixed by the false muzzle and the starter. The false muzzle was then removed. Two shots were fired to warm the gun and settle the telescope in the mounts, after which 5 shots were fired for group, the bore being carefully cleaned after each shot; distance, 186 yards. This group measured: extreme horizontal, $1\frac{1}{8}$ inches; extreme vertical, $\frac{7}{8}$ of an inch; mean radius, 7/16 of an inch. Every shot would have touched a 5-cent piece.

It is most probable that these muzzle-loading target rifles, equipped with telescope sight, set triggers, false muzzles, and bullet-starters, were the most accurate rifles ever made. Very few of the riflemen that were familiar with this type of rifle are living today, but a few old photographs from a camera of over fifty years ago have preserved the pictures of some of the famous old riflemen who upheld the supremacy of the muzzle-loading target rifle to the very last.

Chapter V.

THE RIFLE IN THE AMERICAN REVOLUTION

THE first considerable mention of riflemen in the American Army occurs in connection with the seige of Boston. When the news of Concord and Bunker Hill was spread throughout the Colonies by post riders, and the Continental Congress realized that war had really begun and that the British stronghold of Boston was to be a seat of war, messengers on horseback were dispatched into the sparsely settled western borders, urging the pioneers to assemble and help in the fight against oppression.

Congress could not offer them a reward, nor even guarantee them pay; for it had no funds and no power to raise money by loan or by taxes. But the mid-colonial pioneers were born and bred to fighting. Self-equipped, they responded with alacrity in numbers greater than were called for, and were started in several divisions on the long journey afoot to Boston. As they reached the large towns on their way they stopped to give exhibitions of skill in marksmanship to develop enthusiasm and incite others to enlist.

Accounts of some of these exhibitions, written by eyewitnesses, found their way into the newspapers of the day. *The Virginia Gazette* of 1775 recorded:

"On Friday last there arrived at Lancaster, Pennsylvania, Captain Cresap's company of riflemen consisting of one hundred and thirty active and brave young fellows, many of whom were in the late expedition under Lord Dunmore against the Indians. These men have been bred in the woods to hardships and danger from their infancy. With their rifles in their hands they assume a kind of omnipotence over their enemies. Two brothers in company took a piece of board five inches by seven inches with a bit of white paper the size of a dollar nailed in the center, and, while one held the board upright gripped between his knees, the other at sixty yards without any kind of rest shot eight balls through it successively and spared his brother's thighs. Another of the company held a barrel stave close against his body perpendicularly, while one of his comrades at the same distance shot several bullets through it. The spectators were told that there were upwards of fifty persons in the company who could do the same."

The brothers mentioned in the above were probably the Shain boys who were celebrated as marksmen and also for recklessness.

There is mention, too, in the *Gazette* that three of Captain Cresap's men fired simultaneously at a buzzard flying high overhead, in a demonstration of skill. The bird fell and each man claimed that he had killed it. Examination proved that all three bullets had hit their mark.

On the 18th of July the first company (Nagel's, of Berks County, Pennsylvania) arrived at Boston, and by the middle of August, 1430 men, instead of the 810 required, reported there for duty. They were placed under the command of Col. William Thompson of Carlisle, Pennsylvania, organized as light infantry and assigned to duty in the besieging army.

Shortly after Washington took command of the army he arranged a spectacular review of his riflemen, in order that the fifteen or sixteen thousand New Hampshire, Massachusetts, Rhode Island and Connecticut militia, who had assembled to shut the British up in Boston, might see the novelty of accurate shooting at what, to them, was extraordinary distance, and be encouraged thereby.

It is probable that to New Englanders (with the possible exception of some of the Green Mountain boys and a very few veterans of the French wars who had served with the Mid-Colonials) the rifle was unknown. In the presence of the army drawn up in parallel lines on each side of the range and an immense crowd of spectators, in which a number of British spies were welcome visitors, a pole seven inches in diameter was set up, and a marksman stepped off two hundred fifty paces. At the place where he stopped, a company of riflemen was lined up to show what they could do. The mark was about equal to that a man would present standing sideways and the range was about two hundred yards.

The Rifle in the American Revolution

No New England farmer would waste powder and ball firing at such a mark and distance with his musket or fowling piece, when only luck could account for a hit. But the riflemen, firing singly or at command, so riddled the pole that it was apparent that no enemy could survive an instant.

General Howe, cooped up in Boston, was fully as much impressed as the spectators, and wrote home about "the terrible guns of the rebels."

In the army around Boston, the riflemen were employed as sharpshooters to pick off any British soldiers or officers who were incautious about exposing themselves. This they did to perfection. There is mention of a British soldier shot at two hundred fifty yards when only half his head was visible; of ten men, three of whom were officers, killed one day while reconnoitering; of a rifleman who, seeing some British on a scow at a distance of fully half a mile, found a good resting place on a hill and bombarded them until he potted the lot.

General Howe, thinking that his statement of casualties and American marksmanship might need proof at home, gave orders for the capture alive of one of the riflemen,—together with his shooting iron. Finally such a rifleman was captured and sent to England, rifle and all, and was there exhibited. This stage play of Howe's had an effect upon the British public that perhaps he did not anticipate.

Extract of a letter received in Philadelphia, dated Cambridge, July 31, 1775:

"Last Friday (29th July) we were informed by our out sentries at the foot of Bunker Hill that the enemy had cut down several large trees, and were busy all night in throwing up a line and abatis, in front of it. In the evening orders were given to the York County Rifle Company to march down to our advanced post, on Charlestown Neck, to endeavor to surround the enemy's advanced guard, and bring off some prisoners, from whom we expected to learn the enemy's design in throwing up the abatis in the neck. The rifle company divided and executed their plan in the following manner: Cap. Doudel, with thirty-nine men filed off to the right of Bunker Hill, and creeping on their hands and knees, got into the rear of the enemy's sentries without being discovered. The other division of forty men under Lieut. Miller were equally successful in getting behind the sentries on the left and were within a few yards of joining the division on the right, when a party of regulars came down the hill to relieve their guard and crossed our riflemen under Capt. Doudel as they were lying on the ground in Indian file. The regulars were within twenty yards of our riflemen before they saw them and immediately fired. The riflemen returned the salute, killed several and brought off two prisoners and their muskets, with the loss of Corporal Crouse, who is supposed to have been killed, as he has not been heard of since the affair."

Capt. Michael Doudel's Company was enlisted principally at Samuel Getty's Tavern, now Gettysburg, June 24th, 1775; left York for Boston July 1, arrived at Cambridge, July 25th.

The Committee of Yorktown wrote to the Pennsylvania delegation in Congress on July 1st, 1775:

"Gentlemen: We had the honor of receiving your favor of the 15th ult., enclosing a resolve of the Honorable Continental Congress of the 14th ult. We immediately summoned the committee of this county and laid before them your letter. The committee proceeded to the choice of officers fit to be recommended to the congress and appointed six commissioners to provide necessaries for them. Every resolve passed in committee with the greatest unanimity and the gentlemen of Yorktown, after the meeting, dispersed themselves through the county and assisted the officers in recruiting.

"The officers we take the liberty to recommend to you are: Captain Michael Doudel, Lieutenants Henry Miller, John Dill and James Matson. They are men whose courage we have the highest opinion of. The company including officers and soldiers are beyond the number fixed for this county and as Gen. Gates thought it improper to discharge any, we have sent them all. We hope no alteration will be made in the officers. The captain has behaved very well on this occasion and has done all in his power by advance of money, etc. to forward the important common cause. Mr. Miller is known to some of you gentlemen. The other officers are men of worth and property; they all have wives and families and are entitled to the warmest thanks of their country.

> JAMES SMITH
> GEORGE IRVIN
> JOHN KEAN
> JOSEPH DONALDSON
> THOMAS HARTLEY
> MICHAEL HAHN.

P.S.—The company began their march the nearest road to Boston this day."

There came to me from the above named Lieut. James Matson of York County, Pennsylvania, the first rifle of my collection. He was my ancestor; I inherited the rifle, which has a small barrel of forty-eight inch length. It came to me in early boyhood in almost as perfect condition as when it was used in the siege of Boston. It is still in practically perfect condition after a lifetime with me. Being the first rifle ever owned by me, and also on account of its historic associations, it has always held the foremost place in my collection of firearms.

CHAPTER VI.

ARMS AND AMMUNITION IN THE U. S. CIVIL WAR

WITH the establishment of the Springfield Armory in 1795 and the one in Harper's Ferry the following year, the United States began the manufacture of government arms.

The first arms produced were smoothbore muskets, patterned after the French infantry musket, known as the Charleville model, 1763. This arm had been used in considerable numbers in the Revolutionary War. In spite of the fact that the Revolutionary War had been won largely by the use of the long-barrelled, accurate shooting flintlock "Kentucky" rifle in the hands of the frontiersmen, the manufacture of the smooth bore was continued, and was the principal arm of our regular soldiers until 1840.

A few rifled arms were made in 1800, and were produced in small quantities until the change was completely made to rifled arms.

The year 1840 saw the end of the flintlock musket, which had been the principal arm of all nations for over two hundred years before, but the government had been slow to make the change from smoothbore to rifle.

In 1842 the armories began the manufacture of percussion arms. Also came the invention of Captain Minie, a Frenchman, who brought out the long conical bullet ("the Minie ball") with a hollow base that is to be found in such large numbers on the Southern battlefields.

The principle of this bullet with the hollow base was the expansion of the bullet by the action of the powder gases when the rifle was fired. This expansion of the bullet filled the rifle grooves and imparted a rotary motion that increased the accuracy and range of the bullet. This type of bullet was recommended and adopted to be used in all newly manufactured arms.

In 1856 the United States began the manufacture of rifled arms for all branches of the service, superseding the smoothbore. The caliber was .58.

Arms and Ammunition in the U. S. Civil War

The old model flintlocks were converted to percussion system. With the breaking out of the War Between the States there was a shortage of arms for the great number of soldiers enlisted. Many thousand arms were purchased abroad. The North purchased almost half a million Enfield rifled muskets from Great Britain. Others were bought from France, Germany, Austria and anywhere arms could be purchased.

The South also purchased many arms abroad, but on account of the blockade were not able to use them as extensively as the North.

The South early captured Harper's Ferry arsenal and removed the captured arms and machinery to Richmond. Here they manufactured arms from the captured parts, and with the use of the machinery continued the manufacture until the capture of Richmond and the collapse of the Confederacy.

The cartridges for these arms were of paper, with the powder in one end and the bullet in the other. The soldier tore off the end with his teeth, poured the powder into the barrel and then rammed the bullet down on the powder. Many thousand muskets were picked up on the battlefields. A large percentage of these had anywhere from two to ten loads in them. The old musket lately found in the cliffs of Walden's Ridge, near Chattanooga, is one of the converted flintlocks, and used to arm some of the regiments at the beginning of the war. This old musket is a smooth bore and used a round ball and buckshot. Several regiments almost mutinied and refused to accept them, and those that did accept, disposed of them as soon as possible.

By the time the Union Army reached Chattanooga, smoothbores were being replaced by the later rifled Springfield. The breech loader and repeater were just coming into use at the beginning of the war. The Henry repeating rifle had just been patented and some of them saw service at the Battle of Fort Donelson. The revolving Colt rifle and carbine were also used.

On the Twenty-first Ohio monument on Snodgrass Hill, Chickamauga Battlefield, it states that this regiment was armed with this rifle, which enabled them to hold this position against superior numbers, by firing 43,000 rounds of ammunition.

The Muzzle-Loading Rifle—Then and Now

Of the many arms used by the cavalry, the Spencer was the best, a repeating rifle and carbine of seven shots. Wilder's Mounted Infantry was armed with this repeating rifle at the battle of Chickamauga. Then there were Gallagers, Burnside, Sharps, Maynards, and a dozen other types of carbines. Blockade runners brought in the Whitworth rifle from England, which was used by the Confederate sharpshooters.

The North had various special rifles for this work. The Sharps rifle was used by the sharpshooters of the Union army, as was also the heavy target rifle, often weighing as much as thirty-five pounds. Bullets in numbers can still be picked up on the battlefields around Chattanooga. On the battlefield of Murfreesboro I picked up in one afternoon several hundred bullets, varying in caliber from .36 to .69, some twenty different calibers among the lot, thus illustrating various arms used by the soldiers of both armies.

Bullets and Their Effect in War

From my collection of over five thousand bullets picked up on the battlefields of the War Between the States in Tennessee and Georgia during twenty years (1910 to 1930), an interesting study may be made of the small arms used in that great conflict.

It may seem strange that after many years, so large a number of bullets may still be found. It was only by becoming a student of the military campaigns, by a search of the reports, and by following step by step the movements of the troops along the actual battle lines, still plainly marked in many places by long lines of entrenchments, that this collection was possible.

Records of the ordnance officers of the Federal Army show that at Murfreesboro there were fired by the Federal soldiers two million rounds of small arms ammunition; at Chickamauga two million six hundred thousand rounds; from May 3rd to Sept. 3rd, 1864, there were fired by the Federal Army on the Atlanta campaign twenty-two million one hundred thirty-seven thousand one hundred thirty-two rounds. There are no records available of the ammunition fired by the Confederate Army, but it is probable that they fired almost as many rounds as the Federal Army.

Arms and Ammunition in the U. S. Civil War

Many of these battlefields have never been cultivated but remain just as the armies left them at the close of battle back in 1865.

From Fort Donelson, Shiloh, Murfreesboro, Lookout Mountain (famous for its battle above the clouds), Missionary Ridge, Chickamauga, and the battlefields of the Atlanta campaign, I accumulated an unwritten history of the bullets found. I met many participants in these battles and listened to their recitals of the parts they played. For instance, on the Battlefield of Resaca I met a Federal soldier, a member of an Illinois regiment, that, armed with Spencer repeating rifles had charged a Confederate battery on top of a hill. When within about twenty feet of the battery, a Confederate regiment that was supporting the battery, raised up and opened fire on them,—when they turned and ran down the hill much faster than they went up. Together we located the hill, found the battery emplacements just as they had been left at the close of battle, and, on the hillside up which his regiment had charged, we found Spencer shells and cartridges where they had been dropped during battle. On the ground behind the battery, where the supporting regiment had been lying down, we found Enfield bullets where they had been placed, so as to be in easy reach for reloading.

The line of battle at Resaca was six miles long, covered by strong earthworks. The ground has never been cultivated and one may follow the works the entire distance. There are no markers and it is only by inquiry of the inhabitants of Resaca that one may find battle lines.

The Springfield rifle was the principal arm of the Federal Army, but there were not sufficient pieces to arm the great number of volunteers at the beginning of the war. The United States government purchased arms from every available source, especially from foreign countries: the Enfield from England, and various makes of arms from Austria, Belgium, France, and Germany. The Confederates were much worse off for arms and, also, purchased wherever they could. They, too, bought Enfields from England. Arms were manufactured in many places in the Southern states. Arms captured in battle were repaired and used by both armies.

The Muzzle-Loading Rifle—Then and Now

A few breechloaders were in use before the war, but the army board was unfavorable to their adoption. The Colt, Hall, Burnside, Sharps, and Maynard had been tried, and a few were in the hands of the troops at the beginning of the war. Before the war was over there were twenty or more different makes of breechloaders and several repeating rifles. The Sharps rifle became famous in the two regiments of Berdan's sharpshooters attached to the army of the Potomac, while the Henry repeating rifle, the forerunner of the Winchester, and the only rifle of this war to survive to the present time, was used by Birge's Western Sharpshooters attached to the Army of the Cumberland. The Spencer repeating rifle and carbine was used extensively by both the infantry and the cavalry before the close of the war. Wilder's mounted infantry was, perhaps, the first to use the Spencer rifle in battle at Hoover's Gap on the Tullahoma campaign in June 1861, and I find the first Spencer shells at this place. As the war progressed, increasing numbers of bullets from breechloading and repeating rifles are found. With the beginning of the Atlanta Campaign many of these rifles are in evidence. Birge's Western Sharpshooters had returned from their veteran furlough and brought with them the Henry repeating rifle purchased by the men themselves at $43.00 each, the government furnishing the ammunition. That these rifles and many other new developments in arms were widely in use is verified by the finding of shells and cartridges on all the battlefields of the Atlanta campaign.

At Resaca many Henry, Spencer, Wesson, and Burnside shells were found. That the Henry took a prominent part in the defense of Altoona, when General Hood attacked General Sherman's base of supplies, is made evident by many Henry shells I have found on the works at that place. Again, at Franklin, Tennessee, in 1864, when Hood's army charged the works of Schofield's men and suffered terrible repulse, we find the Henry in action in Cademate Brigade and here in front of that rifle brigade, the dead lay the thickest of all on that battlefield. Some of the arms proved unsatisfactory, as is borne out in the report of Lieut. Granville West of McCook's brigade, where he reports the utter worthlessness of the Ballard rifle with which six companies of his regiment were armed during the raid south of Atlanta. He says a great many became entirely useless during the action.

Every available firearm that was capable of inflicting damage to an adversary was used during the war. The battlefield of Shiloh produces the most varied collection of bullets. A participant in that battle stated that after the fight, arms of every description covered the field, from the old flintlock musket used by Arkansas troops to squirrel rifles and shotguns. In my collection are some forty or more different calibers and shapes of bullets. How it was possible for the ordnance officer to issue ammunition without confusion is beyond understanding. In McCook's cavalry brigade each regiment used a different arm and caliber.

In the report issued June 19, 1864, of the armament and ammunition of the Army of Tennessee, commanded by Gen. Joseph E. Johnston, the following calibers of arms are given: Caliber .69, .58, .57, .70, .54, .52, .56, .44, .37, .51, .36. Among the arms listed were twenty-six Whitworth rifles. These rifles were used by Confederate sharpshooters and had been purchased in England and brought in by blockade runners. There were also listed the Colt Navy and Army pistols, of .44 and .36 caliber.

The effect and force of the rifle fire of the day of the War Between the States can still be seen on the side of the carriage house of the Carter residence on the battlefield of Franklin, Tennessee. On the side facing the Confederate fire and just in the rear of the Federal line of works, on a space 12 x 16 feet can be counted the imprint of two hundred and fifty bullets, the greater number being high, showing a tendency of even veteran soldiers to over-shoot.

The following tables, all taken from official sources, will serve to partially indicate to arms students the wide variety of ammunition and guns that were used in the War Between the States:

The Muzzle-Loading Rifle—Then and Now

TABLE I.

Armament and ammunition report of the Army of Tennessee, commanded by General Joseph E. Johnston, for the week ending June 19, 1864.

	HARDEE'S CORPS	HOOD'S CORPS	WHEELER'S CORPS (Cavalry)	ARMY OF THE MISSISSIPPI	TOTALS
Regiments in command	80	*59	*24	48	§211
Armament					
Small Arms:					
Caliber .69	1,853	1,909	317	1,200	5,369
Caliber .58 and .57	11,420	6,141	2,291	7,245	27,107
Caliber .70		64			64
Caliber .54	2,967	6,207	2,383	4,284	15,841
Caliber .52			799		799
Caliber .56			4		4
Caliber .44	29				29
Caliber .37			6		6
Caliber .51			20		20
Spencer rifles			58		58
Whitworth rifles		3		23	26
Total	16,269	14,224	5,858	12,842	49,193
Pistols:					
Navy			1,673		1,673
Army			1,248		1,248
Total			2,921		2,921

*And two battalions
§And four battalions

Copied from the official records of the Union and Confederate armies. Series I, Vol. XXXVIII, Part LV Washington Government Printing Office, 1891, Page 782, "The Atlanta Campaign".

Arms and Ammunition in the U. S. Civil War

TABLE II.

Report of arms captured, lost and becoming surplus in the Army of the Cumberland for the month of July, 1864:

	Captured	Lost	Surplus
Enfield rifles	303	73	1,146
Springfield rifles	143	274	1,226
Spencer rifles			17
Whitney rifles			6
Colt rifles			2
French rifles	36		
Dresden rifles			14
Austrian rifles	291		1
Harper's Ferry rifles	21		
Total	794	347	2,412

(Page 159 Official Records)

TABLE III.

Report of arms captured, lost and becoming surplus in the Army of the Cumberland during the month of August, 1864:

	SPRINGFIELD RIFLES .58	ENFIELD RIFLES .577	AUSTRIAN RIFLES .54	U.S. RIFLES .58	U.S. RIFLES .54	CONFEDERATE RIFLES .58	DRESDEN RIFLES .58	COLT RIFLES .56	SPENCER RIFLES	TOTAL
										47
Captured	117	219	9	2	1	6				354
Lost	57	57								114
Surplus	197	85								282
	1,019	747		2			3	1	15	1,787

(Page 170 Official Records)

TABLE IV.

List of small arms captured from the enemy and collected from the battlefield during the month of May, 1864:

Small Arms

Enfield rifles, caliber .57	2,072
Springfield rifles, caliber .58	1,110
Austrian rifles, caliber .54	484
Smoothbore muskets, caliber .69	460
Confederate rifles, caliber .58	28
Siege rifles	59
Prussian muskets, caliber .69	3
Sharps carbine, caliber .52	1
Colt rifle, caliber .56	1

(Page 146 Official Records)

TABLE V.

Report of arms, accouterments, etc., captured, lost, and becoming surplus in the Army of the Cumberland for the month of June:

	Captured	Lost	Surplus
Springfield rifles, caliber .58	40	398	475
Enfield rifles, caliber .57	24	418	274
Austrian rifles, caliber .54	73		
Spencer rifles			49
Sporting rifles	4		
Total	141	816	*798

*Rendered surplus by reason of men being killed or wounded and sent to rear.

(Page 152 Official Records)

TABLE VI.

Report of small arms ammunition expended during the campaign commencing May 4 and ending September 8, 1864:

	ARMY OF THE CUMBERLAND Major-Gen. Thomas	ARMY OF THE TENNESSEE Major-Gen. Howard	ARMY OF THE OHIO Major-Gen. Schofield	TOTAL
Elongated ball cart., caliber .57 and .58	11,637,560	7,908,222	1,794,444	21,340,222
Spencer rifle cart.	156,739	180,768	52,815	390,322
Henry rifle cart.	10,240	93,655	23,300	126,195
Colt rifle cart.	10,760		5,000	15,760
Burnside carbine cart.			84,000	84,000
Sharps carbine cart.			16,000	16,000
Smith & Wesson carbine cart.		15,000	68,000	83,000
Ballard carbine cart.			30,000	30,000
Merrell carbine cart.			10,000	10,000
Colt Army pistol cart.		600	28,720	29,320
Colt Navy pistol cart.		1,200	3,000	4,200
Target rifle cart.		7,113		7,113
Total	11,815,299	8,206,558	2,115,275	22,137,132

(Page 126 Official Records Published 1891)

TABLE VII.

Inventory of ordnance and ordnance stores captured by the Army of the Tennessee in Cheraw, S. C., March 3, 1865:

Class vi.

Small Arms—2,345 Springfield muskets (caliber .69), 663 Austrian muskets (caliber .69), 33 Belgian muskets (caliber .69), 70 Enfield muskets (caliber .577), 8 U. S. rifles (caliber .58), 500 muskets (various kinds and calibers); total muskets and rifles, 3,619.

<small>No. 7, Reports of Bvt. Col. Thomas G. Baylor, U. S. Army, Chief Ordnance Officer, Military Division of the Mississippi, Goldsborough, N. C.</small>

<small>Series I., Vol. XLVII, Part I., Reports, War of the Rebellion.</small>

Report of expenditures of ammunition in the campaign from February 1, 1865, to March 23, 1865.

Small Arms

	Rounds
Elongated ball cartridges (caliber .574)	1,223,636
Spencer rifle and carbine cartridges (caliber .52)	213,448
Henry rifle cartridges	38,654
Smith carbine cartridges (caliber .50)	45,000
Sharps carbine cartridges (caliber .52)	112,000
Burnside carbine cartridges (caliber .54)	56,000
Colt Army pistol (caliber .44)	58,800
Colt Navy pistol (caliber .36)	4,800
Total small arms ammunition	1,742,338

<small>No. 7, Reports of Bvt. Col. Thomas G. Baylor, U. S. Army, Chief Ordnance Officer, Military Division of the Mississippi, Goldsborough, N. C.</small>

<small>Series I., Vol. XLVII, Part I., Reports, War of the Rebellion.</small>

TABLE VIII.

Inventory of ordnance and ordnance stores captured in the City of Columbia, S. C., February 16-17, 1865:

ARTICLES	CITADEL	ARSENAL	TOTAL
Yager muskets	960		960
Palmetto rifles	500		500
Remington rifles	100		100
Mississippi rifles	200		200
U. S. muskets, caliber .69	1,740	1,700	3,440
Enfield rifled muskets	1,200	700	1,900
Enfield rifles (short, sword bayonet)		2,000	2,000
Austrian rifled muskets (old)	60	500	560
Whitney rifles (old)		50	50
Springfield rifled muskets		100	100
Morse rifles (South Carolina)	400		400
Total muskets and rifles, serviceable			10,210

No. 7, Reports of Bvt. Col. Thomas G. Baylor, U. S. Army, Chief Ordnance Officer, Military Division of the Mississippi, Goldsborough, N. C.

Series I., Vol. XLVII, Part I., Reports, War of the Rebellion.

Chapter VII.
MY GUN COLLECTION

I HAVE been interested in guns and their makers, have shot guns and remade them, all my life. I have owned hundreds of guns which came into my possession as gifts, by purchase and inheritance.

When I began, many years ago, to collect firearms, my motive was not to see how large a collection I could get together, but rather how good a collection I could make. My chief interest has been in reclaiming rifles and in shooting rather than in collecting as a hobby or as a business.

I have gathered rifles from all sorts of places and in every condition possible. Most of the guns in my collection were not in shooting condition when I obtained them, but every one has been conditioned and put in good order.

Always when reclaiming an old firearm, I have tried to vision how it looked when new, and it has been my chief ambition to restore it as nearly as possible to its original condition, or just as it came from the shop of the maker. I have cleaned, rebored, and repaired, and moulded my own bullets. I have even put pieces of two decayed guns together and made a fair rifle.

Moreover, I have shot every gun I own, not once but many times. In fact I have never listed a gun that was not tested out by me personally. All of the work on these guns has been done by me, not with a view to selling them, but for the purpose of putting them in good shape for my own study and use.

The evolution of American firearms and their place in the development of our country, has been a most interesting study.

Among the guns I have particularly cherished is, of course, the rifle used in the American Revolution which I inherited from an ancestor, mentioned in another chapter.

I like the gun Meredith Wolfe, of Chattanooga, made in his youth. He was a locksmith for the city for many years, and his shop on Georgia Avenue was a sort of mecca for gunsmiths or for rifle shooters seeking expert repair of old firearms.

My Gun Collection

A favorite of mine is a double-barreled rifle made by Benjamin Mills, of Harrodsburg, Kentucky. He was a gunsmith who made guns for the United States in the Harper's Ferry Armory, and an outstanding craftsman.

I have a good gun make by the famous gunsmith of the Confederate Army, J. P. Murry, of Columbus, Georgia.

To mention another, I have always loved a single-trigger flintlock smoothbore, very early gun, .45 caliber, 41-inch barrel, hand-forged lock, sliding wood cover on patchbox, with the name *"Watson Piper"* faintly written on the cheek-piece beneath the finish. This was probably the name of the first owner, for whom the gun was made, rather than the name of the maker.

My collection includes a Spencer repeating rifle, which was one of the first repeaters to be used in the United States Army. Spencer rifles were used in the East Tennessee campaign by Wilder's brigade of mounted infantry, and were also used in Barber's first battalion of Ohio Sharpshooters. I am not sure in which my gun was used, because both units were equipped with Spencer rifles. On the hill where the battle of Resaca took place I have picked up cartridges for this gun; in fact, I have a large collection of these bullets.

I have a fine English gun of 1863 which was used in the Confederate Army.

My collection of match target rifles (muzzle-loaders) and some seventy-five or more pistols, is a good one; a pair of duelling pistols are as handsome, I believe, as any of the kind I have ever seen.

I do not deem it necessary here to list in detail all of the arms which I have accumulated over the years. As I have already explained, I have always regarded myself primarily as a shooter and student of arms rather than as a collector, but I have always possessed an inherent love for antique arms of character and merit, and I have a great respect for the great army of collectors down through the ages who have preserved and cared for these old pieces.

In 1929 I decided to list for sale about half of my arms and later, in 1940, I listed for sale more arms from my collection, in-

The Muzzle-Loading Rifle—Then and Now

cluding my match rifles and also the beloved "Long Tom", which had been my companion of many shoots.

My collection was not listed without certain pangs of regret because of my long association with these faithful old pieces, but it has long been my belief that after owners of antique arms have enjoyed their collections over the years, they should arrange to dispose of them in a manner so that these old guns may fall into the hands of other collectors and shooters who can in turn enjoy their possession and study their details. It is on account of that belief that I was constrained to part with my beloved possessions.

In addition to my collection of arms, I have endeavored to accumulate a small library of worth while books on guns and shooting, which I likewise listed for sale. It is my sincere belief that many collectors miss a great part of the joy of their hobby by not assembling a gun history and military library along with their collection of arms. Knowledge of the history and use of arms is necessary for their full appreciation, and this knowledge is best obtained by reading worth while books and source history, manuscripts, and records.

A well-selected collection of antique arms, together with a carefully assembled group of books, constitutes a hobby which can afford great joy and pleasure to the owner and to the host of friends which the hobby will enable him to make through the years.

CHAPTER VIII.

MODERN VS. OLD-TIME METHODS

SO WIDE is the interest in the muzzle-loading rifle that the question of accuracy is the prevailing topic wherever a few enthusiastic riflemen get together.

Following a National Muzzle-Loading Rifle Match at Portsmouth, Ohio, I decided to go into the question thoroughly and to use as the basis of my research:

(a) Files of information gathered by personal contact with the riflemen of the muzzle-loading days, and preserved for many years;

(b) The theories of early writers, preserved in publications, the oldest of which dates back to 1808;

(c) The ideas of the living gunsmiths, still keen of mind and active in their work.

I had a good accumulation of data with which to begin my accuracy experiments.

The great questions that confronted me were:

1. In order to attain the greatest accuracy, what should be the length of barrel, the caliber, number of grooves, width, and depth of said grooves, pitch, powder charge, patching, size of bullet for a certain bore, how tight the bullet should load, the sights and weight of rifle.

2. What is the cause of the occasional off-shot, which still is the bugbear of the modern rifleman?

3. Does modern machinery and equipment produce a more accurate muzzle-loading rifle than the old methods of years ago which produced the handmade rifle?

I was very fortunate in having a friend who is an enthusiastic muzzle-loading rifleman, Mr. Carlin Shackleford, sales manager for a large manufacturing concern, which is equipped with the very finest of modern machinery. Incidentally, Mr. Shackleford can make nearly anything that it is possible to make with modern machines.

One evening, sitting in his office, I brought up the subject very tactfully and told him what I had in mind. It just happened that

The Muzzle-Loading Rifle—Then and Now

I spoke at an opportune time. Somewhere back in the Cumberlands, "Shack", as he is affectionately called by his friends, had found a muzzle-loading rifle and had talked the owner out of it. He now began to question me as to the best methods of rebuilding it and, of course, I recommended the long bit and a few of the old tools that had proven satisfactory in the days gone by.

He did not think much of them, although he did make a long bit. But as the grooves in the barrel of his rifle were only a half pitch and had been dressed out numerous times and the lands had been flattened out, the long bit chattered badly. He made me a present of the long bit and said he could remember it without having to look at it.

"Now I will grind you some reamers," he said, "and with our modern machinery we will rebuild some of these old rifles and make them shoot as they never shot before!"

We eventually used ten rifles in our tests. For our first effort to learn what modern machinery would do we selected a rifle from my collection called "Tellico", named for a little town in the mountains, "Tellico Plains." This rifle had a 48-inch barrel, caliber .416, narrow grooves, a pitch of one turn in the length of the barrel and weighed 16 pounds. I had cut the grooves deeper.

Mr. Shackleford had ground a beautiful reamer with four flutes and then at the other end he had left a collar .0005 inches less than the flutes, which measured .421. We were about three hours getting this reamer through the 48-inch barrel and the result was nothing to be elated over, as the reamer did not cut smooth although we had a perfect cylinder bore. This barrel as finished was caliber .421. The pitch of the grooves was one turn in the length of the barrel (48 inches), with the width of the grooves one-third the width of the lands. A telescope was mounted on the rifle and the best we scored on the standard small-bore fifty-yard target was one 47 and two 48's five shots each. While this was encouraging, it was not fully up to expectations.

So another reamer was made. While on the same lines as the first, it had a taper to the cutting edges of the flutes of about .001

Modern Vs. Old-time Methods

of an inch in three inches, and was expected to cut a very smooth bore. It was necessary to make a special feed for this reamer, as the slowest speed of the lathe was too fast for best results.

The barrel selected for this attempt was 48 inches in length with a caliber of .440. As finished the reamer measured .452. It is not necessary to go into a description of this process, but we were twenty hours getting this reamer through the barrel and then finally finished it with the long bit. This rifle weighs 14 pounds, caliber .453, seven grooves one-half the width of lands, with a pitch of one-half turn in the length of the barrel. This rifle gave excellent results, shooting 48, 49, and possibles with a scope.

An interesting development occurred while we were using this rifle. All at once it began to scatter its shots. An examination of the patches showed that it was cutting them and the bullets were going wild. On examination, the barrel showed that a rough place had developed in the breech. We cut two inches off that end and re-breeched it. With one and one-half drams or 41 grains of King's Semi-Smokeless FFG powder, this rifle gives fine accuracy. The patching used is of linen, the so-called coat linen, measuring .015 in thickness.

Of the ten rifles used in these tests, five were selected as outstanding in accuracy. Fifty shots were fired from these rifles under ideal conditions for a test; ten shots each, in five-shot strings. The result was that of the fifty shots, all were in or cut well within an inch circle.

Four of these rifles had 48-inch barrels. Two of them had a pitch of one turn in 48 inches. One had a half turn and one a three-quarter turn. The fifth rifle was a stranger to the others, being a precision match rifle, of .421 caliber, with a 36-inch barrel, six grooves, a gain twist ending in one turn in thirty-six inches. This rifle was recut by William Large, of Ironton, Ohio, and was an excellent job. It weighed 18 pounds and was equipped with peep sights. It was in a class by itself and shot possibles right along. It is a difficult job to recut a gain twist, as there is a constantly changing pitch and the long bit cannot be used. It requires great skill and patience.

Since these tests two other rifles have been tried out successfully. The first is an eight-grooved barrel with narrow lands and wide grooves, with a pitch of three-quarters turn in a 42-inch barrel, caliber .480. This rifle is very temperamental, and a load of ten grains of black FFG powder as a priming charge and one dram King's Semi-Smokeless FFG is the only charge that we have found that will give accuracy. The other rifle is a forty caliber, weighing 11 pounds, which was the lightest of those tested; it has grooves which are the same width as the lands, with one turn in a 48-inch barrel. These last two rifles have never fired wild shots and will group well within an inch circle at fifty yards.

We also tried a flintlock rifle which shot right up with the percussions. It might be well to add that we tried out another rifle in our tests, one of the best looking and the finest of all in workmanship. But in spite of all the work we put on it, using all known methods, we have never succeeded in getting it to group under two inches at fifty yards. We have not discovered the reason for this.

Our deductions from this group of tests which were under way for more than a year are as follows:

We have found, just as the riflemen of the muzzle-loading days found, that a barrel of soft charcoal iron is the best where a patched round bullet is used. Each barrel used was tested under the Scleroscope for hardness and uniformity. All the barrels which showed the greatest accuracy were around 18, 19, or 20 Scleroscope test. Steel barrels run around 26 to 30, the old cast steel and our cold rolled steel being about the same test.

The barrel must be straight and the bore perfect. Any number of grooves from five to ten is satisfactory. The pitch of the rifling may run from one-half to one full turn in 48 inches. The half turn makes a splendid match rifle for sixty yards and is the least susceptible to variations in powder charges. A round ball has very little bearing on the lands and more velocity can be attained in a half pitch barrel.

In our tests with rifles of this type, variations in powder charged up until the recoil became unpleasant, only changed the center of impact and did not increase accuracy. We found some of the steeper

PLATE 11

Match Riflemen from the Highlands of Sunny Tennessee

Rube Swafford

A Sale Creek Shooter

Mysinger of Soddy

R. D. Holt, Pikeville

Arthur Kelly

Jenkins of Soddy

PLATE 12

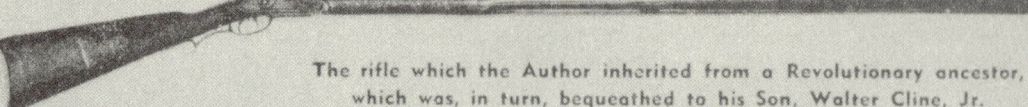
The rifle which the Author inherited from a Revolutionary ancestor, which was, in turn, bequeathed to his Son, Walter Cline, Jr.

Sam Houston, an idol of the author, typifies the sturdy frontiersman of the late Indian Wars.

This bright-eyed youngster is Walter M. Cline at the age of five years, at which time he started his gun collection by inheriting the ancestral flintlock of '76

Walter and his two children, Sara Antoinette and Walter, Jr., examine some of the thousands of bullets which Mr. Cline picked up on the Civil War battlefields of the South.

PLATE 13

Views at "Piney Nook" (near Chattanooga), where the Author enjoyed his own private shooting range and where he said he spent the happiest days of his life.

PLATE 14

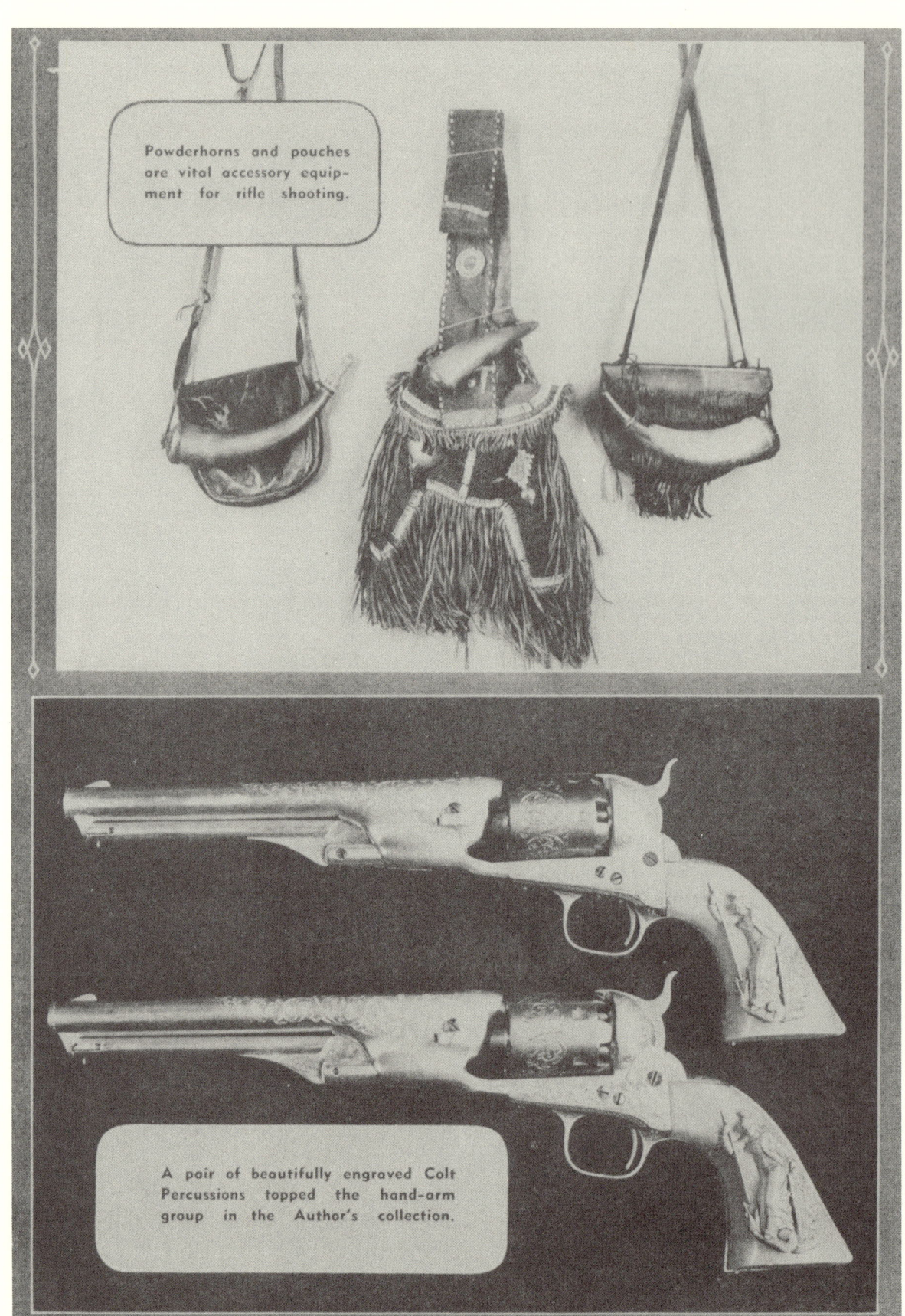

Powderhorns and pouches are vital accessory equipment for rifle shooting.

A pair of beautifully engraved Colt Percussions topped the hand-arm group in the Author's collection.

PLATE 15

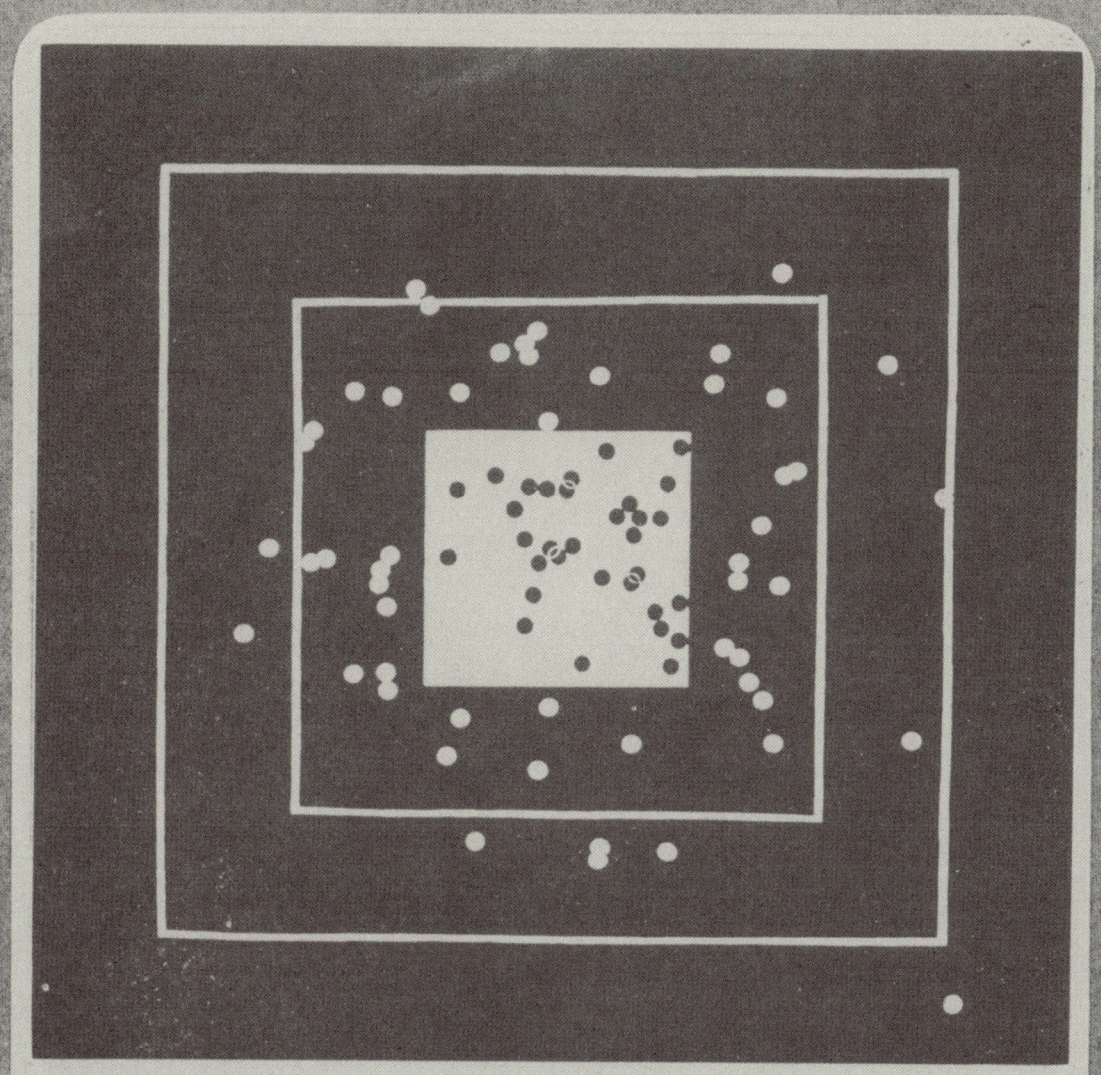

TARGET MADE BY TWELVE MEMBERS OF THE
SONORA RIFLE CLUB,
Seven shots each, resulting in three ties, of 32 points out of possible 35.
APRIL 1, 1879.
DISTANCE, 100 YARDS; SIZE OF TARGET—BULLS-EYE, 12 INCHES; CENTRE, 24 INCHES; INNER, 36 INCHES; OUTER, 48 INCHES.

PARTICIPANTS:

JOSEPH PHELPS,	S. S. BRADFORD,	JAMES BELL,
JOHN SHAW,	M. B. MOODY,	B. L. RADOWICH,
H. H. ROWELL,	C. F. SMITH,	E. A. RODGERS,
A. GRAHAM,	H. NELSON,	FRED. SUTTON.

PLATE 16

A half-dozen of the many muzzle-loading medals and trophies which Mr. Cline won during his shooting career.

PLATE 17

A GROUP OF TENNESSEE MATCH SHOOTERS

First row (left to right), Arthur Hale, Cold Springs; Frank Ferguerson; an unidentified gentleman; Hugh Mansfield; and Bob Freeman. Back row (left to right), John Clifton; John Wheeler; Rube Swafford; R. D. Holt (gunsmith); Bird Freeman, of Sequatchie; and an unidentified gentleman. In the above photograph there are four rifles that were made by Eph Terrell, three by Enoch Hardin, and two by R. D. Holt.

PLATE 18

Some Southern Mountain smiths utilize a mere "lean-to" or "shelter" for their gunsmithing activities. Here are two examples. Holding the rifle above is Robert Freeman, of Sequatchie Valley, rated as one of the best makers of rifle stocks in Tennessee.

pitches vary in accordance with variations of the powder charge. The length of the barrel does not affect accuracy, but a long barrel has a big advantage in using open sights. The weight of the barrel may run from 9 to 20 pounds. Our preference is a rifle weighing from 12 to 14 pounds with a 48-inch barrel.

The width of the grooves and lands apparently does not affect accuracy, as every rifle we used was different in this respect. Narrow grooves are much easier to cut, but a barrel with narrow grooves requires much more care to get the best results than one with the wider groove. The depth of grooves, which does not affect accuracy, varies with the width. The narrow grooves are a little deeper and the wider grooves may be less deep, but they must be cut with the circumference of the bore. The grooves must be sharp and of equal depth. The depth of grooves may run from .008 to .010 inches.

The caliber of the rifles from which we secured the finest accuracy run from .400 to .480. We tried out calibers from .320 to .600. With a caliber under .400 the bullet is very easily affected by wind currents, and rifles with calibers of .500 or over are difficult to manage and get good results. Ninety-five per cent of all match rifles are made between .400 and .500 caliber.

The much discussed question of bullet size for the bore and also the thickness and material for patches underwent a thorough test. Starting with a bullet that would just drop through the bore, the size of the bullet was increased by lapping the moulds and increasing the size of the bullet .001 inch at a time, until the greatest degree of accuracy was secured. Also round and out-of-round bullets were tried out. As it is impossible to cut a perfectly round ball mould cavity with a cherry, Mr. Shackleford pressed out a mould, using a steel ball, and succeeded by very careful measurements in getting a mould which would cast a ball that was only out-of-round less than .001 inch. We tried this out in one of the rifles with a bullet which was out-of-round over .005 inch. If there was any difference it was in favor of the out-of-round ball! Still we are not convinced but that the more perfect is the best; at least we feel better when using it.

The Muzzle-Loading Rifle—Then and Now

All of the best known materials for patching were used, and we finally decided, after many trials, that linen was the best. We used what is commonly known as coat linen, that is, material used for ladies' coats. For the narrow grooved rifle we used a soft weave as it will fill the grooves better than any other. For the wider grooves we used a finer, harder weave. The thickness of the linen used for both was .015 inch. We decided in favor of linen because it was of more uniform thickness and would absorb the saliva better, giving a more uniform lubrication than any other material.

Regarding bullet size, the old rule still holds good; a bullet that will go through the barrel under the weight of the ramrod is a good rule to follow. The tightness of the bullet and patch should require from 18 to 20 pounds of pressure to seat the bullet down on the powder, and the patch should fill the grooves. We arrived at this by unbreeching the barrel, then pushing a patched bullet through until the imprint of the grooves on the patch showed that it was filling them to the bottom.

We arrived at the powder charge in the following manner. Starting at one dram we increased the load one-quarter dram until the limit of accuracy was reached. With the various calibers that we were using, we found that FFG Kings Semi-Smokeless gave the best results. The old rule—"one-fourth the weight of the ball in powder"—is still a good one to go by. This has been the rule handed down for more than a century. This amount of powder will give a velocity of around 1,400 feet and is about the highest velocity that can be attained with a round patched ball and still retain accuracy.

Slow ignition is another factor which affects accuracy. The long sweep of the hammer and the blow to the nipple has an important bearing on accuracy. We discovered with the use of the telescope that the blow of the hammer moved the barrel in spite of the steadiest hold, using muzzle and elbow rest.

The percussion cap is slow and when the ignition takes place through a slender tube some time elapses before the complete ignition is achieved. We speeded up the lock-time by shortening the

Modern Vs. Old-time Methods

throw of the hammer and by using a very stiff mainspring. This was the English method, but it seems never to have been taken up by the gunsmiths in America. We also used the nipple with the cone-shaped opening, the large part of the cone up and the small hole next to the powder. When the cap explodes, this converges the flame, and it is driven through the small hole with a very intense heat, which quickens the ignition. Powder residue is continually changing the shape of the powder chamber and unless the rifle is wiped out carefully this has an effect on the results of the shots.

We wiped the bore carefully after each shot, being certain that the wiping rag was uniform and reached the bottom of the grooves. We moistened the rag, either with saliva or water, and when we inserted it in the bore were sure that it followed the grooves. We pushed this down very slowly, so that the fouling would be moistened. After reaching the breech, we allowed it to remain several seconds so that the powder residue would be softened, then carefully removed the rod, allowing it to follow the spiral of the grooves. We found that the powder fouling in the grooves was moistened as the rod was pushed down and came out very readily as we removed the patched wiping rod. We were always careful to wipe the barrel the same way every time. This is one of the most important operations in using a muzzle-loader.

A starter was used to seat the bullet the same depth in the bore each time. The old method of cutting the patching off with a knife each loading insures the exact centering of the bullet in the patch. The bullet is seated about three-sixteenths of an inch in the bore before the patch is cut off. We tried both methods of seating the bullet, neck or sprue down and up, but could not find any difference in accuracy. The bullet should be seated in the same position each time, however. In these tests we used either peep sights or telescope and found that there is very little difference in fifty yards, the peep sight getting just as good groups as the telescope.

We also found that a very slight taper bore gave better accuracy, but this should be not more than .001 inch or less larger at the breech than the muzzle. If too large, it will cause the patch to slip and this is one of the chief causes of off-shot. When the bore is not perfectly wiped out and the fouling accumulates at the breech, this will cause the bullet to slip its patch. One of the most common causes of variations, especially where an old barrel has been dressed out, is the condition of the bore at the breech. In looking through the bore, it seems to be all right, but from corrosion and lack of care the iron at the breech often has become porous and soon gives away with use and either cuts the patch or causes it to slip.

In working over barrels for these tests the special reamers were used on two of them. The others were cut by the old method and one barrel was rebored and rerifled. We used the cast in the bore with saw for cutting the grooves deeper, using tissue paper for raising the saw. In the slow pitch grooving, we used longer saws with more teeth, but in steeper pitches, like one turn in four feet, we used not more than four teeth. These were set two each way and made to cut both ways. The saw must be carefully set in the cast or it will cut one side of the groove deeper than the other. A lead cast working through the bore will wear and have a tendency to cut the groove wider. We also used a land saw for cutting the lands. To secure the best results in cutting the bore by this method, it is recommended that brass guides be set in the cast so that they may guide the cutter in the groove and counteract the natural tendency to cut wider. The saw for the groove and the saw for cutting the lands can both be used at the same time and it is better to use them in this manner as a truer bore will be achieved. When the bore is finished, a few slight cuts from the breech to the muzzle will relieve the bore at the breech. tending to make for greater accuracy.

The great question of whether modern tools and machinery can build a better and more accurate muzzle-loading rifle has been settled in our minds, at least, and we contend most emphatically that they cannot.

Modern machinery, gas welding and electric furnaces can fashion the old tools more easily and perhaps better than the old hand

Modern Vs. Old-time Methods

methods. But these tools, handled in the old way, are still supreme, and we found that it was necessary to use the old long bit on all but one barrel to get the best results. The long bit has come down from the dim past and is one of the oldest gun shop tools. It was known in the distant past as the Armorers Bit; and so far there has not been anything developed to take its place. In the boring of the long barrel or in cutting down the lands, there is no other tool that will give the highly polished surface to the bore. The long bit requires skill and knowledge to handle correctly, but when once mastered, there is nothing quite equal to it.

CHAPTER IX.

PROVING ACCURACY BY TESTS

THE famous scout of Tennessee pioneer days, Abraham Castleman, possessed a rifle he loved, he said, as much as if it were a sweetheart, and he gave it the name "Betsy". The remarkable things "Betsy" had done and would do in the shooting game were often related by Castleman. One of his stories was that on one occasion "She girdled a white oak, nicked the epidermis of an Indian's back, knocked over a catamount, brought down a flock of turkeys from the tree tops, laid out a buffalo, blazed a section of land, split enough boards to cover a shanty."

I have never claimed so much for any gun I have owned, even my "Long Tom",—but I believe in the accuracy of the old rifles. In an article published in the *American Rifleman,* January 1926, Captain Richard related the incident of the Kentuckian Kirk's shooting of an Indian across the Maumee River, at a distance of six hundred yards, when Fort Meigs was besieged by the Indians.

I believed the story. Many riflemen expressed doubt as to the possibilities of the old muzzle-loading flintlock rifle accomplishing such a feat, and to those not familiar with the capabilities of these old rifles this narrative may well seem incredible.

I decided to try out a flintlock rifle at the range at which Kirk made his celebrated shot. I have a number of flintlock rifles, but the caliber of the rifles I possess are not as large as I thought necessary for this experiment. Therefore I rebored and rifled a barrel of a caliber I thought would be best suited for this attempt. I selected a flintlock rifle which weighed 11 pounds.

The bore of the rifle selected had seen its best days, so I rebored and recut the grooves as nearly like the original as possible. This gave me a 40-inch barrel of seven grooves, the pitch of the grooves being one turn in 48 inches, and carrying a bullet of 220 grains.

The result of the trial was surprising as to range, penetration and accuracy.

Proving Accuracy by Tests

The trial was made on a lake a few miles out of Chattanooga, where I was able to secure the elevation.

The rifle was first loaded with a priming charge of 25 grains of FFFG black powder, followed by 50 grains of FG black powder. On top of this a ⅛-inch felt wad was placed. Then the bullet was patched with heavy drilling greased with tallow.

With the old rifle loaded I offered the first shot to any one of my friends who would volunteer for the honor. All declined. I had taken a great deal of kidding about the test, and numerous remarks had been made, such as:

"The bullet won't go half-way."

"The old thing won't make even a splash in the water."

"How are you going to tell where the bullet goes?"

"When you shoot, I'll walk around the lake and be there when the bullet gets there and see where it hits."

Only I had faith in my rifle and the trial.

With the sight raised to the highest elevation, I touched the set trigger. Following the report, there was a splash in the water about a foot under the target which had been put in place at the distance of 600 yards. This showed my confidence had not been misplaced. I fired ten shots before inspection was made of the target. Of these, *four would have hit a man*. The others were close to the target.

This trial was a demonstration of the fact, beyond doubt, that the Kentuckian, Kirk, got his Indian.

One of the bullets penetrated into the ground six inches and it was the opinion of an army rifleman, who was present, that this bullet would have put a man out of commission at much longer range than the 600 yards.

Now, for the remaining part of this chapter, I am going to leave the story of muzzle-loading target rifle accuracy to the capable pen of my friend Captain Philip P. Quayle, of the Peters Cartridge Company, who writes as follows concerning the test which he has made with a favorite rifle from my collection:

The story has been told of a gentleman who visited a museum after imbibing too freely and who, when confronted by the mounted

The Muzzle-Loading Rifle—Then and Now

skeleton of a dinosaur, some 60 feet in length, is reported to have said, "G'wan, y'ain't real."

With similar skepticism the shooting fraternity, as a whole, has received evidences of unusually accurate targets fired with muzzle-loading rifles.

In books such as Cleveland's *"Hints to Riflemen"* and Barber's *"Crack Shot"* and others, are reproduced targets fired at ranges varying from 110 to 220 yards, the shot groups of which appear to be absolutely incredible in comparison with breechloaders.

However, at ranges up to 200 yards, at least it is highly probable that the most accurate shooting which has ever been done has been accomplished with heavy, muzzle-loading target rifles equipped with telescopic sights, set triggers, false muzzles and bullet starters.

A test was made of Walter Cline's N. Whitmore rifle, which is one of the finest examples of the handmade target rifle. This rifle is a cased set, made by N. Whitmore, and is complete with original mould, swage, bullet starter, wiping rod and other accessories.

This N. Whitmore rifle has the following specifications:

Length of barrel 31¾ inches, over all, including false muzzle and patent breech.

The rifling is cut on a gain twist which measured every 30 degrees reads as follows:

Angle	*Distance from the breech*
30 degrees	6 1/2 inches
60 degrees	11 13/16 inches
90 degrees	16 1/2 inches
120 degrees	21 inches
150 degrees	24 7/16 inches
180 degrees	27 3/4 inches
Bore diameter	0.432 inches
Rifling or groove diameter	0.448 inches
Depth of rifling	0.008 inches
Width of rifling groove	0.103 inches
Width of rifling lands	0.069 inches
Weight of the rifle including false muzzle	16 1/2 pounds

Proving Accuracy by Tests

The bullets of the flat-end picket type were cast, hammered and then swaged after which they were weighed and only those selected which were within 0.5 of a grain of the standard bullet weight used which, in this case, was 225 grains.

For the best results with one of the muzzle-loading target rifles of the type tested, the bullet, which is cast of pure lead, should cut about half way into the grooves, the patch filling the remaining space.

The caps used were those of the Winchester Repeating Arms Company, No. 12 Foil Lined.

The patch was of fine linen $\frac{7}{8}$-inch in diameter and 0.008-inch thick.

The powder charge giving the most uniform velocity consisted of 64.7 grains of FFG King's Semi-Smokeless giving a mean muzzle velocity of 1,638 feet per second. All powder charges were weighed to within 0.1 of a grain.

This rifle was equipped with a set trigger of the single type and a full length telescope having a magnification of approximately 12 diameters. The telescope is adjustable for windage by means of a dovetailed piece let into the barrel at the muzzle. Changes in elevation are made by a finely cut elevating screw at the breech end of the telescope.

In all the tests made with this rifle the bore was scrupulously cleaned after each shot.

As to the gain twist on which the rifling of the arm is cut no importance attaches to it as such but rather to the fact that the final twist of one turn in approximately 40 inches was particularly suited to the ball and charge combination of this rifle.

As to the gain twist, it has its slowest pitch where the velocity is lowest and its greatest pitch where its velocity is a maximum. Furthermore, the ball starts with one pitch on loading and has another when loaded, the process being reversed when firing.

If the bullet does not strip or cut its patch when it leaves the muzzle the only effect of the rifling governing its flight is the pitch or rate of turning with which it left the barrel.

This principle was recognized by Busk and other eminent writers of the period of transition from muzzle to breech-loading arms.

The Muzzle-Loading Rifle—Then and Now

After some experimenting in the laboratory with various powders and carefully measuring the velocity by means of our precision oscillograph, a charge of 64.7 grains of King's Semi-Smokeless powder was selected.

With some of the powder charges the variation in velocity was such that a vertical dispersion of over five inches would have resulted from their use.

It is of course evident that when the proper load is determined, as it was in this case, the arm in question has every advantage over those in which the "cut and try" methods must be used due to lack of the proper equipment.

Much depends upon finding the charge which is best fitted to the arm in question, for a powder which gives excellent results in one rifle may be productive of great errors in another.

A charge of powder which gives excellent results in a given arm with one weight and configuration of bullet may produce very unsatisfactory results if the bullet is appreciably modified.

In loading the rifle used in the test, a felt wad 3/16-inch in thickness was seated on the powder. This wad was of such diameter as to fit snugly into the barrel.

For the test the N. Whitmore rifle was taken to the range in its case and there assembled. The bore was carefully wiped out and a cap snapped on the tube to be sure that it was clear. In this connection Forsyth, in his excellent book *"The Sporting Rifle and Its Projectiles"*, says of the double rifles then in use, "Snap a cap on each, barrel, pointed downwards at a straw or such like, and if this is blown away by the gas, I load." This is exceedingly good advice to heed in loading a percussion arm.

When it was determined that the barrel was clear, one of the weighed charges of 64.7 grains of King's Semi-Smokeless powder was poured into the muzzle using a small wooden funnel provided for the purpose. The felt wad was then seated down on the powder but never *rammed*.

It is, of course, to be understood that the false muzzle is always in place except when firing.

Proving Accuracy by Tests

Having properly seated the powder charge, and wad, a linen patch 0.008-inch in thickness and ⅞-inch in diameter was first wet with saliva and then accurately centered in the depression in the false muzzle provided for this purpose.

One of the weighed bullets was then placed accurately in the center of this patch, the bullet starter set in place and the bullet seated down into the rifling of the barrel by striking the plunger of the starter with the palm of the hand. The bullet starter on this rifle was so made that it would fit only in a certain way, but on many of these old rifles the starter may be turned through 360 degrees. With starters of this latter type both plunger and guide should be lightly marked, say with a center punch, and the punch marks always turned towards the sight or some other fixed position when loading. This precaution will eliminate variations due to any lack of concentricity in the starter itself.

When the bullet and patch were seated in the barrel by the starter they were then seated down on the powder wad with a loading rod having a flat end. A loading rod having a concave end or a cavity fitting the nose of the bullet should not be used since such a rod is apt to alter the axis of the bullet as determined by the false muzzle and bullet starter.

Here again the bullet is merely firmly seated on the powder. It is never rammed under any circumstance. In regard to this matter Busk says, "The instant the bullet is felt to have reached the powder, the rod should be withdrawn—no second stroke, however, should be given."

Having completed the loading operation the loading rod is withdrawn, the falze muzzle removed, the cap placed on the tube and the arm is ready to fire.

Loading in this manner, two shots were first fired to warm the gun and to settle the telescope in its clamping rings after which five shots were fired for record.

All firing with this rifle was done with a muzzle and breech rest since the maximum accuracy of the rifle was what it was desired to determine.

The Muzzle-Loading Rifle—Then and Now

This target was the only one fired, and while the result was by no means the best ever obtained, it is certainly very remarkable. All the shot holes may be covered by a silver dollar and all touch a five-cent piece.

The extreme horizontal measures 1⅛ inches, the extreme vertical measures ⅞ inch and the mean radius is 7/16 inch.

When it is considered that a width of 1⅛ inches in 186 yards represents an angle whose tangent is about one in 6,000, the accuracy of this rifle and telescope combination appears well nigh incredible.

The aiming point used in firing the target was approximately 15 inches below the group but as the group size was all that was wanted no attempt was made to shift the center of impact.

It is realized that an inspection of the target will, in many circles, provoke the remark of the gentleman alluded to in the first paragraph of this article. However, it should be realized that the best of the target rifles of the 60's were related in name only to their muzzle-loading contemporaries of the common type.

In conclusion, it is realized that while the type of shooting thus described may be considered impractical by many, still, if the object in view is to hit the target with a minimum dispersion, then the Whitmore type of rifle on which this test was made appears to be most satisfactory.

CHAPTER X.
HUNTING IN THE GREAT SMOKIES

I WAS a young man when I went to hunt in the Smoky Mountains, for the first time, and I went with all the enthusiasm and expectation of a young man.

I had hunted from early boyhood in the country in which I was born, but the great forest of the southern mountains where such men as Boone, Crockett and the long riflemen hunted, challenged me and called until at last I found it possible to make my dream become a reality.

At this time, in 1900, no one could find his way in the unbroken forest of the Great Smokies without a guide born and reared in the mountains. My guide was L. G. Moore, known in the Smokies as "Daddy," a hardy mountaineer who had carved out a home and a living from the steep slopes of the mountain forest. Daddy was a veteran bear hunter who could find his way over dim trails, hidden by laurel, rhododendron and the running green brier, which is a bane to the stranger in the wilderness.

Daddy was to become my guide, teacher, boon companion, and friend in the years which were to follow my entry into the Smokies. He was to teach me that which no man may learn from books, the quest of game and the secrets of the woods. I drank deep of an invisible cup which has sustained me since that time. I came to the forest on horseback. I entered it on foot.

One eats of the kill on the hunt, and corn cake which is taken along. At the cabin there may be sweet potatoes, sorghum with the corn pones, and coffee or something stronger. In the cabin, too, a squirrel, or deer, or bear, or rabbit may fry or roast. On the hunt, one may have a wash-up in a creek or not, as he may wish. But on the hunt one hunts from dawn (the false dawn at that), until late. There are animals one hunts in the night. There are trails where bears frequent; there are waters where deer come to drink. On the hunt, one must learn to see on the trail the bear tracks; one must learn to hear the whistle-grunt of the wild pig, and one must endure hardship. No slacker may handle the long rifle.

The Muzzle-Loading Rifle—Then and Now

A bed of leaves under a cliff, a fire of brush in front, rifles carefully laid aside,—no more was given by the night except sleep for the regeneration of a body racked by trail climbing. Daddy taught of the frontier life, of pathless forests and the hunt, where only marksmanship could save a man from death.

I have owned a percussion rifle, secured from Elisha Green of the Great Smoky Mountains, which was a typical Southern mountaineer's rifle. Its barrel was a 43½-inch octagon; it was .45 caliber, with full-length stock of black walnut. It was plain iron mounted. Its weight was 9½ pounds.

One so like it only an expert would distinguish the difference in weight, I was shouldering the day I shot my first bear and qualified for promotion in the eyes of Daddy Moore. To him I was on the trail to a hunter's goal; but to the outside world I became "a big game hunter."

Three years after I entered the Great Smoky forests for the first time, I again took the Little River Road to the fork where Daddy Moore waited for me. Once there we shouldered our packs and hit the trail up the middle prong, our destination being a herder's camp ten miles back in the mountains. We passed Daddy's cabin on the way, where his son Ashley joined us, with three bear dogs. I think that the ten miles to camp were the longest ten miles I ever traveled. We finally reached our destination near night. It was close up under the high tops of the Great Smokies. After a supper cooked over a campfire, we turned in and slept the sleep of the weary.

Ashley took the dogs and made an early start before daylight the next morning, to get over on the other side of the mountain in order to begin the drive, since bear is hunted the same way one hunts foxes. They are known to have crossing places in the low gaps, where, if started on a certain mountain side, they will always cross. Daddy Moore stationed me on a crossing place, with the instruction to keep still, and when I heard the dogs to keep a close watch so I could tell if they were coming my way. He showed me a rock on the trail and told me that he had killed two bears there the year before. All I had to do, Daddy said, if the bear came that way, was to wait till he was crossing that rock and then whistle. When I whistled the bear would stop and look around, so I could shoot him. Daddy told me to shoot the bear in the white spot under his throat. It sounded easy, but one feels differently about it when it's a first bear hunt and one has not seen a bear previously outside of a circus!

Daddy went away and left me there alone. I told myself I was not afraid, but I found I was near a most likely looking tree, which gave me comfort. Before long I heard the dogs yelp occasionally. This went on for some time, to be broken by a chorus yelping which told me that they had located a feed trail, which meant that in chestnut time the bear laps the trees, as the mountaineers call it, because the bear climbs the trees, breaks off limbs, then gets down and eats the chestnuts out of the burrs. A bear will work one tree as long as the chestnuts last. We had climbed about four thousand feet above the camp to a place where Daddy had located this bear in a chestnut grove. The clouds were down and it was dark and misty. Finally I saw a dim outline of something moving. Daddy appeared beside me. "Shoot," he whispered. "Take him right behind the foreleg."

I shot, and my first bear was dead on the trail! He weighed (so Daddy estimated), 450 pounds.

We struck a new trail after my shot, because one bear often means another. Near the top of the trail, a yearling bear crossed in front of us at about 150 yards. Daddy killed it with his first shot. We were then about four miles from camp, on the head waters of Shut-In Creek. This is one of the most difficult sections to penetrate and we had a 125-pound bear to get out. By crawling and dragging the bear we reached camp. Daddy had had on a pair of overalls, but he left that garment, piece by piece, on the briers. He made the last two miles in his undergarments. I was scratched until I looked as if I had been in a fight, but bear, men and rifles came at last to camp.

The big job: How to get *my* bear out was now before us. Daddy and I had rolled him down about half way to the open woods when Daddy proposed securing help from below, at Bill Stinnett's cabin. He returned after a half hour without Bill but did bring an ax. He had decided to dress the bear and carry him away on a pole.

The Muzzle-Loading Rifle—Then and Now

That afternoon was spent in cutting up the bear and getting it ready to pack out. We stayed at Stinnett's that night, Daddy and I sleeping on the puncheon floor before the fire. Bear steak, corn bread, and coffee make a splendid supper for toil-worn men.

Daddy maintains that I know nothing of what a scare may mean to a man. He told me of the time he went on a bear hunt; it was his turn to take the dogs and drive; he had a bear up and going and decided that he could reach the crossing before the bear did. He reached the crossing at the same time the bear did. He insisted this is a real "fix" for any hunter. The bear, instead of leaving the field, chased Daddy round and round a tree. Daddy made a dozen revolutions around that tree trying to find time to reload the muzzleloader. He yelled for the dogs as he ran. Finally, after spilling a half dozen charges of powder, he managed to reload. The dogs came and closed in. Daddy was given a chance to shoot, and he killed his bear.

"Muzzle-loaders ——" I began.

"None better on earth!" interrupted Daddy positively and firmly.

* * * * *

For ten years I hunted each year in the forest of the Smokies before I made a trip to Clingman's Dome, going in by way of Townsend and the old Anderson Road to the crest of the Smokies, which was sixteen miles west of the dome. Daddy met me this trip at the fork of the Little River, and told me that on account of the failure of the mast (no acorns and chestnuts) bears were gone from the forest, unless there might be some among the beech groves on the mountain tops.

The first night we spent at the Spence cabin, west of Thunderhead. There we could have a fire and shelter; but the second night was not comfortable because we could have only one blanket each and a few provisions, and the climb was so steep there was no sheltering cliff to bed beneath. The third day we reached Clingman's Dome, densely wooded with balsam. That night the earth and everything above it froze solid. I felt as if I had frozen, and I yet wonder how we survived that long night of cold and hunger. The

Hunting in the Great Smokies

Cherokee name for Clingman's Dome is "Kuwahi", meaning the Mulberry Place, but I saw no berries nor bears that day.

As is often the case in the Smoky forest, the weather was milder next day, and we descended to a lower level and to a cabin, where a hot hearth and coffee and corn pones drew the ice from our bones.

Daddy smoked in contentment for sometime before he said it was squirrel season and we'd better hit the trail, and forget bears for the time being.

Audubon, writing about Kentucky sports in the early days, mentioned that he once went hunting with Daniel Boone near Frankfort. On this trip he was introduced to the art of "barking" squirrels by this veteran marksman. This, Aubudon states, calls for the greatest skill and accuracy in the use of the rifle.

I wanted to try squirrel barking. I had seen it done many times by old riflemen using the long-barreled muzzle-loader, and shooting close enough so that the squirrel was killed by the concussion of the ball against the bark of the tree, (hence, the term "barking"). A rifle carrying a half-ounce ball is the best size. I had brought with me a beautiful flintlock rifle. I had recut the grooves and smoothed out the barrel, and mounted a three-power telescope and set it for thirty yards.

Daddy was much interested in this flintlock rifle.

"I have hunted many a day with one," he said, "killed many a bear and deer."

Daddy, however, scorned the telescope. He said he did not want "nary one of them things on my rifle". And he did not, he could bark squirrels without it. He said he would show me how it was done. He told me that when squirrels were plentiful in the forest in the early days of his people, one could stand in a cabin door and shoot them for the pot.

"We barked squirrels then just to keep our hand in," he assured me with a solemn nod of his head.

On our way to Chestnut Ridge, a half mile from Daddy's cabin, where squirrels could always be found, we were joined by Queen, one of the best squirrel dogs I ever worked with. Half way up the ridge, Daddy decided to wait for squirrels to put in an appearance.

The Muzzle-Loading Rifle—Then and Now

The old dog lay at our feet as we sat on a log, seeming to know that there was nothing doing as yet. After a half hour, suddenly just below us there appeared a squirrel, sitting, as did we, on a log.

Holding the cross hairs just under him at what I thought was the proper distance, I touched the trigger. There was a click, a puff of smoke, and splinters flew,—so did the squirrel! When he lit, he lit a-running with the dog a close second, but he beat her to an old dead snag with a hole in it, and that was the last we saw of that squirrel. An examination of the log showed that I had held too low. The half-ounce ball had torn a splinter a foot long out of the log just under where the squirrel had been sitting, but too low; I had only shocked the feelings of that squirrel!

Daddy told Queen to "hunt 'em up" and it was only a few minutes until she barked "treed"! Daddy went to the tree. "I'll see," he said, "if there is a hole in the tree. If there is not I'll turn him up for you. Then you shoot so that the ball will just cut the bark under and behind his foreleg."

Daddy walked around the tree, shaking the bushes as he went. Suddenly there was a slight scratching and about 75 feet up the tree appeared the squirrel. This time I had a good rest for my flintlock and 75 grains of FFG black powder sent the half ounce of lead true,—and the squirrel went off the tree as if a cyclone had hit him. He struck the ground at Daddy's feet. I had barked my first squirrel! There was not a drop of blood to be seen.

I barked two squirrels that day as perfectly as Daniel Boone himself could have done, but, as Audubon said, it calls for the greatest skill and accuracy with the rifle, and there were three other squirrels shot that morning that I did not bark.

The environment of the lonely Smoky forest means that the rifle must provide the kill for the table. Bear must be salted and smoked for the winter meat. Deer must be treated after the Indian fashion. Turkey, squirrel, rabbit, each in season, must be brought in for the pot on the hearth. The rifle is the hunter's only defense from starvation for those for whom he must provide. Rifle accuracy in the forest of the Great Smoky Mountains is amazing, deadly, and sure.

Hunting in the Great Smokies

"Necessity, the mother of invention," is responsible for the crafts of the Smokies, which are gun making, metal working (even in silver), weaving of great beauty, skin tanning, curing of furs, pottery making, hammering of pots and kettles from iron in the mountain forges, chair making, etc.

Without the rifle there could be no homes in this beautiful virgin forest.

* * * * *

When I sold my collection, there passed from my ownership the "turkey call," used in the mountains to "fool 'em and catch 'em" as I was told on the Cumberland Plateau. It was a cedar box call I sold for ten dollars.

I have fooled wild turkeys and caught them with a shot through the head. I have found them good roast on the trail. But Daddy Moore told a better campfire story about a turkey call than any one of my own or any one I have heard.

Daddy Moore lay in front of a fire in the Smoky Mountains one night, quietly smoking when I said I hoped we shot turkey next day. Daddy was silent for a long time before he said: "A turkey box once came near costing me my life!"

I waited.

Daddy Moore said that one morning he went out before daylight to watch a turkey roost he had located. He hid on an oak stump that had bushes grown up around it and waited for the turkeys to move preliminary to getting down from the roost. Then he began turkey calling, thinking what a splendid turkey roast there would be for his family that day. The turkeys listened and one came slowly and inquiringly a few paces. Daddy reached for his muzzle-loader and was in the act of shooting, when something hit him a tremendous blow in the back, knocking him off the stump and sending his gun skywards. From the ground where he landed he looked to see what had hit him, and found himself looking into the eyes of a catamount. The beast had heard him turkey calling and thought the imitation a real turkey in the bushes. He had pounced for a turkey breakfast.

The Muzzle-Loading Rifle—Then and Now

Daddy Moore never told a lie, nor for that matter overstated a fact. He said the catamount and he looked at each other for a long minute—no more—and then each went his own way as rapidly as possible. The turkeys scattered.

"That catamount," drawled Ashley, "knew about a man and he knew about a muzzle-loader, but he couldn't quite connect the two with a 'turkey call.' He musta reasoned with himself a minute and then decided that he could get more turkeys without runnin' the risk of Pap gettin' the muzzle-loader in action. I allus say that a catamount has got sense."

CHAPTER XI.

MOUNTAIN SMITHS AND THEIR CRAFTSMANSHIP

(Editorial Note—Mr. Cline, at the time of his death, had not completed this chapter giving short biographical sketches of early gunsmiths. Through the courtesy of Mr. Henry Howard, of Chattanooga, Tennessee, we are privileged to introduce this chapter by Mr. Howard's description of early gunsmithing in the mountains. He has firsthand knowledge of the making of rifles in the Great Smokies where he lived in his youth, and he often helped the smiths to construct the earth furnaces for the smelting of iron and he has always been interested in the craftsmanship of the early gunsmiths of the Southern Mountain areas. So it is from the pen of Mr. Howard that we offer you the following contribution to this work, "Methods of Early Gunsmiths," after which will follow some random notes and sketches taken from the files of the incomplete manuscript which Mr. Cline left.)

* * * * *

Early Gunsmithing

THE earliest settlers in the southern mountains were dependent on rifles for both food and defense. Not long after settlement some of the pioneers began to look around for means of supplying these much needed rifles.

Iron was made by our forefathers in the mountains of the South. It was made in little furnaces, called water blasts. The pioneers had some knowledge of one of the earliest known ways of smelting iron,—a hollowed out place in the ground, with a tube running into it to provide means of blowing in air. This originated in the Province of Catalonia in Spain and was known as a Catalonian forge.

Iron ore was discovered in many places in these mountains and charcoal was burned for use in smelting. This charcoal was simply mixed with iron in small earthen furnaces near some waterfall. A few split boards and a hollow log provided a crude vertical standpipe, in which water poured from as much elevation as they were able to use. This water carried with it a considerable amount of air, which was compressed as the water reached the bottom of the pipe; and as it neared the discharge, this compressed air was trapped in a box-like chamber at the discharge point and from this it was directed into the mixture of iron ore and charcoal.

When the blast was completed and the furnace cleared, a small amount of charcoal iron suitable for gun barrels would be found in the bottom. The early gunmakers would then reheat this iron in small forges, where the air would be provided by the well known bellows, and the bellows were also easily made by these early gunsmiths.

In most instances the iron would be hammered into flat bars little longer than the wanted gun barrel. After the laborious, hand process on their crude anvils, the smiths would start the final welding of this flat bar around a small iron rod which provided the first rough bore. After this first rough bore, the barrel would be in crude octagon shape, or round, whichever way the smith preferred.

After the weld was completed and the barrel hammered to such finish as the smith desired, it would be taken to his boring machine, which was but a hewn log on which notched pieces of wood were attached by hand-hammered spikes or drift bolts. The barrels were clamped into the notches of these timbers with wooden wedges, at the same time aligning the barrel with another set of notched timbers, which would hold their rods and rifling machines for the completion of the boring and rifling.

The boring was carried on with an armourer's bit, which is simply a square of steel slightly smaller than the desired bore and anywhere from a few inches to a foot long. This was welded on the end of a round rod slightly smaller in diameter than the bit. The bit would be sharpened on grindstones made from sandstone found in sections of the country.

Mountain Smiths and their Craftsmanship

The early smiths could provide their cutting bits by hammering their charcoal iron thus producing a low carbon steel. This was chilled to sufficient hardness by heating and dropping into water.

The smith would bend a crank or attach a handwheel by binding to one side of his squared bit a strip of hickory wood which he would make oval to approximately the curve of the original welding rod. This piece of hickory would be attached or bound at the ends only in order that the smith could make the bit sufficiently tight in the barrel to make a slight cut in the barrel metal as it was twisted with a rotary motion slowly forward and backward through the barrel.

After each cut the smith would slip a piece of paper or very thin fiber between the bit and the hickory strip each time he wanted to enlarge the bore, and this would be repeated until the bore was completed in accordance with the idea or intention for that particular rifle.

Upon the completion of the bore to the exact caliber desired, the barrel was then ready for the rifling. This was accomplished by two methods even in the earliest attempts to make an accurate shooting gun. Some of the earliest rifling was accomplished by the use of another barrel similar to the one in process of making. This barrel would be clamped on the same log as the one to be rifled and a small iron rod, slightly longer than both barrels when in position, would be inserted in the barrel, which had been previously rifled, with the end of the rod just about ready to enter the new barrel. A slug of lead would be poured around the rod at the rear end of the barrel which had been previously rifled from a guide for the rod and it would twist as it was pushed forward in exact relation to the rifling in the previously completed barrel.

The cutting bit for the new rifle was a small piece of steel which was about one-sixth inch thick, about one inch long, and contained from three to five cutting teeth, which were merely points with straight cutting top edges and looked very much like teeth on a hand saw. This piece of steel would be let into a short piece of hickory

The Muzzle-Loading Rifle—Then and Now

which had been fitted to the bore and which would be pushed backward and forward through the two barrels,—the new barrel receiving the rifling cut and the old barrel doing the guiding.

The groove in the piece of hickory to hold the cutter bit would be cut at an angle as near as possible to the twist of the rifling. This would be raised many times during the cutting process by lifting the cutter bit out of the groove and placing under it a piece of paper or fiber in order to press the bit against the iron for the cut in the barrel.

To start a new rifle the gun-maker would pull the rod out far enough to clear the lead slug from the rear barrel and he would then turn the slug to the next rifle in the old barrel which would provide the necessary guide for the next rifle to be made in the new gun barrel. The other method of rifling barrels was by using the rifling machine (a grooved cylinder and head block) described and illustrated elsewhere in this volume.

There was no standard for the number of rifles or lands,—neither was there a standard for the gain or twist, nor the depth of cut to be given the rifle. Each gunmaker had his own notion. Most of the old rifles would turn out to be very accurate in the hands of expert marksmen. There was always considerable argument at the "turkey shoot" or "matches" about all these points, and much pleasant argument wherever a number of the marksmen got together.

While the means and methods of the earliest gun-makers in the mountains of the South were always crude indeed when viewed from the standpoint of modern precision metallurgy and machinery, yet it remains a fact that those old guns were very accurate even when compared with the finest of the present day rifles.—H. H.

Random Notes From Cline File

Gunsmiths were the greatest artisans of colonial days. They were ironsmiths, silversmiths and woodworkers all in one. While artisans usually were skilled in only one medium, the pioneer gunsmiths of America excelled in all three. The same smith was able to make the barrel for a gun out of iron, then construct a stock of wood, and finally decorate this artistically with silver or brass.

Mountain Smiths and their Craftsmanship

No two rifles were ever made exactly alike. Each was made to order, and was made particularly to suit the person who would use it. The gunsmith put a part of himself into each rifle. He loved the rifle he worked on and the owner in turn took it into his affection. In fact it has been said that the pioneers cherished their rifles more than any other possession and often even more than they cherished members of their own families.

The maker's name, if shown at all, was usually on the top flat of the barrel, near the rear sight. Not often was the name on the lock the name of the maker of the gun. Sometimes the name of the rifle, Killdeer, Long Tom, Castor Oil, Sudden Death, or other designation to suit the fancy of the maker or original owner, appeared on the barrel or in some other prominent location. One barrel by Sherman, of Portsmouth, Ohio, bore a script *"Fool Killer, I Am Looking for You"*, in two places, written on with acid. The barrel surface on this rifle was badly eaten away except where this acid had been used.

The handmade gun in America reached the height of its development in the period from 1750 to 1820.

Norman S. Brockway

Norman S. Brockway, of Bellows Falls, Vermont, one of the most remarkable riflemakers of his time, and famous for his superbly accurate percussion target rifles, died only a few years ago after living to be nearly one hundred years old.

Since the revival of muzzle-loading rifle matches, the Brockway rifles, in the hands of their fortunate possessors, have been winning new laurels to add to the many won in the matches of over three-quarters of a century ago. To Norman S. Brockway the riflemen of today owe a debt for the preservation of much unwritten history of the American match rifle, together with evidence of the indisputable accuracy of this famous weapon. To Willis E. Wooster, a neighbor and friend of Mr. Brockway, I am indebted for the following information.

Norman S. Brockway was born in South Charlestown, New Hampshire, on March 13th, 1841, the family moving to Bellows

Falls, Vermont, in the year 1844. Here Norman grew to manhood, and with the breaking out of the Civil War he went to work in Springfield Armory as a filer, starting on mainsprings. Springfield at that time employed 349 filers. Sickness caused a short absence from work, and on his return he was put on the two-leaf sight for the Springfield rifled musket.

In February, 1864, he went with the Norwich Arms Company, which had a contract from the government for rifled arms. Here he was in charge of the mainspring work. His father was also employed at this place.

In March, 1865, Norman went with Smith and Wesson, where he operated a turret lathe, cutting out steel blanks for revolver cylinders. It was here that an incident occurred which foreshadowed the knowledge and skill that were to make him famous in years to come. Norman observed that the speed of his lathe was too high for fine work, and asked the chief machinist to reduce it, but the latter refused to shut the shop down to change the pulleys. However, during the noon hour Norman made the change himself, with the result that the breakage of tools was reduced, as well as the amount of cutting oil required, which latter (sperm oil) cost two dollars a gallon. His rule for maximum lathe speed was that the chip must hold together.

Brockway was working at Smith and Wesson's when President Lincoln was assassinated. The shop and all business closed, and there was great excitement among the people.

In May, 1866, Norman went to Bellows Falls, Vermont to help his father build a house. Here he also built his own shop, and started his riflemaking business on May 1st, 1867. His specialty was fine target rifles, with false muzzles, bullet starters, swages, and all the other equipment that went with them. He made all his own machinery and tools, as well as a steam engine to drive them.

He made his barrels from cast steel blanks, that were bored in his steam-driven lathe. He used a regular twist drill welded to a shank, the breech end of the barrel being held in the lathe chuck while the muzzle end was supported in a steady rest. The drill was run through a steadying die in the tool post, and was fed by the tail

Mountain Smiths and their Craftsmanship

stock. A tool resembling a pair of wooden pliers was used, clamped around the shank of the drill to prevent it from turning, yet if it got jammed it could be instantly released and allowed to turn with the barrel. Every quarter inch the drill was taken out and the chips removed, and every two inches Brockway took a mirror and threw light into the barrel to see if the drill were running off center. If it were, he ran the lathe slowly to see just where to strike the barrel to straighten it, after which he removed the barrel from the lathe, laid it on an anvil, and struck it a heavy blow with a lead hammer. This was repeated as often as necessary until the boring was finished.

After the barrel was drilled it was planed octagon in shape, and to the desired dimensions and weight. Holes were then drilled for the false muzzle, which was cut off and the pins fitted. This was then clamped in place, and the barrel was ready for reaming. For this operation all gunsmiths, including Brockway, used the so-called long bit, which was a square reamer backed with wood. A thin piece of paper was inserted between the reamer and the wood when it was necessary to raise the reamer. This tool was run through the bore twenty or thirty times, until the finish was perfect, after which the barrel was straightened. To locate the crooked places, Brockway used a piece of ground glass with a black line across it. When looking through the barrel at this glass, against the light, the black line was reflected in the surface of the bore, and wherever the line was broken there was a crook in the bore. This was removed by striking with a heavy lead hammer. After the barrel was straightened the reamer was run through again from both ends.

Norman Brockway's first barrels were rifled with a gain-twist guide loaned to him by L. Amadon, a jeweler of Bellows Falls, who was also an enthusiastic rifleman and who also made rifles. Brockway was not an advocate of the gain twist, maintaining that a bullet in passing through such a barrel was constantly undergoing change. He said that he wanted the bullets to get out of his barrels as easily and with as little difficulty as possible. He soon discarded the gain twist, and as he was familiar with the rifling guides used in Springfield Armory, he designed one according to his own ideas, with uniform pitch. He conducted many experiments with various twists, widths and depths of grooves, etc. He developed a different type of bullet from that commonly used at the time and found that one turn in 16 or 18 inches suited this long bullet of his, though he never knew one to strip even with as short a pitch as 9 inches.

The writer has three bullets as used by the Brockway rifles. One is .50 caliber and measures 1½ inches in length; one is .38 caliber and measures 1 3/16 inches in length, while the third is .34 caliber and measures 1⅛ inches in length. Test shooting on a windy day, checking against a rifle using a shorter bullet, has proved that there is much less drift with the longer bullets than with the shorter ones.

Brockway found that the number of grooves has very little to do with accuracy, and he used both six and eight grooves. Depth and width of grooves *does* affect accuracy, wide grooves and narrow lands being best. Lands should never be more than half the width of grooves. In rifling barrels Brockway used a steel rifling head similar to the one used in Springfield Armory, except that where the Armory head had two curved cutting edges, Brockway used only one. This cutter cuts in both directions, and is raised by a wooden wedge carried in a hole through the center of the rifling head, the cutter resting on this wedge. A plate on the rifling bench carries a small screw, which, when turned in, strikes the wedge at the end of the stroke, the screw being turned in each time it is necessary to raise the cutter. Only one cut at a time was made in a groove, but the cutter was run through each groove two or three times before raising. Brockway cut his grooves .005 inch deep. A fine barrel made by him measures as follows: bore, .380; pitch of grooves, one turn in 16 inches; width of grooves, .145; width of lands, .058; weight of rifle complete, 20 pounds.

After the grooves were cut to the proper depth a lead cast was made in the bore, and the latter lapped smooth with emery dust. The bore was lapped from the breech end, and all emery was put on the cast at that end, the lead cast never being permitted to go clear through the bore and out at the muzzle. After the bore had been given a perfect polish, a few strokes were made to within two inches of the muzzle, so that there would be no chance of the bore being larger at the muzzle than elsewhere. Brockway believed that the last two inches of the bore had everything to do with the accuracy, and that if this were perfect the rifle would be accurate.

Brockway made rifles in calibers from .22 to .50. To get the proper diameter for the bullet, a lead slug was pushed through the bore. The mould and swage were cut with a tool shaped like half a bullet. It was necessary to use a different form of patch with the long bullets in order to get proper lubrication, so Brockway designed the two-strip paper patch, and later the three-strip, and designed a false muzzle for loading them—a most ingenious arrangement. The paper patches were lubricated with sperm oil. As in the case of all new developments, the riflemen of that day were skeptical until Brockway demonstrated the fine accuracy of the long bullet and the strip patch. He had also tested out the long composite or two-piece bullet with hard point and soft lead base, so made in order that the bullet would not upset beyond the patch.

Brockway found that bullets cast in a mould and then swaged were not uniform. He made a trip to New York and investigated the making of lead wire in a lead-pipe factory, but found that this wire could not be used for making bullets; so he came home and built a press to work the lead cold, and press out lead wire from .22 to .50 caliber. This machine, Brockway estimated, would exert a pressure of about 64 tons. To use it he first cast a cylinder of bullet mixture 1½ inches in diameter and 5 inches long, which was then pressed into lead wire of the desired caliber. The wire was cut into lengths, weighed and then swaged. To test the performance of bullets made in this manner Brockway recovered many bullets after firing into wet sand, and also snow banks, sometimes having to dig 30 or 40 feet into the snow to reach them. He found that these bullets upset uniformly, and shortened up as much as ⅛-inch.

He used as much powder as the rifle would burn, which amount was determined by firing the rifle over snow. If any unburned grains were found on the snow the load was reduced until the entire charge was consumed. There was much discussion about the granulation of powder, but Brockway used FFG Hazard, Kentucky. He considered loading one of the most important parts of rifle shooting, and exercised great care in cleaning the bore after each shot. The first patch was used wet, and pushed slowly down the bore to dissolve the burned powder. However, the patch could not be too wet or water and powder residue would run down into the patent breech and cause misfires. The ramrod was of such length as to not quite reach the chamber in the breech. Then the bore was wiped dry with two or three dry patches, and oiled with a patch saturated with sperm oil. He found that a grain of powder left on the muzzle would start a bullet crooked in the bore; also that after each shot the powder marks extending across the muzzle must be wiped off before loading again as the force exerted by the starter in seating the bullet was enough to injure the rifling. One of the best rifles he knew of was injured in this manner, and could never again be made to shoot accurately.

Brockway lined (or "bushed" as it was called in his day) many barrels by drilling and rifling his own liners and soldering them in the barrel with soft solder. He is positive in the statement that the most accurate barrels are made this way. He also made telescope sights, boring the tubes from the solid bar, and grinding the lenses. The power of these scopes was from 4X to 10X, and they had a clear field.

Brockway made a device for determining the recoil of a rifle, and what part, if any, of the recoil took place before the bullet left the barrel. This device consisted of a brass rod attached to the rifle, with a knife mounted above it. A fine wire running across the muzzle of the rifle held the knife from touching the rod. When the rifle was fired the wire was broken and the knife dropped down on the rod, where it made a scratch the length of the recoil.

Brockway's stocks were made as straight as possible. He maintained that a stock with too much drop would flip the muzzle and tend to cause the rifle to shoot high, making it hard to hold. His stocks were made without cheekpiece or fore-end and were fastened to the barrel with a pin through the patent breech.

Norman Brockway joined the National Rifle Club in 1868. He won the medal in the years 1877, 1883, 1886, 1889, 1890, 1892, and 1899—seven years in all. He was elected secretary in 1881, and served until the last match held by the club, in 1906; this being the 49th year of the National Rifle Club matches.

He always attended the shooting matches near Bellows Falls, especially the turkey matches, where they shot at live turkeys at ranges of from 40 to 80 rods. Though the party putting on the shoot always advertised it as being at a certain number of yards, the actual range was not within 30 rods of that advertised. Brockway said that he never paid much attention to the distance, but would usually sight-in on some object even with the turkey but off to one side, such as a stone—getting laughed at by the crowd for hitting a stone instead of the turkey. But on the next shot he usually got the turkey. At one turkey shoot he watched a weather vane on a church steeple, and as it was a very windy day he was able to dope the wind and shoot when it was in the same direction as it had been for his previous winning shots. He won all the turkeys that day. At one of the most difficult turkey matches he attended, the turkey was placed on a stand set in high swamp grass, with not a thing to sight-in on. He fired twenty-two shots and never touched a turkey. At another match, which lasted for two days, the man that held the shoot moved the stand about 20 yards during the night, and Brockway said that there were plenty of misses the next day.

Brockway was always a great woodchuck hunter. The greatest number of chucks he ever bagged in one day was twenty-two. On three different occasions he killed two chucks with one shot, and always hoped to be able to kill three at one shot. He killed a chuck on his ninetieth birthday.

Norman S. Brockway is the last of that group of skilled workmen back in the percussion period who gave to the American rifleman that wonderful weapon of precision, the American target rifle, the performance of which has not been surpassed even in the present day.

Jonathan Browning

Sometime in early 1800, a gunsmith of Tennessee left the mountains and rivers of the state and followed Joseph Smith into the West, joining the Mormons at Nauvoo, Illinois. There he established a gun shop. Later he went with Brigham Young toward Utah. On this march westward a stop for the winter was made on the Missouri River near Kanesville, Iowa, and another gun shop was established by the Tennessee gunsmith. He advertised this shop in a pioneer newspaper of Kanesville, in the issue of September, 1849. It read:

"Gunsmithing

The subscriber is prepared to manufacture to order improved firearms, viz: revolving rifles and pistols; also slide guns from five to twenty shooters. All on an improved plan and he thinks not equaled this far East (farther West they may be). The emigrating and sporting community are invited to call and examine Browning's improved firearms before purchasing elsewhere. Shop eight miles south of Kanesville on Mosquito Creek, half mile south of Trading Point.   Jonathan Browning."

Jonathan Browning made enough from his trade to take the trail to Utah in two years, more or less, and very shortly afterward he opened the third gun shop in Ogden, Utah. Adjoining the shop was a small building where he made a home for himself and wife and where, in 1854, a son was born, who was named John Mose Browning.

The whole world knows the story of John Mose Browning, who at twenty-four years of age sold his first patent,—a model which was to become the Winchester single-shot rifle, and to establish a long connection with the Winchester Repeating Arms Company;—but few know that he was the son of a Tennessee gunsmith who sold his "Improved firearms" to the Forty-Niners and who went West to follow and join the Mormon faith.

John Selvridge

John Selvridge was a noted pioneer gunsmith of eastern Tennessee, who had a combined blacksmith and gunsmith shop near Cleveland, where he settled as a young man in 1826. His shop became one of the best known in the state. In 1845 he took as his apprentice Meredith Wolfe, who later became the excellent gunsmith of Chattanooga.

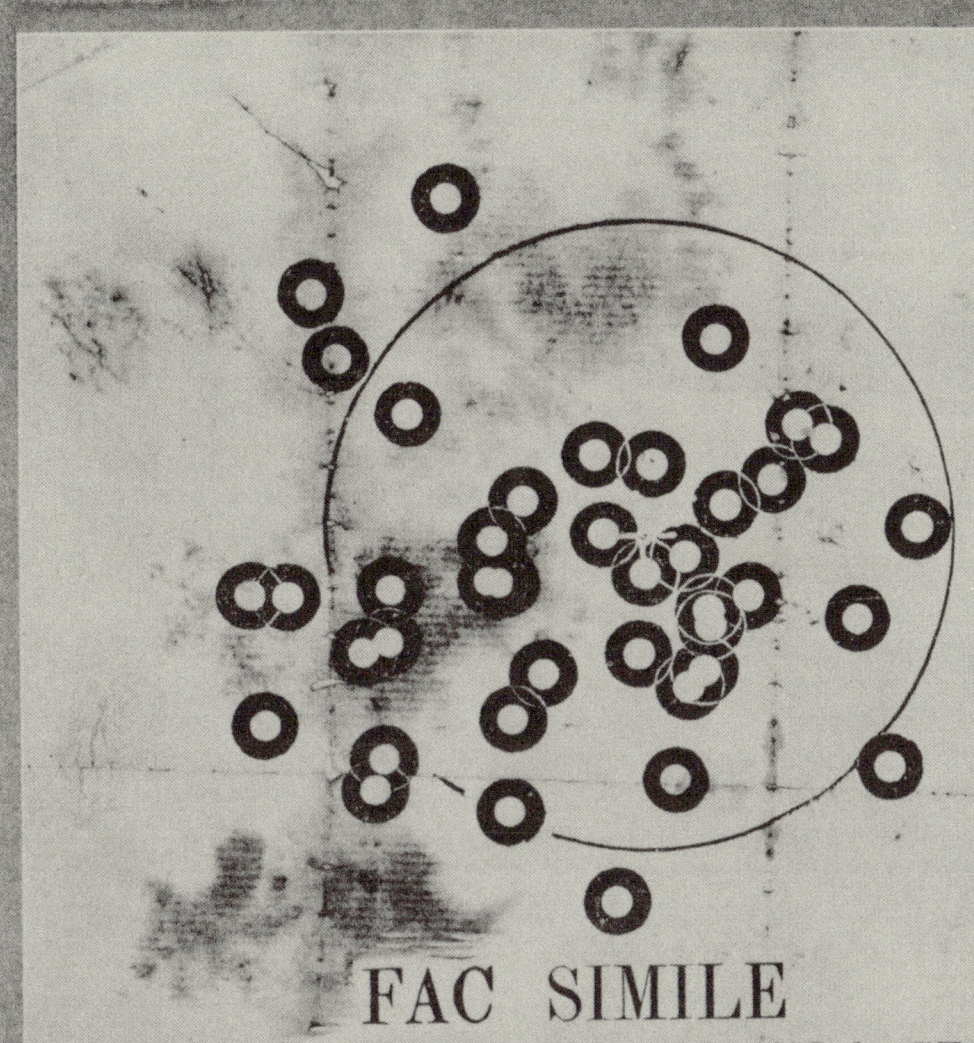

PLATE 20

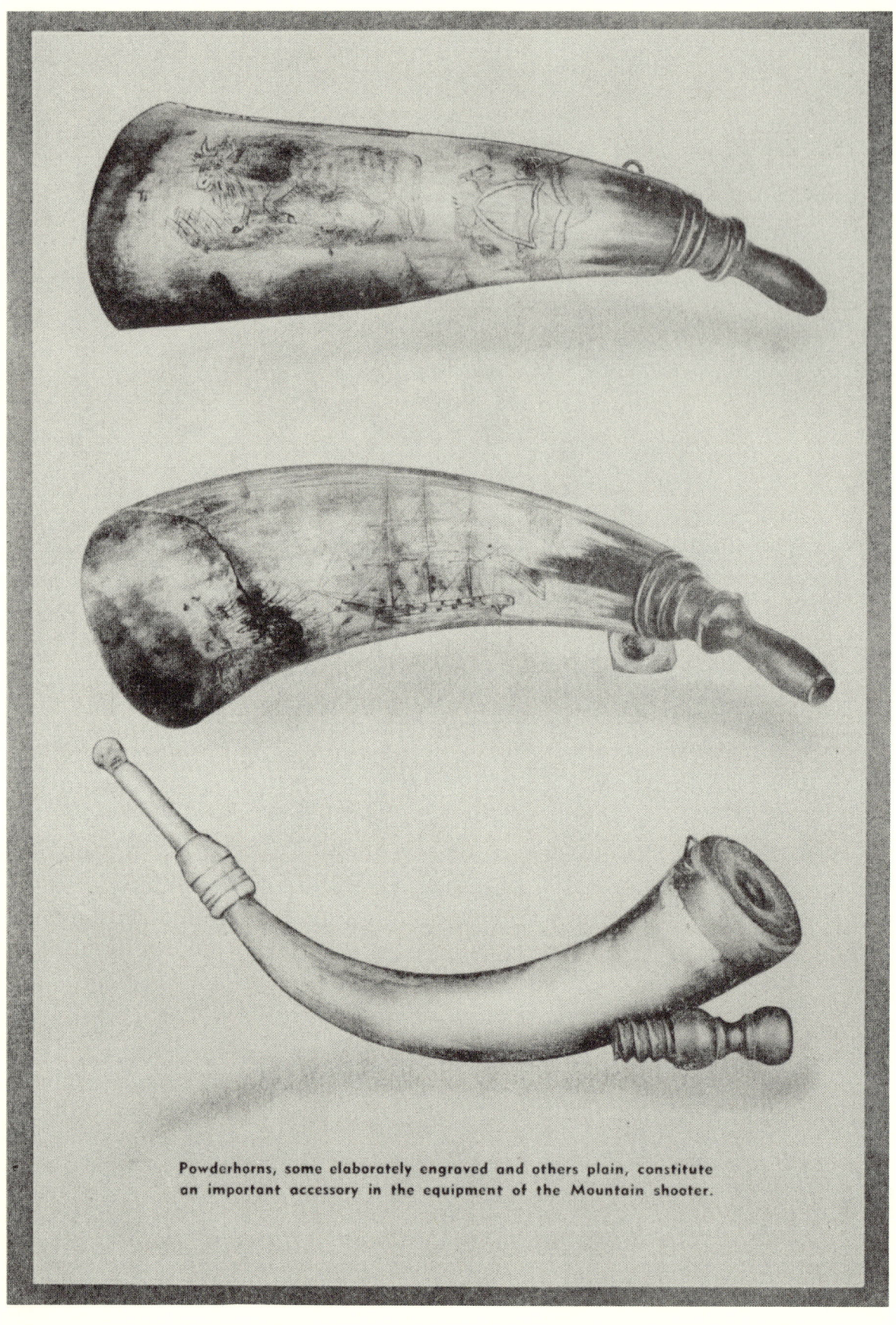

Powderhorns, some elaborately engraved and others plain, constitute an important accessory in the equipment of the Mountain shooter.

PLATE 21

Above is shown a team of marksmen which brought the National Rifle championship to Joliet, Illinois, in June, 1889, by scoring 1,288 points out of a possible, 1,500 in a match held at Indianapolis. Heavy calibre Schuetzen rifles were used and the match was shot at 200 yards, standing. In the above picture are shown (left to right, standing): John Spelter, who was a gunsmith as well as a shooter; Joseph Braun, Jr.; and Al Robinson. Shown sitting (left to right) are: Fred Beuttenmueller, Sr.; Henry Pipenbrink; and Louis J. Sehring.

Above is another picture of the famous Joliet gunsmith and marksman, John Spelter, taken June 21, 1889. His rifle is a 32-40 Ballard Remington. The stock of this unusual gun, which Mr. Spelter made himself, consists of 550 separate pieces of seven different kinds of wood; namely, walnut, cherry, lignum vitae, white holly, rosewood, ebony, and maple. The best target he made with this rifle was 228 x 250, shooting 200 yards off-hand at the 25 ring German target, with globe and peep sight.

A GALLERY OF NOTABLE SCHUETZEN SHOOTERS OF JOLIET, ILLINOIS, IN THE YEAR OF 1866

Conrad Schweitzer

On this and the following pages are presented the pictures of 21 remarkable shooters who made up the famous Joliet, Illinois, Schuetzen club in the year 1866,—just one year after the end of the Civil War. At this period, the Joliet club was in the hey-day of its popularity. In 1866, John Spelter, Joliet shooter and gunsmith, whose picture is shown on a previous plate, was only a lad of 13 years, but even at that age he was busily engaged as the target-keeper at the Joliet Schuetzen club. Mr. Spelter recalls that the barrels of the rifles used then were homemade, but he cannot remember the names of the makers. They always shot at 200 yards on the 25 ring German target, 10 shots to each match. He cannot recall the past scores but he thinks that the highest averages ran about 200 x 250. At the age of 13, Spelter did not shoot but he then absorbed the smell of gunpowder in his veins which prepared him for his prize-winning achievements of later years. In 1889, when Mr. Spelter had become a shooter, he used a Ballard action 32-40, but he recalls that all of the other shooters of that date used a 38-50. Most of the barrels in 1889 were Remington but there were two Pope barrels in the club. Charles J. Kellem, close friend of the Author, through whose courtesy these photographs are furnished, says that two or three of these rifles are still in existence and that on a recent occasion he himself shot the Piepenbrink rifle, using ammunition that was loaded by Mr. Spelter nearly 50 years ago. The powder was semi-smokeless, FG, and after the rifle was sighted in, Mr. Kellem made 10's easily at 100 yards on the standard target. Mr. Spelter generously loaned this remarkable group of photographs to Mr. Kellem for use in this volume. The names of most of the shooters are as "Schuetzen" as the guns they used.

On this page is shown Conrad Schweitzer and on the following five plates are shown the photographs of the other twenty members of the Joliet Schuetzen club of 1866.

PLATE 23

PLATE 24

PLATE 25

PLATE 26

PLATE 27

PLATE 28

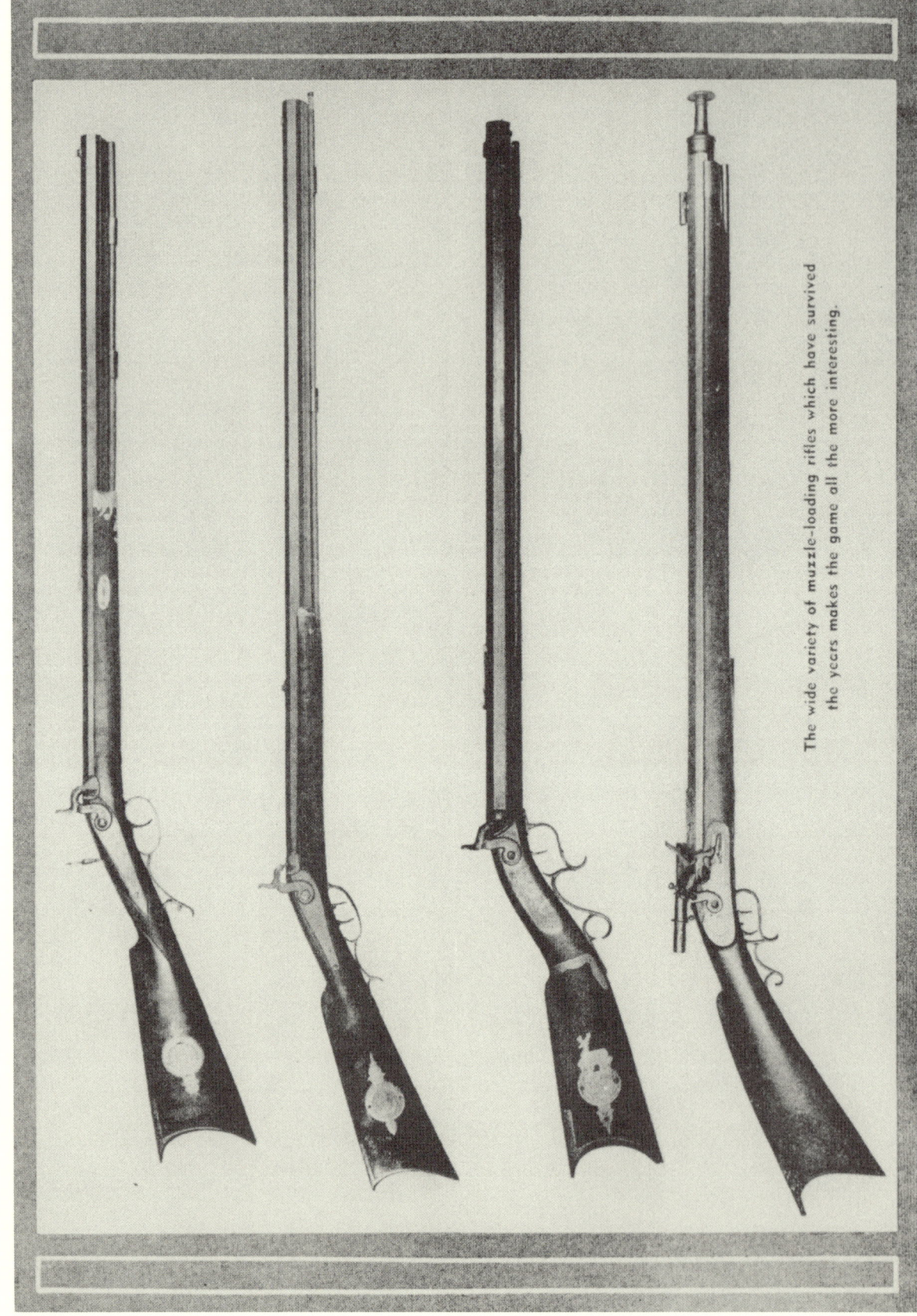

The wide variety of muzzle-loading rifles which have survived the years makes the game all the more interesting.

PLATE 29

L. G. (Daddy) Moore, picturesque bear hunter and guide of the Great Smokies (See chapter ten).

A combination of ingenuity and patience is required in the hand-welding of a rifle barrel.

PLATE 30

Plate 31

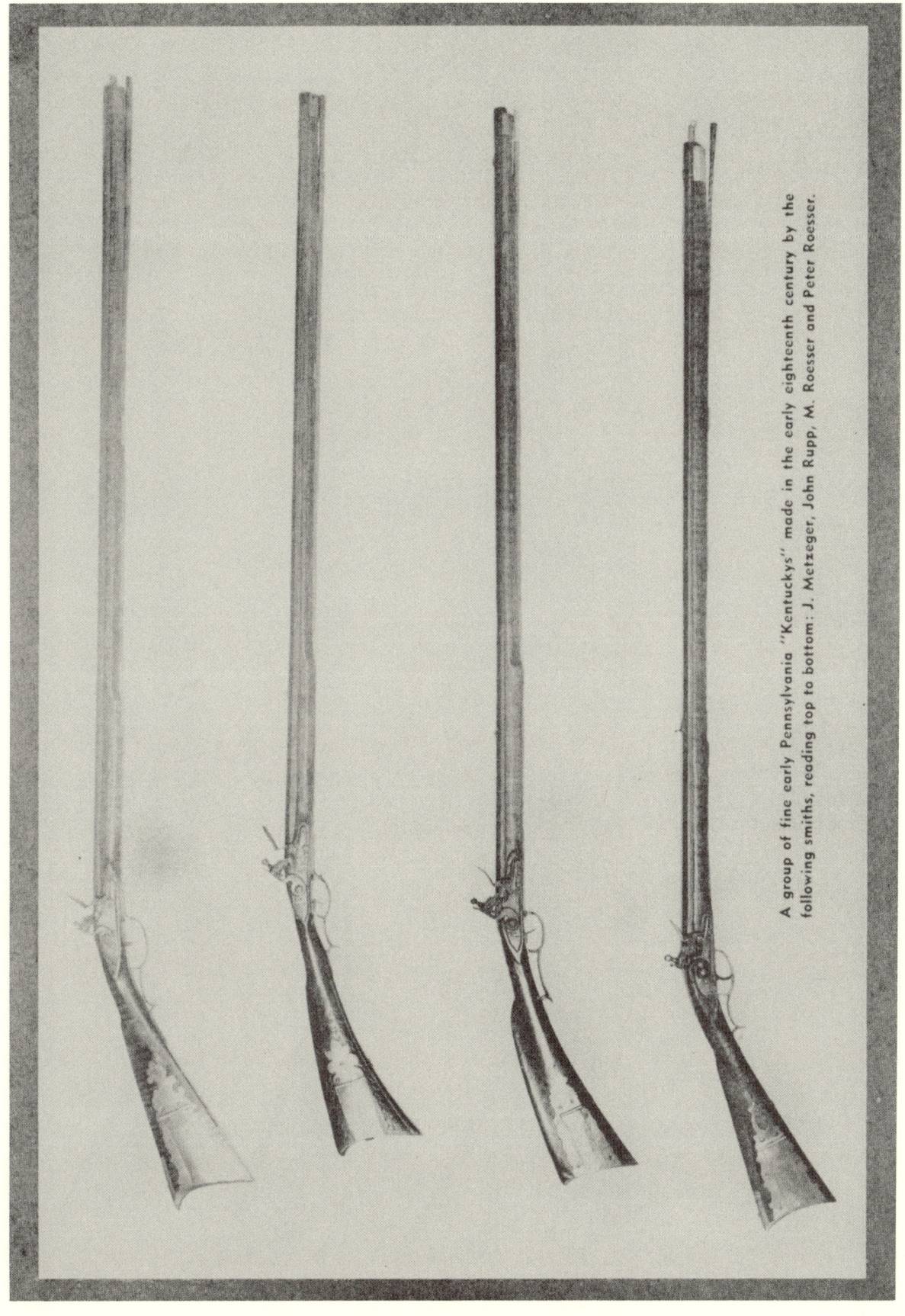

A group of fine early Pennsylvania "Kentuckys" made in the early eighteenth century by the following smiths, reading top to bottom: J. Metzeger, John Rupp, M. Roesser and Peter Roesser.

PLATE 32

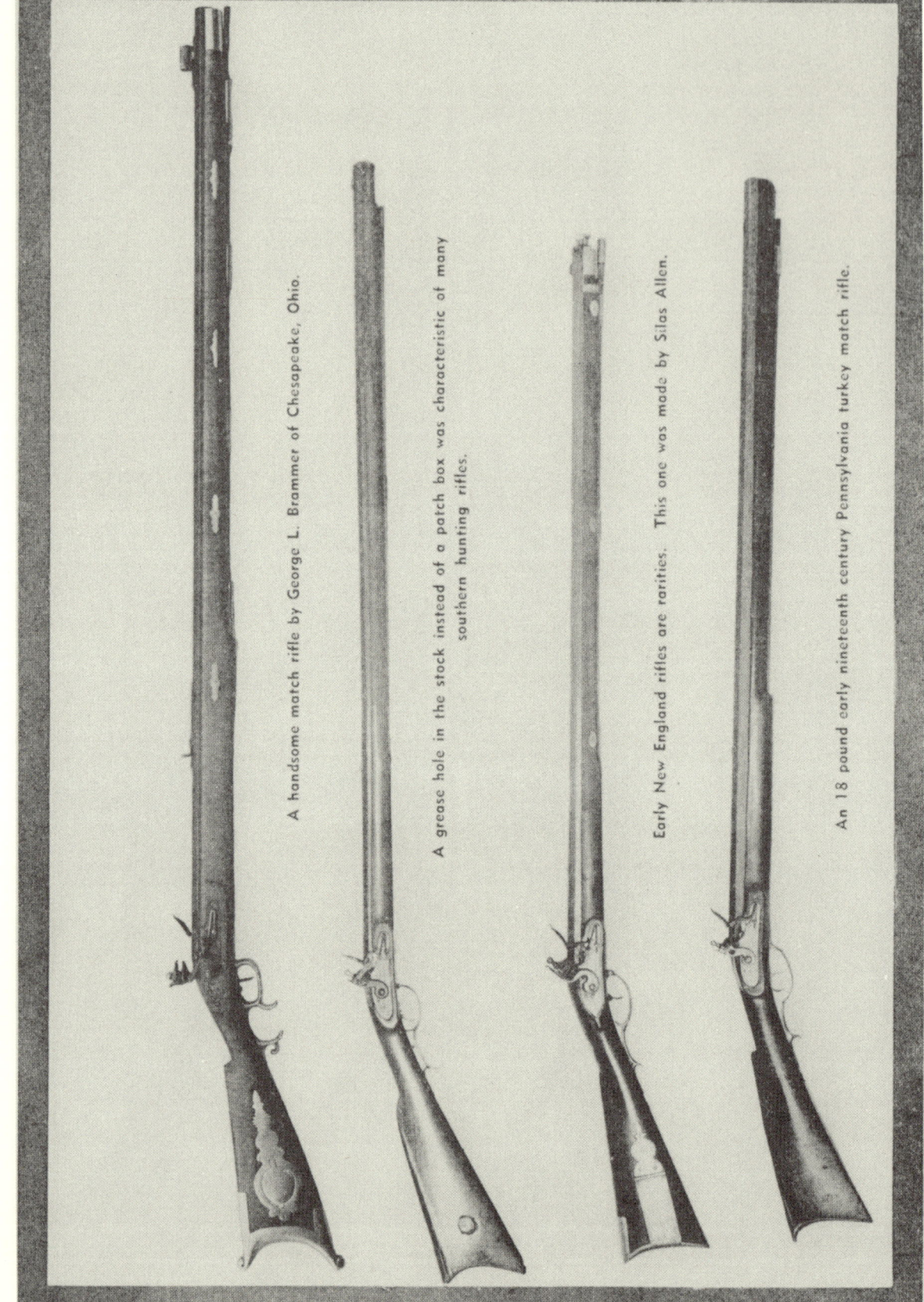

A handsome match rifle by George L. Brammer of Chesapeake, Ohio.

A grease hole in the stock instead of a patch box was characteristic of many southern hunting rifles.

Early New England rifles are rarities. This one was made by Silas Allen.

An 18 pound early nineteenth century Pennsylvania turkey match rifle.

PLATE 33

William Walker, Walker's Valley, Blount County, Tennessee hunter, has killed more than one hundred brown bears in the Smoky Mountains.

Henry Howard of Chattanooga learned his gunsmithing under the old masters.

"Nothin' takes the place of Mountain Shootin' with me."

PLATE 34

The National Rifle Club at Vernon, Vermont, June, 1886. Norman Brockway is shown sitting in center in shirt sleeves.

A group of modern shooters with ancient methods. They still adhere to the muzzle-loading rifles of their forefathers in preference to the arms of today.

Mountain Smiths and their Craftsmanship

In his book *"The Kentucky Rifle"* Captain John G. W. Dillin included four illustrations of Selvridge's tools, rifling guides and boring machines made from actual photographs which I took in Selvridge's shop.

Meredith Wolfe

Meredith Wolfe, who was born in McMinn County, Tennessee, September 3, 1833, and who died in Chattanooga February 8, 1930, was a maker of muzzle-loader rifles. I have owned many of his handmade guns,—good, accurate rifles. At one time I owned a muzzle-loader with a 45-inch barrel, caliber .40, walnut half-stock, brass oval patch box, weighing 10½ pounds, which was typical of his work.

Even as a boy he was so interested in rifles that he apprenticed himself to the famous gunsmith, John Selvridge. It was to this gunsmith's skill in the trade that Wolfe later attributed his own remarkable handiwork. He married Elizabeth Selvridge, his instructor's daughter.

Meredith Wolfe had an amazing life. When he was twenty-one years old he made an overland journey from Sweetwater, Tennessee, to New Haven, Illinois, in a one-horse wagon, crossing mountains and rough roads. He visited a sister there and became known as a match shooter in the vicinity. He never ceased to chuckle over a match with a rifleman who, being sure that he could out-shoot the Tennessee gunsmith, wagered a Negro slave. The target was the head of a tack at a distance of ten paces; the number of shots was decided to be thirteen in straight time. The competition ended with the Illinois rifleman missing on the thirteenth shot and with Wolfe hitting the tack head thirteen times.

After the war Between the States and a period when he served as United States Marshal of Bradley County, Tennessee, Meredith Wolfe came to Chattanooga and opened a lock and gun repair shop in 1881. It was a famous rendezvous for riflemakers, that shop where Wolfe repaired old muzzle-loaders and reminisced. There I could find any missing piece for a flint or muzzle-loader; there I could learn, in my youthful days, of rifles new and old, and of the days when Tennessee was a pioneer country.

Wolfe said that the reason he came to Chattanooga to live was that he saws skins of bear, deer and other animals spread on the roofs of the houses of the then small hamlet, and he thought that where there were so many skins there were also many hunters, who would need a gunsmith. He was right; he was never without work. He had been a hunter himself from boyhood, and always included two long hunting trips in a year's calendar. For many years a stuffed wolf, victim of a muzzle-loader in Wolfe's hands, hung as a sign outside his shop. Wolfe's four sons followed his trade, and there are no better gunsmiths in the state than John, James, Frank and Robert Wolfe.

Meredith Wolfe told me that he had seen only one muzzle-loader barrel that did not need straightening. He had fifty years of experience when he made that statement. He also maintained, after a long life experience, that in many respects the handmade guns are superior to the machine-made ones of today.

Today there are yet many Meredith Wolfe handmade guns in use in the Cumberland Mountains. I have never seen an inferior muzzle-loader of his make.

W. S. Blankenship

W. S. Blankenship is a gunsmith of the old school who, as this is written, is still working in his shop at Hot Springs, North Carolina. He is now seventy-five years of age and has been a gunsmith for fifty-six years. Mr. Blankenship is a shooter as well as a builder of mountain rifles and match rifles, and he won all honors and two-thirds of the prize money at the Raleigh State Fair in 1925. He likes to recall the sixty dollars that he won once in a night match at Greeneville, Tennessee, in 1919, in which match he confined his shooting within a one-half inch target lighted by a lantern, at 15 yards distance. He won twenty-four matches at one dollar a shoot at Melvin Price's store, Wolf Creek, Tennessee; and two night matches at 38 yards, all dead centers.

Blankenship is known to his friends as "Champion of the Mountains." He once walked and trotted 54 miles in 12 hours. He estimates that he averaged about 12,000 shots per year from the old rifles when he was in his prime.

Blankenship made his last prize rifle in 1917, a splendid gun which weighed 27 pounds and was 71 inches over-all. The barrel was welded around a core from one piece of iron and was 53 inches long. The caliber was .38, 1⅛ twist to the rifling. He said that two weeks were required to complete this rifle and that he made the walnut stock from a tree on his own farm. The screws in the stock were the only pieces not made by hand—even the tools were all handmade by him. Since Blankenship was left-handed, this rifle carries the lock on the left-hand side of the stock.

D. C. Addicks

In D. C. Addicks, gunsmith of Rome, Georgia, I found a friend and sympathetic companion,—one who cared for the old rifles as I did. I have spent many delightful hours in his shop in conversation about rifles and the men who made them. He repaired many of my own rifles and I sent many riflemen to him and they, like me, found him to be a gentleman and a craftsman of unusual ability.

If you had a muzzle-loader gun problem that needed expert attention, you did not have to go further than the shop of Addicks, located at the rear of his garage. The shop itself was well equipped with lathes, grinder, small tools, rifling machine, boring machine, drills, etc. He employed gears on his boring machine to reduce or increase speed, as required. For rifling he preferred the gain twist. The work he did was varied,—everything from minor repairs and replacements to converting cap-and-ball revolvers to cartridge arms and manufacturing outright precision match rifles.

He was an unusual machinist and tool-maker and, therefore, had a wonderful background of ability and experience to become the remarkable gunsmith that he was. He was apprenticed to a gunsmith when he was a mere boy, and he never lost his love for the old-time shooting irons. I do not know of another smith more careful or skillful than he.

The Muzzle-Loading Rifle—Then and Now

And when he died in 1941, I was more saddened than I had been in years. My grief was for a friend who loved the old rifles of the frontier as I did. He understood my language. He always had an attentive ear and sympathetic heart for any topic that had to do with the making and shooting of these arms of olden days. My friend, Addicks, surely typified the sterling qualities and character that I have found were common to nearly all of the smiths of the old school.

Salola—Cherokee Gunsmith

Tradition is one thing and fact may be, and often is, another; therefore I am giving a record Charles Lanman, librarian of the War Department, left in his book *"Letters From the Allegheny Mountains",* published in 1849 by Putnam, New York. Mr. Lanman saw and visited Salola in May, 1848, and his is a sympathetic sketch of the Cherokee gunmaker. He wrote:

"On my arrival in this place, Qualla Town, North Carolina, which is the home of a large number of Cherokee Indians, I became the guest of Mr. William H. Thomas, who is the 'guide, counsellor, and friend' of the Indians, as well as their business agent.

"Qualla Town is a name applied to a tract of 72,000 acres of land, in Haywood county, which is occupied by about 800 Cherokee Indians and 100 Catawbas. Certain celebrated Cherokee Indians are deservedly considered as among the particularly bright stars of the nation.

"Salola—'the Squirrel'—is now living in Qualla Town. He is quite a young man and has a remarkably thoughtful face. He is the blacksmith of the Indian nation, and, with some assistance, supplies the whole of Qualla Town with all their axes and ploughs; *but what is more, he has manufactured a number of very superior rifles and pistols, including stock, barrel and lock;* and he is also the builder of grist-mills, which grind all the corn which his people eat.

"A specimen of his workmanship in the way of a rifle may be seen at the Patent Office, in Washington, where it was deposited by Mr. Thomas. I believe Salola is the first Indian who ever manufactured an entire gun. When it is remembered that he never received a particle of education in any of the mechanical arts, but is entirely self-taught, his attainments must be considered truly remarkable.

"That he labors under every disadvantage in his most worthy calling, may be shown by the fact that he uses a flint-stone for an anvil and a water-blast for a bellows.

"In every particular he is a most worthy man and though unable to speak the English tongue, is a very good scholar in his own language. He is the husband of a Catawba woman, whom he married before he could speak one word of her own tongue or she could speak Cherokee; but they have now established a language of their own by which they get along very well.

"Salola, upon the whole, is an honor to the country, and one whose services in some iron or steel establishment of the eastern cities would be of great value.

"Is there not some gentleman in Philadelphia or New York who would take pleasure in patronizing this mechanical prodigy of the wilderness?"

* * * * *

Editorial note—If Mr. Cline had lived to complete his biographical sketches of early gunsmiths, he would doubtless have included many, many others, among them such men as the following, whose names we find mentioned in the rough drafts of the notes he left:

William Large, of Ironton, Ohio; Ben Hawkins; P. I. Spence, of Marietta, Ohio; Win Woods; Wyatt Atkinson, of Hidalgo, Kentucky; W. Ed. Faust, of LaFontaine, Indiana; Luther Ackley, of Sharon, Ohio; Eli McGregor, of Lebanon, Ohio; Alvin Wagner, Jackson, Missouri; McElhaney, who died twenty years after the War Between the States; Elijah Bull, who lived on Turkey Creek, Morristown, Tennessee, and who made a gun for Donaldson; Postman Manny, Blairsville, Georgia; Bill Smith, Elizabethtown, Ken-

The Muzzle-Loading Rifle—Then and Now

tucky; E. L. Davis, Hinckly, Illinois; John Battls, Whittier, North Carolina; Fred Johnson, of Illinois; Goff Bailey, Kincheloe, West Virginia; Hacker Martin, of Jonesboro, Tennessee; George L. Brammer, of Chesapeake, Ohio; etc.

Especially have we searched in vain for his completed manuscript on John Shell, Kentucky gunsmith featured in *"The Kentucky Rifle,"* by Capt. John G. W. Dillin, but the following memorandum is all that we can locate:

"I was in Leslie County, Kentucky, in September, 1920, and interviewed John Shell, who said he was born in Tennessee in 1788. He talked of the cap-lock rifles he was making, of rifles he had made and of guns he had handled in the long-ago-past. He told me he had reached the advanced age of 130 years. I was amazed and bewildered at his story."

CHAPTER XII.

BUILDING TWO RIFLES FROM A JUNK PILE

FROM an accumulation of parts of old rifles of a period long since passed, I built two rifles. One is a flintlock, a type which was in use in various forms for over two hundred years. It is typical of the American long-barreled flintlock that was developed by the pioneer gunsmiths of Pennsylvania early in the eighteenth century. It is representative of the first accurate rifle in the world and with it the American pioneer set a standard of marksmanship in battle that has never been surpassed. The other rifle is of the percussion type that followed the flintlock, but had a much shorter life.

Many years ago, before the old gunsmiths had closed their shops, I learned the use of the long-barreled muzzle-loading rifle. With it I made my first hunting trips; then, only a boy of twelve years, I killed my first squirrel, although I had to stand on a stump to load my rifle.

The love of the rifle and its associations remain after all these years. I have owned many modern rifles and have killed my share of game with them, yet not one has taken the place of the old frontier rifle.

It was but natural that I should preserve from the wreck of time many fine specimens of both the flintlock and percussion rifles, together with the tools that fashioned them and a knowledge of how to use them. In my travels here and there no rifle or part ever escaped me. So from the accumulation of many years, I selected the parts to make these two rifles.

I made the percussion first, incorporating in it some modern developments; I even employed the pistol grip, although the pistol grip was used a hundred or so years ago by a celebrated maker in Philadelphia by the name of Constable. The barrel used in the percussion rifle I found under an abandoned log cabin in the Cumberland Mountains while on a hunting trip. It was a mass of rust and dirt, and what remained of the stock was rotten. I had walked many miles that day and had a long tramp ahead of me, but something made me pick it up. I strapped it to my pack and it was with me when I reached camp that night. At the end of my vacation it came home with me. The back strap came from an old flintlock by Keller, who lived over one hundred and twenty-five years ago. The trigger guard and butt plate came from an old rifle from Alabama. The lock, tube and cylinder came from an old gunsmith's stock that I had stored away.

Beginning on the barrel, I dug the dirt and rust out of the bore. I smoothed the lands with the long bit of the old gunsmith days. I found enough of the grooves remaining to carry a guide. Casting a guide on the end of the rod, I set a saw in it and went to work. It was beautifully working iron, and in about two months, working spare moments, I finished a fine bore of .340. A friend in a lumber plant furnished the cherry and walnut planks for the stocks of both rifles. The cherry was used on the percussion rifle and the walnut on the flintlock. By draw filing, I finished the outside of the barrel, and this was real work!

Inlays were sawed out with a jeweler's saw. I made the inlay of the squirrel in the cheek piece from a reproduction of a photograph of a pet squirrel that belonged to my children. I reduced the photograph to the required size by photographic process and transferred it to German silver.

Out of the foothills of the Unaka Mountains came the wreck of what once had been a beautiful flintlock rifle, a masterpiece of gunsmith's art. Only a trace of its former beauty remained. The stock was shattered, but a silver patchbox was intact. The butt plate, barrel and some inlays of silver remained. The flintlock had been taken off but was still preserved. In hopes of being able to reproduce something like the original rifle, I inspected the bore and found that long use and repeated scouring had caused it to become funneled at each end, so there was nothing else to do but rebore and re-rifle the barrel.

Building Two Rifles from a Junk Pile

To bore out a barrel by hand is somewhat of a job and it was only by taking my time that this was accomplished. All boring or reaming was done with the long bit. Then using an old rifle guide or lead with a pitch of one turn in four feet cutting seven grooves, I rerifled the barrel. The finished bore measures .380; lands and grooves are of equal width. (The grooves are not cut out, but scraped out. It takes about one hundred scrapes to make a groove. Seven hundred for this job.)

The most essential qualities in building a rifle are patience and confidence. It can not be done in a hurry. In making the stocks the barrel is first let in, then the lock, butt plate, set triggers and trigger guard. The only tools needed in making the stock are a rasp, files, two or three chisels, a good knife, a brace and several bits, handled *with lots of patience!* If one has the design of a stock in mind, it can be done rapidly. I used a cast fore end on the stock as this is the easiest way to make one. The soldering of the ramrod pipes and the rib on the under side of the barrel requires care and some knowledge of the process of soldering. The moulds I recherried from old ones that were for a smaller bore; then lapped them smooth. It is impossible to make a perfectly round spherical ball in this way. One of the moulds cast a ball that is only out .003 inch; the other one a little more. Both rifles are good-looking and are admired by all who have seen them.

The old saying that "the proof of the pudding is the eating thereof" may apply to the rifle in that the shooting thereof is the proof.

Testing the percussion rifle with scope sights, muzzle and elbow rest, the first three shots broke together at fifty yards and I was highly elated. The next few shots went all over the target. An inspection of the inside of the barrel showed that a slight rough place had appeared on one of the lands near the muzzle and it was cutting the patches. This was corrected by running the land saw through a few times. Now I have a rifle that will make an inch group of five shots at fifty yards three times out of five, which is not bad for a homemade rifle.

The Muzzle-Loading Rifle—Then and Now

The flintlock is just a little better, having a heavier and longer barrel.

"But, what does all this have to do with the subject *'The Muzzle-Loader—Then and Now,'*" you ask. Well, I asked myself that selfsame question. Knowing the hearts of the rank and file of the muzzle-loading shooters as I think I do, I concluded that I should share with my friends of like sentiments the joy and fun that I had in playing the role of gunsmith myself and building these two pieces.

CHAPTER XIII.

FRONTIER RIFLEMEN IN AMERICAN HISTORY

Colonel Ferguson and Kings Mountain

THE British Army at Kings Mountain was commanded by a soldier who was regarded in Europe as second to none in marksmanship. Lieutenant-Colonel Patrick Ferguson of the British Service, who was killed by the Watauga riflemen, had acquired skill in the use of the rifle by a long and large experience in war, which should not be belittled by one attempting a fair appraisal. He had invented a rifle to be loaded at the breech, which it is claimed he fired with precision seven times a minute. I have wondered many times if he was carrying this rifle the day he has recorded in a letter which he wrote to his relative, Dr. Adam Ferguson, a Scottish historian, and in which letter he stated he believed he could have shot Washington before the battle of Brandywine.

The letter is as follows:

"A rebel officer, remarkable by a hussar dress, passed toward our army, within a hundred yards of my right flank, not perceiving us. He was followed by another, dressed in dark green and blue. mounted on a bay horse, with a remarkably high cocked hat. I ordered three good shots to steal near to and fire at them; but the idea disgusting me, I recalled the order. The hussar in returning made a circuit, but the other passed within a hundred yards of us, upon which I advanced from the wood toward him. Upon my calling he stopped, but after looking at me, he proceeded. I again drew his attention and made signs to him to stop, leveling my rifle, but he slowly cantered away. As I was within that distance at which in the quickest firing I could have lodged half a dozen balls, I had only to determine—but it was not pleasant to fire at the back of an unoffending individual, who was acquitting himself coolly,—so I let him alone."

It is American tradition that Ferguson was told later the identity of the "cool rider." He paid a generous appraisal to Washington in his curt comment, "The American, eh? Well,—I am not sorry I did not know who it was."

The Muzzle-Loading Rifle—Then and Now

The American frontier riflemen at Kings Mountain filled Ferguson's body with lead and with him lay two hundred and twenty-five British dead and some two hundred wounded to testify to the accuracy of the backwoods rifles of the Southern country. A linen hunting shirt which Ferguson wore over his uniform is said to have identified him to the frontier marksmen.

I have climbed Kings Mountain often and I never fail to remember what might have happened without the accuracy of the American frontier backwoods riflemen of the Southern mountains. Washington's own record in his letter to General Reed, just before the Kings Mountain battle, is evidence of the marksmanship of the woods. "I have almost ceased to hope," he wrote. In his letter to Steuben it is recorded: "The prospect is gloomy and the storm threatens————." But in spite of such adverse prospects, the backwoodsmen turned the tide.

The enemy's testimony to American marksmanship is found in the *"Memoirs of Prevost,"* an English Captain, published in 1802:

"These Americans had riflemen—they could hit a man anywhere they liked at two hundred paces distance. We came to dread *them* far more than the *regular Continentals*. At Kings Mountain they destroyed us."

John Sevier—Sharpshooter

When one reads Theodore Roosevelt's *"Winning of the West"*, pages 182 and 340, Vol. 1—wherein he condemns James R. Gilmore (Edmund Kirk)—one can but feel a large price has been paid for too great a degree of hero worship. Few Tennesseeans would acknowledge that too much praise could be given the first elected governor of the state, especially when the contested record consists of rifle supremacy.

Sevier himself was a frontier sharpshooter who demanded accuracy of rifle fire from the men he led in battle, both for reason of conserving bullets, which were handmade in the settlements, and for the reason that accuracy meant efficient fighting. His terse order to his men at Kings Mountain was:

Frontier Riflemen in American History

"Now, boys, single out your men, take sure aim, and fire." His tactics and military genius were exceptional, but the key to his success in battle was accurate sharpshooting.

At Kings Mountain Sevier led his men of the backwoods up the mountain against the enemy's center to the summit where a barricade of rocks gave protection. I have climbed the path he went up. I know the British firing at him and his men were shooting down hill and over-shot the Sevier band, because I found British bullets in tree trunks eight or more feet from the ground and only there. The bullets of the backwoodsmen (DePeyster's "Yelling Devils") were found on top the mountain.

Sevier commanded the right wing; Cleveland and Williams the left wing; and Shelby and Campbell the center column; soldiers of all commands were driven by British bayonets save Sevier's men, who could not be approached from behind their barricade of rocks. The settlers did not have bayonets, and fought the Kings Mountain battle with long rifles.

Sevier was only one of the commanders,—but he was the most staunch advocate of sharpshooting and it was into his band of backwoodsmen that Ferguson, when he realized all was lost, spurred his horse directly therein to break through and escape down the mountain, or die. A sharpshooter, named Gilliland, recognized Ferguson but, too badly wounded to fire himself, he called: "In the linen shirt —Ferguson—get him!" The Watauga riflemen shot. DePeyster raised a flag of truce. The British commander, one of the finest marksmen of the world of that period, died by fire from the long rifles of Sevier's men—the frontier sharpshooters.

The General Assembly of North Carolina at its first session after the defeat of Ferguson, passed a resolution that a sword and pair of pistols should be presented to Shelby and to Sevier. Sevier's sword—so presented—hangs in the Tennessee Capitol at Nashville. He had many rifles, he moulded his own bullets and he thought *accuracy* worth more than the make of a gun or the certain mould of a bullet. He died a sharpshooter while on a mission to the Creek Indians near Fort Decatur, Georgia, September 24, 1815.

The Muzzle-Loading Rifle—Then and Now

Daniel Morgan

Daniel Morgan, who commanded the first organized corps of riflemen in the American Army, was born in Maryland in 1736. His first military experience was with Braddock in 1755, where he was a teamster. He had moved from Maryland to Virginia and lived at Charles Town (now West Virginia) at this time. He took part in all the Indian wars before the Revolution. In 1773 he was a captain in Dunmore's War. In 1775 Morgan was captain of a company of 96 riflemen. He marched from Winchester, Virginia, to Boston in 21 days. His men were strong and of great endurance; many of them were more than six feet tall. They wore leggings, moccasins and homespun hunting shirts. Each carried a long rifle, a hatchet and a hunting knife.

Between the twenty-fifth of July and the seventh of August, 1,400 riflemen arrived before Boston. They were the first troops levied under the authority of the Continental Congress. They played a prominent part in the siege of Boston and were from Maryland, Virginia, and Pennsylvania.

After the siege of Boston, Arnold was sent to join Montgomery before Quebec. Three companies of riflemen were included in the detachment, one from Virginia under Morgan and two from Pennsylvania. Morgan was sent first to clear the path. In the assault on Quebec, Morgan's riflemen gained the only advantage, capturing a battery, but the success was only temporary and he and his men were soon captured.

In August, 1776, Morgan and his riflemen were sent from Quebec on parole. Washington hastened his exchange and recommended his promotion. Washington selected 500 men from his army and organized the first corps of riflemen in the American forces, which he sent to General Gates before the battle of Saratoga.

Daniel Boone—Syndic

When Daniel Boone, the long-gun hunter of Kentucky and Tennessee, met with reverses in the loss of his Kentucky home by a flaw in the title, he shouldered his rifle and crossed into the territory to the westward, then known as Louisiana and under the rule and ownership of the Spanish. Furs from the hunt, he knew, would provide the wherewithal necessary to live and prosper; the forest would receive him again and hold him safe.

Boone became famous in a short time in a section the Spanish called "Femme Osage;" his skill with the rifle reached the Spanish owners' ears and they gave him a place as a director in the development of the fur trade, which had enriched the English and the French to the north. They advised him that if he would bring in settlers for the valley, they would give him land for a home in the section. He selected a site on the top of a ridge, commanding a valley view of forest and rugged hills, and went eastward for one hundred Kentucky families who were only too glad to share the valley with him.

The group of stone dwellings which the Kentuckians built stand in the valley about two miles from the Ozark foothills. Boone's house was built of white limestone and faced east and west on top of the ridge. To the south and north the fertile valley beneath, a mile in width, stretched to the Missouri River. It is a beautiful house, even today, and when I visited it I wondered if Boone, because of black walnut rifle stocks, chose black walnut for the interior mantels and finish. There must have been memories of the Kentucky colonial style of building, for the house is of that type of architecture.

Boone's tenure in the hill country became permanent when the Spanish government, through its Governor of the Spanish province, made him Syndic. He undertook the job, although he knew nothing of law technicalities; he established his court under a large elm tree, which became known as the Judgment Tree and opened sessions of his court by repeating the Golden Rule, "Do unto others as you would have them do unto you." There was no appeal from his decisions. He represented the Spanish crown and was the civic authority of the vast district. The settlement of disputes, questions of boundary limits and frontier regulations, and rulings in settlement affairs were made and accepted by the frontier settlers. How well he did his job is testified to by the fact that after the Louisiana Territory was purchased by the United States, the pioneers ignored federal courts and still sought justice under the Judgment Tree Court of Boone.

What Spain had given the United States took from Boone. He had been Syndic from 1798 to 1803—the date President Jefferson acquired Louisiana. The United States did not recognize a Spanish title and once again Boone and his long gun were adrift in the forest. He prepared a memorial to Congress—and after some half dozen years Boone and his rifle were again safe. His prayer was granted in part—"the one thousand arpents of land" (the original Spanish grant) were his in absolute title.

"Simon—You Are a Fine Fellow"

Simon Kenton, hunter, Indian fighter, scout, spy, and marksman, was not excelled in these five paths of his existence. A Virginian by birth, being born in 1755 of Scotch-Irish parents, he became familiar with Indian warfare, the ambush, the raid, and cruelty of capture. From the South through Kentucky and Pennsylvania, he eavesdropped at council fires and learned in advance of plans and raids.

His spy work with Lord Dunmore, Virginia Governor, earned him the lasting hatred of the Indians.

In 1777—when Kenton was twenty-two years old—he made Boonesborough, Kentucky, headquarters for his activities. His only companion, so he stated, was a trusty rifle. In that year Harrodsburg and Boonesborough were besieged by Indians half a dozen times and the situation was serious even for such Indian fighters as Boone and Kenton. It had become impossible to travel the Wilderness Road, which was covered with Indians in ambush.

Perhaps due to the fact that the Indians were in almost daily forage, the hunters became too careless; for a trick of the Indians, well known and often practiced, led to an almost fatal attack.

As it was, several small groups of Indians made the attack—which was a decoy to lead pursuit to a hundred or more Indians hidden in the grass. Realizing the trap too late, Daniel Boone shouted to his men to wheel and go back to the fort in a hand-to-hand conflict.

PLATE 35

The author sat in homemade hickory chairs to shoot on his range at "Piney Nook."

Four important smithing tools, reading from top to bottom:

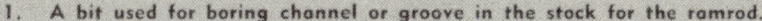

1. A bit used for boring channel or groove in the stock for the ramrod.

2. A rifle cutter or "saw" in place in a hickory "rifling head."

3. A short bit for roughing out of the bore after welding.

4. A long bit for smoothing the bore, shown with hickory guard on the opposite side of the cutter, which prevents the borings from scratching the barrel.

PLATE 36

John S. Sumner, Newton, Massachusetts, member of the Massachusetts Rifle Association at Walnut Hills, in 1879. He won the long range championship of the United States at Creedmoor.

A wild pig of the Great Smoky Mountains.

The wild boar hound used by the author and "Daddy" Moore.

Powder and bullets are oftentimes kept in gourds. The hunter places the young gourd between two boards so that it will grow flat, making the appearance of a bottle, as shown in the illustration to the left.

PLATE 37

Pictures of the famous Whitmore, cased with all original accessories, with which Mr. Cline won the coveted Boss Johnston Trophy shown.

PLATE 38

On his way to the matches.

E. M. Farris, efficient secretary of the National Muzzle-Loading Association.

Enoch Hardin, Tennessee gunsmith.

This group is measuring carefully to determine the results of a close match.

PLATE 39

A Tennessee blockhouse, used years ago by frontiersmen, still standing. Note the "portholes" for rifle barrels.

Molding bullets while on the chase was an art that the frontiersman had to learn.

Women have taken up the sport of muzzle-loading shooting and many have become good marksmen.

Gordon Morgan, of Waldon Ridge, Tennessee, can employ a simple leaf from most any tree in an emergency to imitate a turkey call.

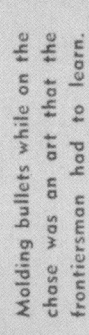

PLATE 40

Sergeant Alvin York, a hero of World War I (see Chapter Thirteen).

Boss Johnston, President of the National Muzzle-Loading Rifle Association.

Charles J. Kellem, Joliet, Illinois, enthusiastic follower of the muzzle-loading game.

In bad weather, ulsters and rain jackets are a necessary part of the paraphernalia of the match shooter. This group is heading for their favorite Tennessee range.

PLATE 41

John Shell, Leslie County, Kentucky, reputed to have lived one hundred thirty-five years, told the author that he made rifles in his earlier days.

This grim visaged mountaineer typically portrays his tribe in this unstudied pose.

David Crockett, hero of the southland, who died in the battle of the Alamo in Texas (from a painting "In the Alamo.")

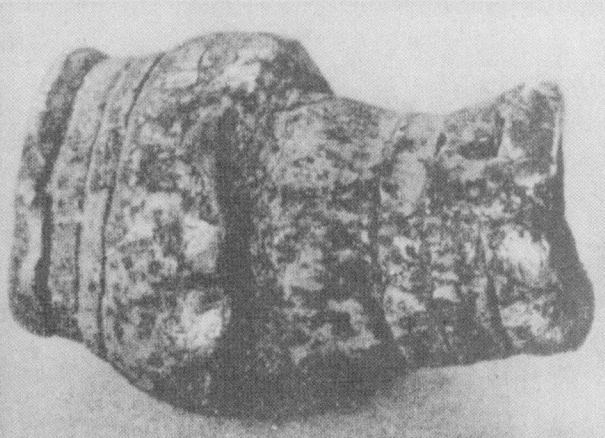

The above portrays two Minie bullets which met head-on and were welded together in the battle of Resaca, Georgia, and were unearthed only recently,— a grim reminder of the days of 1864 when General Sherman was fighting for the possession of Atlanta. These two bullets were found near a spring where a Confederate Sharpshooter had concealed himself, knowing that the Union soldiers would come to this spring for water. He wounded two or three men and a Union sharpshooter was sent for and a desperate duel was waged by these two marksmen, which was won by the Union soldier. It is reasonably conjectured that these two bullets were fired by these two men. A question for the puzzle-minded: if these two bullets had just missed each other, would either of the men that fired them, or both, have been hit?

PLATE 42

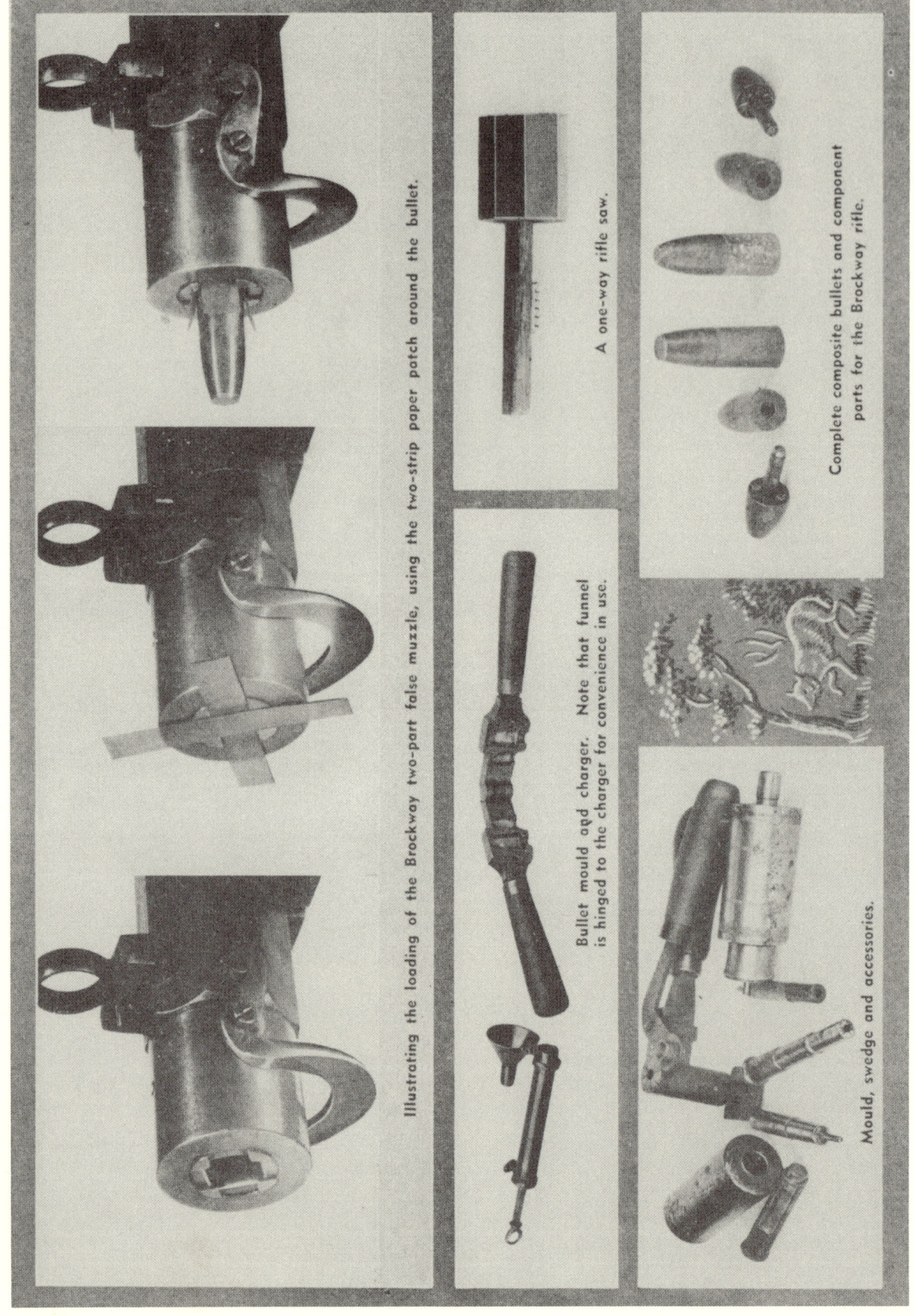

PLATE 43

Getting ready for the shoot.

Prone position—mountain style.

Riffling a barrel.

Boring a rifle

On the firing line.

Plate 44

A token of many matches.

The end of a perfect day.

Three mountain musketeers.

PLATE 45

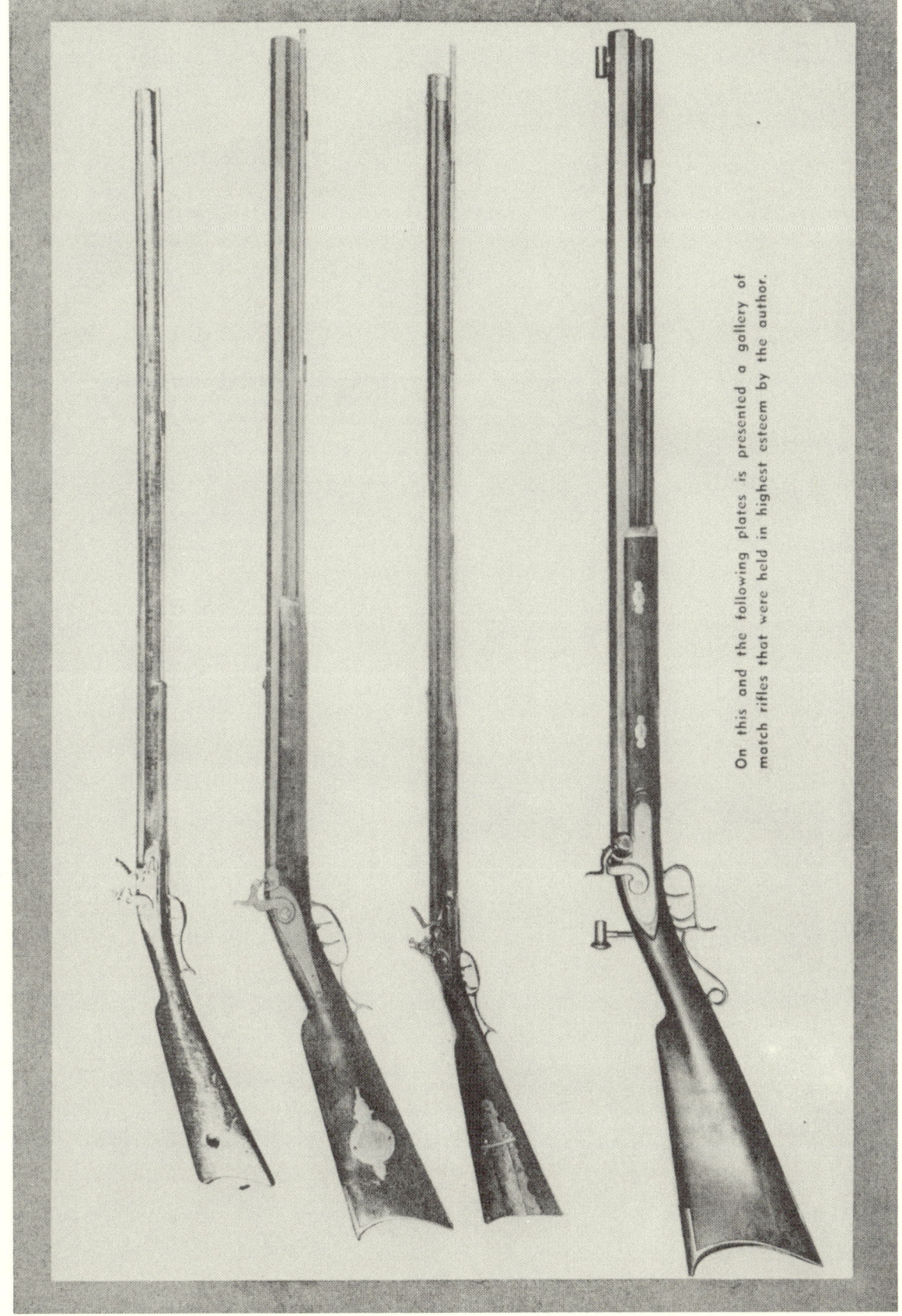

On this and the following plates is presented a gallery of match rifles that were held in highest esteem by the author.

Plate 46

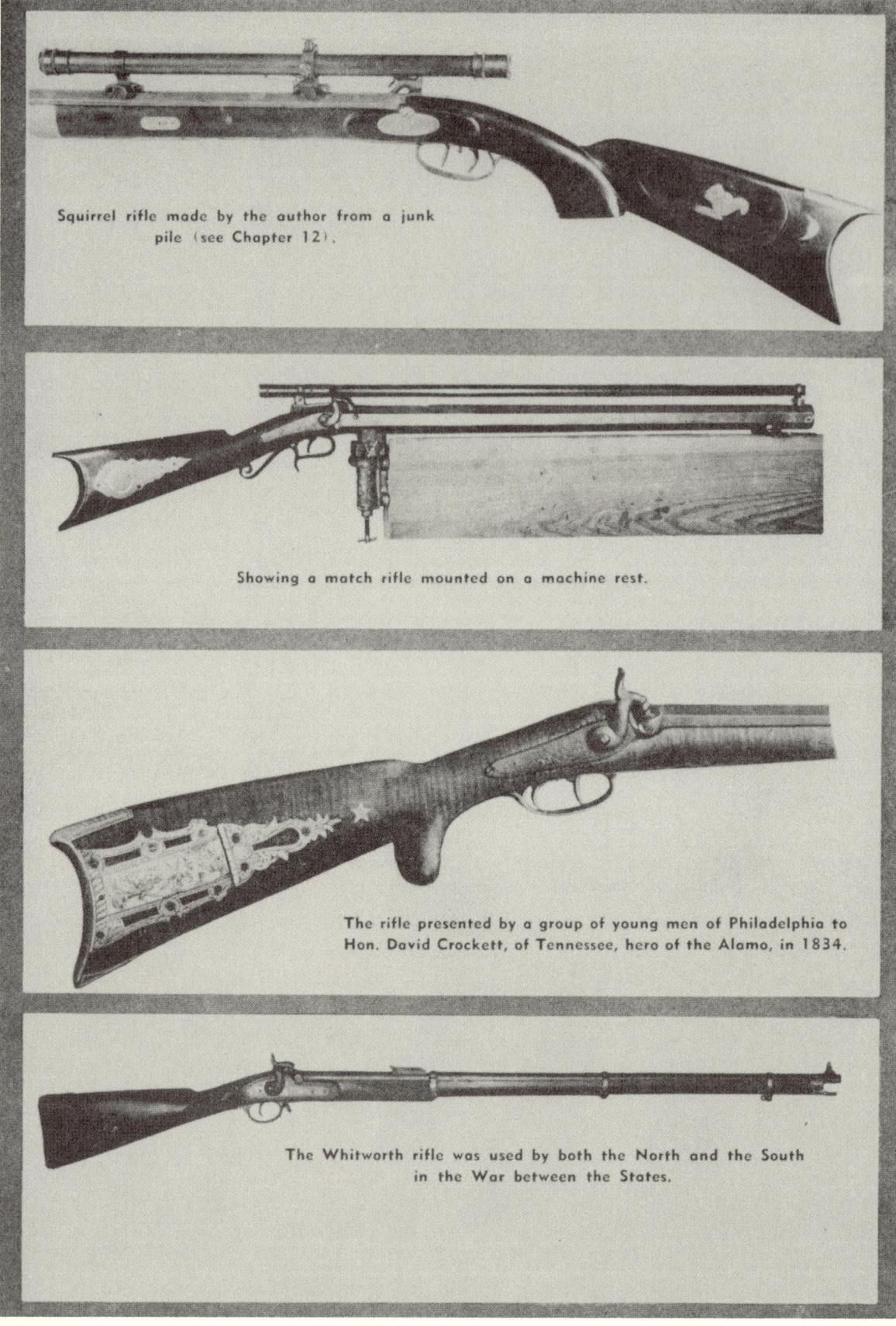

Squirrel rifle made by the author from a junk pile (see Chapter 12).

Showing a match rifle mounted on a machine rest.

The rifle presented by a group of young men of Philadelphia to Hon. David Crockett, of Tennessee, hero of the Alamo, in 1834.

The Whitworth rifle was used by both the North and the South in the War between the States.

PLATE 47

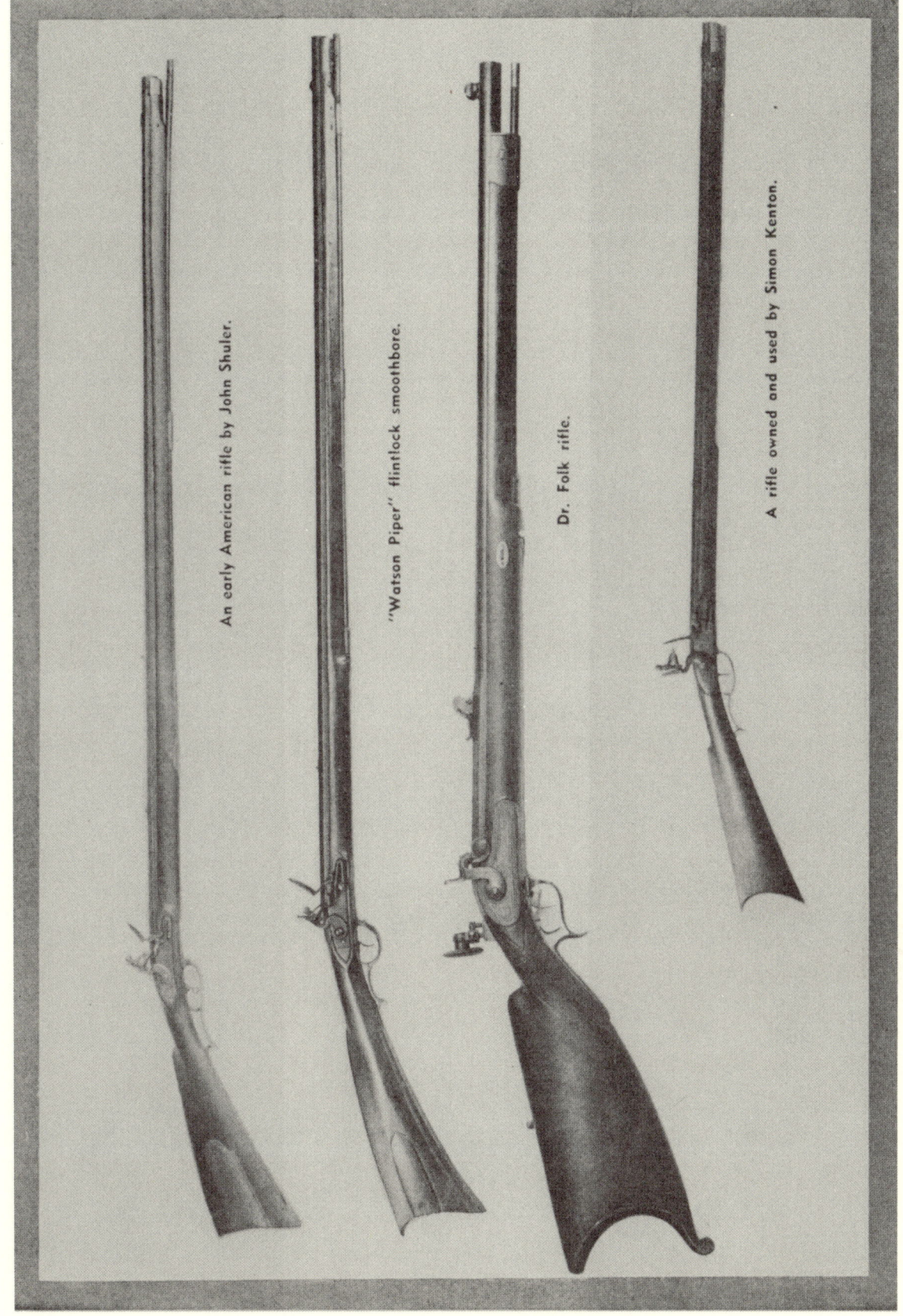

An early American rifle by John Shuler.

"Watson Piper" flintlock smoothbore.

Dr. Folk rifle.

A rifle owned and used by Simon Kenton.

PLATE 48

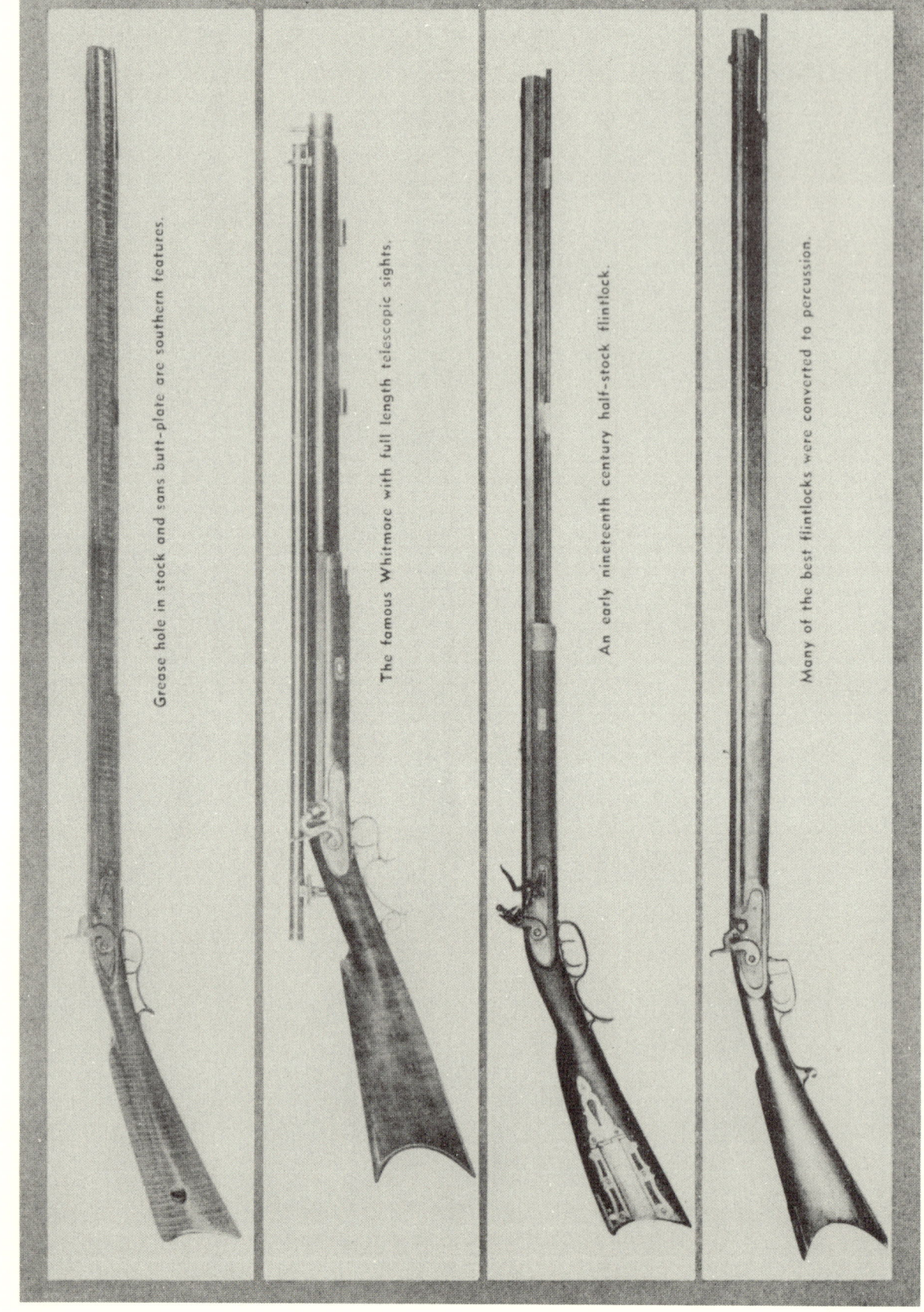

PLATE 49

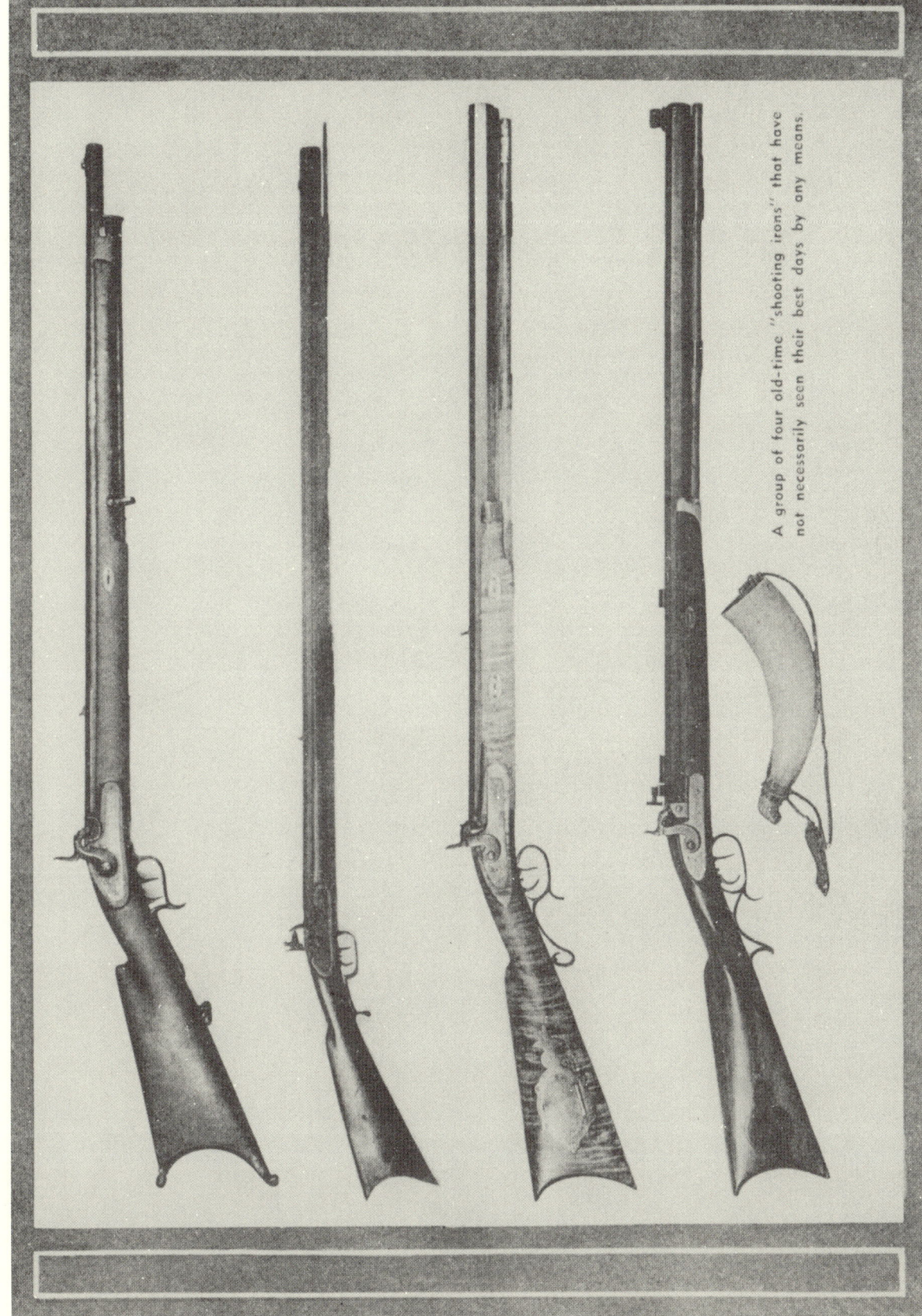

A group of four old-time "shooting irons" that have not necessarily seen their best days by any means.

PLATE 50

Above are shown nine shooters at a Southern match held at Jamestown, Tennessee, on July 4, 1942. This part of Tennessee is the home of Sergeant Alvin York, World War hero, to whom this volume is dedicated. Shown in this group are (left to right): Sam York, E. M. Farris (Portsmouth, Ohio), John Sowders, John Conatser, Sergeant Alvin C. York, Joe Young, Judge Roy S. Tinney (New Jersey), George Randall (Portsmouth, Ohio), and Henry York. The matches held here at "Three Forks of Wolf" are regular events.

Frontier Riflemen in American History

Boone's leg was broken by a bullet and he fell. An Indian leaped with tomahawk to finish him. Simon Kenton, shooting as he ran, saw Boone fall and shot the Indian who was hovering above the hunter. Lifting Boone, Kenton carried him into the fort and returned to the fight, which continued until the Indians fled.

When Kenton came into the fort, Boone thanked him in a terse backwoods statement for the saving of his life, "Simon, you are a fine fellow!"

Neither Boone nor Kenton thought that history would record the saving of Boone as the preeminent act of Kenton the scout.

Kenton was one of the foremost of our frontier riflemen during the last quarter of the eighteenth century. One of the rifles he used is still preserved in the collection of a West Virginia collector who lives near the Big Sandy River, where Kenton camped and hunted on two of his expeditions to the Kentucky country.

Andrew Jackson at Horse Shoe Bend

In his *"Constitutional History of Tennessee"*, Joshua W. Caldwell wrote of U. S. President Andrew Jackson: "The inauguration of Jackson brought a new class of men into leadership and marks the beginning for good or evil of a distinctly American order of politics, begotten of the crude forces of a new nationality. A change of political weather long preparing had set in——."

A change always set in wherever Jackson might be, whether in battle, politics, or the ordinary routine of existence. He was a dead shot with rifles or pistols, and he was a leader of men. The extraordinary reputation of Jackson is said by historians to have obscured men worthy of record; but from the time he was appointed Attorney General for the Tennessee district of Mero, and almost immediately received his first military appointment, in his twenty-fifth year (Sept. 10, 1792) and became Judge Advocate for the Davidson regiment, there can be no controversy over his place as leader.

I have handled guns of Andrew Jackson's soldiers; have looked over his pistols and rifles treasured in museums; and have stepped over the ground of his battles, but none gave me the thrill with which Tohopeka fired me.

The Muzzle-Loading Rifle—Then and Now

It was a day of high, cold March wind when I stood as Jackson had the day of his battle, looking at the bend of the river Tallapoosa, where, in the shape of a horse shoe it surrounds the land. This place the Indians thought inaccessible, surrounded by the river save for a narrow neck of land three hundred and fifty yards wide, which led into the place, and which the Indians had barricaded by placing large tree trunks across in rows, even making portholes for their rifles, after the manner of the white settlers. The 1,200 Indians behind the barricade of tree trunks felt secure.

From any other commander, perhaps, there might have been security, but to Jackson it was not a place of security but a pen, a pen where he would slaughter Indians as if they were pigs in a trap. "Corralled for slaughter" was evidently written above the pen Jackson visioned, a pen made of eighty to one hundred acres.

The plan of battle which Jackson prepared to accompany his report to superior officers is to me one of the most accurate and illuminating maps of battle line I ever have seen. I looked it over for an hour, thinking of what carnage followed in the pen, where between eight and nine hundred Indian braves met death. The rifles of that day were sufficient unto the task. Jackson lost forty-nine men, and one hundred fifty-four men were wounded. The Indians' power in a last stand was utterly broken by the accurate shots of the backwoods guns. Jackson himself was a dead shot.

After an hour I went over the site of the breastworks of the Indians,—tree trunks, now buried beneath years of accumulated mud. I was lucky: to my great joy I found several bullets of Jackson's soldiers in decayed wood many feet under ground. Half frozen, I waded out and added new bullets to my collection.

The Indian, Chief Tecumseh of the Shawnees, plotted to unite the Western tribes of Indians, from the Gulf of Mexico to the Great Lakes, in confederation against the white race,—and this scheme was forever crushed by Jackson. Tecumseh instructed Red Eagle, or William Weatherford as he was called by the white people, to close the enterprise.

After the muzzle to muzzle contest through portholes there was the wail of Red Eagle, "my warriors can no longer hear my voice." On Jackson's side there was the death of Major L. P. Montgomery, for whom the capital of Alabama was afterwards named, and there was a wounded soldier named Sam Houston; but there remains forever, above all, the accuracy of the backwoodsmen's rifles —the accuracy without which rifles are useless even in the hands of brave men.

The Friendship of Two Riflemen

The friendship between Andrew Jackson and Sam Houston, which began when Jackson saw a young boy, lying wounded on the battleground of the Horse Shoe Bend, and ordered a soldier to pull an Indian arrow from his thigh, has seemed to me one of the strongest and fairest formed by two noted riflemen. Andrew Jackson never forgot the young wounded Sam Houston who stormed the Indian tree fortification, stopped two bullets in his shoulder, and was left for dead in the charge.

From that time Sam Houston was a favorite of Jackson's and was backed by his powerful political influence. The tragedy which befell Houston in the second term of his governorship of Tennessee was made into a triumphant finale by an act of Jackson, which gave Houston the chance for a brilliant comeback.

When a young boy, Houston lived for three years with the Cherokee Indians in the Hiwassee country and was adopted by the chief, Oolooteka, who gave Houston the Indian name Colonneh, meaning "The Rover." When at the zenith of his success in Tennessee, having resigned the gubernatorial chair, Houston went again to the Cherokee nation, and to his Indian foster-father, who had moved with his tribe to Arkansas. Here Houston was witness to certain injustices which the Indians bore due to the misappropriation of funds from a government appropriation for their benefit. Oolooteka is said to have bitterly resented the injustice to his people.

Finally Houston agreed to intercede by placing the matter before Andrew Jackson, who was then President of the United States.

The Muzzle-Loading Rifle—Then and Now

Houston appeared at the White House in tribal dress and appealed to Jackson, who promptly referred the charges to the U. S. head of Indian affairs. The result was not satisfactory. Houston's charges were belittled.

However, as the two friends talked, Jackson convinced Houston that he should return to civilization and recover his former standing. As a first step Jackson offered Houston a small job, which was to take over the adjustment of the affairs of the Comanche Indians, who were raiding American settlements. This meant the assignment of Houston to Texas, then a part of Mexico, to act as a peacemaker.

"You know Indian life, Sam," Jackson insisted; "you are even an adopted son of the Cherokee Indians, and, in my opinion, you can do what no man I know could-do for me. I want that trouble attended to: it's more serious than the politicians think."

The settlers of Texas desired separation from Mexico and were lead by Sam Houston against Antonio Lopez de Santa Anna, president of Mexico, in a decisive battle at San Jacinto, where the battle cry "Remember the Alamo", rang from the throats of the settlers, and the hero of Texas found that the loss of his soldiers was six killed and twenty-five wounded. The Mexican loss was six hundred thirty killed, two hundred eight wounded, and seven hundred thirty prisoners.

Sam Houston, in a brilliant comeback, became the first president of the independent Republic of Texas. Behind this comeback I ever vision the friendship of Jackson—and I see the ring of rifles and riflemen—and, not least, I vision the unrecorded work of the army smith shop and the gunsmiths who were present on the eastern side of the Brazos, where Houston found two six-pounders which, he records, were "a present from some patriotic men in Cincinnati, which the smith's shop and gunsmiths employed in repairing the arms of the troops, were immediately occupied in making ready for use. All the old iron in the vicinity was cut into slugs and formed into cartridges." (Page 70, *"Life of Houston"*, by William Carey Crane).

Frontier Riflemen in American History

The Crockett Rifle

Of the many rifles that have been preserved from the days of the pioneer, none have a more interesting history than the rifle presented by the young Whigs of Philadelphia to the Hon. David Crockett, when he made a tour of the Northern states after his election to Congress in 1834. This rifle is now the property of Miss Beth Crockett of Little Rock, Ark., who is the great-great-granddaughter of the illustrious Davy. The rifle itself is in the State Capitol Museum at Little Rock.

There is no doubt of the genuineness of this famous rifle. On a silver plate near the lock is the name of the maker, Constable. His shop was at Second and Walnut Streets, Philadelphia, Pa. He was a wonderful workman and made very fine rifles and pistols. There is inlaid in the barrel in gold letters,—"Presented by the Young Men of Philadelphia to the Hon. David Crockett of Tennessee", and the words "Go Ahead". On the silver patch box, engraved by Hollyland, New York, is the picture of a coon, which is, no doubt, the one that said: "Don't shoot, Davey, and I'll come down."

Crockett states in his biography that this was the most beautiful rifle he had ever seen.

After returning to Tennessee from his travels in the North, Crockett went hunting to try out this rifle and he killed a deer at the distance of one hundred and thirty yards. One of the unusual features of this rifle is the pistol grip,—something ordinarily not found on the rifles of the earlier days. It has a percussion lock which was just coming into use at this time,—and this, perhaps, was the reason that he did not take it with him to Texas. He evidently preferred one of larger caliber and a flintlock, as flints could be obtained anywhere, while percussion caps might be difficult to obtain on a distant frontier.

Crockett was born in Greene County, East Tennessee, in August, 1786,—and his rifle shots rang in every forest of the state during his life. As late as 1926 a lone grave in a forest near Winchester, Tennessee, was identified as that of Crockett's beloved wife, Polly. There had been no record of Crockett's life in which the Elk river homestead had been chronicled,—but a search resulted in finding old letters which revealed that he had lived there with Polly and that when she died and he had buried her in the forest beneath a top crude marking of small boulder-like stones, he shouldered his flintlock and walked a trail southward. That flintlock was, without doubt, the rifle he shot last in the Alamo. Of this rifle there is no trace. Crockett was put to death by order of Santa Anna, March 6, 1836, and the rifle became war plunder.

Alvin York

I made a photograph of Sergeant Alvin York's marriage in the mountains where he was born, reared and learned to shoot with frontier rifles. He knew and handled the muzzle-loader as did his ancestors, and he has been a match shooter from his youth.

"Were those Germans like squirrels or a match shooting target, in your Tennessee mountains, to you and your aim?" I wanted to ask him; but it was not a fitting day on which to inquire about the flintlocks and muzzle-loaders which are numerous in the hills back of York's house.

York's spectacular accomplishment as a soldier in the First World War caused him to be acclaimed one of the greatest heroes of the war. In the Argonne on October 8, 1918, armed only with a Springfield rifle and an automatic pistol, York single-handedly killed twenty Germans, captured a strategic hill, and compelled the surrender of 132 Germans, including a major and three lieutenants, as well as capturing thirty-five machine guns.

General Foch called this feat "the greatest thing accomplished by any private soldier of all the armies of Europe." York was awarded the Medal of Honor by the United States government, and the Croix de Guerre by General Foch personally.

York's outstanding marksmanship was acquired by long practice in match shooting in the mountains of his native Tennessee, where he won fame as one of the best shots with the highland rifle. In shooting matches at a range of forty yards, which was just the distance from which he fought the Germans, he would put ten rifle bullets into a space no larger than a man's thumb nail. Even as a small boy he had aimed his rifle at the bobbing heads of turkeys that had been tethered behind a log so that only their heads showed. In comparison, therefore, hitting the German heads and helmets, which loomed large before him, seemed a simple matter to York. Truly, the outstanding hero of the First World War was a product of the kind of rifles and the kind of shooting that I have attempted to cover in this book.

CHAPTER XIV.

MATCH SHOOTING TODAY IN TENNESSEE

"I WOULD rather go to one of the old matches than any other kind of sport. We have great times down here at the matches. They use the same old method that was used one hundred years ago," I wrote my close friend Guy Burch, of Macedonia, Illinois, and how true that is, it comes from my heart.

Philip P. Quayle wrote me not long since: "I had not the least idea that these old rifle matches were still or rather even recently held. I have often wished that I could attend one. However, after noting the kind of shooting you and your friends do I would only want to be a spectator . . ."

The long, heavy, soft metal-barreled match rifles of an old and pioneer day are used in these matches, and guns of four to seven generations in age often appear on the shooting range, having been handed down from generation to generation in one family or related group. I have shot in matches in the Cumberland Mountains for many years and have known gunmakers; the art or trade of making match rifles is handed down from father to son in most cases.

The match of which I wrote in an earlier chapter of this book is typical of all matches. They are conducted today as they were in the first matches, and there is little, if any, change in the men, the rifles, or the shooting of yesterday and today.

Raven Rock is still a favorite match shooting range of many years past, and will continue to be for many years more, despite the close approach of highways of recent days.

In 1934 I took with me to the National Muzzle-Loading Rifle Matches held at Portsmouth, Ohio, February 21-22, four match shooters with whom I had shot over a period of many years, each Saturday afternoon, if the weather permitted, near Raven Rock, Tennessee. The four, Arthur Kelley, Jim Kelley, Bird Fann and Gilbert Angel, were Cumberland Mountain match shooters of great accuracy. I expected the shooting of these men would be at least of first grade, and I was not disappointed, for Gilbert Angel, using

Match Shooting Today in Tennessee

my 15-pound, 31-inch barrel Whitmore rifle, (mentioned elsewhere as tested by Philip Quayle), won first place with a score of 46 out of a possible 50 at 220 yards.

Angel's comment was that of a Southern mountaineer, "I went nine hundred miles to shoot five holes in a piece of paper," but he was proud of the target and of winning the 220-yard match. It was no better shooting than he did many a Saturday under a Tennessee sky.

As I have previously stated, the match rifle differs from the hunting rifle in length of barrel, weight and caliber. The shooting match rifles which are used in the Tennessee mountains are all originals, most of them having been in the families of the men using them for, perhaps, over a hundred years.

I have owned several hundred of these match rifles, and my favorite, "Long Tom", was made by Enoch Hardin, a gunsmith whose guns excelled in correctness of sight placements and the quality of the materials used in the making. Enoch Hardin lived in Birchwood, Tennessee, at one time, later coming to Soddy, within a few miles of Chattanooga.

A description of only six Tennessee mountain match rifles from my collection will serve to illustrate the typical rifle used by the shooters with whom I have been associated in match shooting in this state. They are all handmade by the mountain gunsmiths of Tennessee and the barrels welded of the very softest iron. The match rifle of Tennessee is noted for accuracy. Each rifle has a name and is known by that name among the rifle shooters. There are few exceptions when a rifle has not been used in matches at sixty yards.

(1) "Long Tom"—54-inch barrel, caliber .42, full-length black walnut stock, weight 20 pounds, seven grooves, pitch one-half turn in 48 inches. Will shoot center at 60 yards. Made by Enoch Hardin.

(2) "Jack Henderson"—weight 16 pounds, 50-inch tapered barrel, caliber .46, full-length black walnut stock, double triggers, seven grooves, pitch one turn in 48 inches. Made by Enoch Hardin.

(3) "Old Scaley"—so-called because the outside of the barrel was never dressed. The welding scales still remain just as when it

came from the forge. 46-inch barrel, caliber .47, pitch of rifling one turn in 48 inches, weight 14 pounds. It holds a record group at 60 yards, five shots measuring one-quarter inch from center to center of bullet holes. A famous match rifle made by Enoch Hardin.

(4) "Uncle Bob"—45-inch barrel, caliber 48, full-length black walnut stock, weight 12½ pounds, German silver patch box, narrow lands and wide grooves. I do not know the maker.

(5) "Shackle Stock"—43-inch barrel, caliber .48, full-length black walnut stock, weight 13 pounds. Made by John W. Clement, one of Tennessee's noted gunsmiths prior to the War Between the States.

(6) "Old Flint"—a match rifle of unknown age but very old, changed from flint to percussion lock. Has 43-inch barrel, caliber .52, full-length maple stock and weight 18 pounds.

I have written many articles from time to time eulogizing and glorifying the rifle matches I enjoyed so much, and it occurred to me that perhaps some additional eyewitness' testimony or evidence would be in order, so I have asked my friend, Charles J. Kellem, of Joliet, Illinois, to report his findings. Mr. Kellem has often accompanied me on my Saturday shooting matches. His article follows:

My First Long Rifle Shooting Match

"Having been invited by Mr. Walter Cline, I attended my first old-fashioned shooting match on the Jim Barker Kelley farm in Sequatchie Valley, near Pikeville, Tenn., Saturday, December 10, 1927, where only the muzzle-loading rifles with open sights were used.

There were eleven contestants, including Mr. Cline, J. G. Gauntt of Chattanooga, Gilbert Angel, Jack Morgan, Rudolf Holt, Bird Fann, Bird Freeman, Arthur Kelley, Jim Barker Kelley, myself and one other whose name I did not get.

Two kinds of targets were used. (1) A piece of white cardboard about four inches by five inches tacked on a charred board about 8 inches by twelve inches. On the charred board two lines were cut at right angles, over which the cardboard was placed. The

Match Shooting Today in Tennessee

object was to cut the cross or the intersection of the lines. (2) An inverted cut was made in a piece of white cardboard and the apex placed directly over the intersection of the lines cut in the charred board.

The shooting was at 60 yards, prone position, and muzzle rest. One man acted as target keeper, placing each shooter's target, in his turn, against the backstop, which was an old tree.

When a shooter cut or came close to the intersection of the lines, new lines were cut on the board for the succeeding shots and the cardboard was moved so as to place the point of impact on the white card over the intersection of the new lines, thus avoiding grouping of the shots on the board and making it easier to measure the accuracy of each shot. Also, when a shot cut the intersecting lines such expressions as "center", "four points", "first choice", "ham and eggs" were heard, meaning that the shooter had placed a winning shot even before inspecting his target.

At the close of the match Arthur Kelley gathered up the targets and by the use of a pair of dividers he measured very accurately the best scores to determine the winners. This operation was most interesting. A half bullet was placed in the bullet hole in the charred board, the flat surface flush with the charred board. Cross lines were cut on the flat surface of the bullet to determine the center, then the crossed lines on the charred board were extended on the half bullet, the intersection of these lines cutting the exact center of the point of impact. By placing one point of the dividers on the center of the half bullet and the other point on the center of the point of impact, the accuracy of the shot and the best scores were determined. Nothing was left to the eye or to guess work. Some of the scores looked as if they were tied, but this method of measuring showed them to vary by several thousandths of an inch.

The shooting was finished just before dark. One of the men killed a hog, a fine big Duroc Jersey, with one shot from a long rifle placed well between the eyes. The hog was then thrown across the back of a horse and one of the men rode to hold it from slipping off while another led the horse to Mr. Kelley's house. A kettle of water

The Muzzle-Loading Rifle—Then and Now

was heated in the yard and in the light furnished by the headlights of two automobiles, Bird Freeman dressed and divided the meat among the winners.

The prizes were portions of this freshly butchered hog, which was paid for by entry fees of $1.50. Each shooter was allowed seven shots and the hog was divided seven ways as follows: first and second choice, hams; third and fourth choice, shoulders; fifth choice, backbone; sixth choice, spare ribs; and seventh choice, the leaf lard and head.

Gilbert Angel took first choice, Rudolf Holt second choice, Mr. Cline and I tied for third choice, and I also won seventh choice.

Mr. Cline permitted me to shoot one of his best rifles, "Long Tom." This noted rifle was made by Enoch Hardin, of Soddy, Tenn. The barrel was 54-inches long, caliber .42, seven grooves and pitch one-half turn in 48 inches. The stock was full-length black walnut and the rifle weighed 20 pounds.

It is needless to say that this match not only initiated me into the pleasures of long rifle match shooting, but also into the company of a group of the best sportsmen it has ever been my pleasure to meet. My heart has been in match rifle shooting ever since that experience. —C. J. K."

Reading again my friend Kellem's report in the foregoing paragraphs brings vividly to my mind other shooting experiences I enjoyed with him, but I shall take time to record only one:

August, of 1928, on the grounds of the Chattanooga Rod and Gun Club, near Hixson, Tennessee, an old-fashioned shooting match was held. Many of the marksmen were men of the mountains and each was accompanied by his trusty muzzle-loader and each carried a bandolier of supplies, which was certainly necessary, about his neck. There were "mountain men" F. B. Fann, of Pikeville; J. E. Weigle, Pikeville; Gilbert Angel, Pikeville; Jim Kelley, Pikeville, and "city fellers" Charles Kellem, Dr. W. F. Morgan, Prof. M. O. Hill, J. W. Oliphant, Roy Painter, and Walter M. Cline.

Match Shooting Today in Tennessee

The targets were at a distance of sixty yards from the marksmen and the position was prone. I took my five shots at the beginning of the match and split my cross on the first bullet. I won the silver cup; F. B. Fann won second and fifth prize, a silver cup and a flashlight; Roy Painter won third prize, which was a box of cigars; J. E. Weigle, of Pikeville, won fourth and tenth prize, which consisted of a watch chain and a very handsome pocket knife; Gilbert Angel was so busy helping everyone else that he did not shoot with his usual excellence, but he won sixth prize, a pocket knife; Dr. Morgan won seventh and eighth prizes, a knife and a pipe; Prof. Hill won ninth prize, a knife; Charles Kellem won the eleventh prize, which was a first aid kit, and Jim Kelley who only half tried to shoot, won twelfth prize, which was a necktie.

It was a most enjoyable match and I recall most pleasantly the laughter, the jokes, the serious handling of rifles, and the keen interest of those taking part in the competition. The papers headlined the event as a "Colorful Affair"—well, it was all of that and more!

Chapter XV.

THE REVIVAL OF THE MATCHES

THE modern revival of the muzzle-loading matches began February 22, 1931, in Portsmouth, Ohio, with a match sponsored by the Norfolk and Western Railway Y. M. C. A. Rifle and Revolver Club. It was instituted at the suggestion of Oscar L. Seth, president of the club, when the accuracy of the muzzle-loading rifle was being discussed by some of the old-timers, who contended that at short ranges the old rifle compared favorably in this respect with the modern arms.

From this small beginning of sixty-seven enthusiastic riflemen, the National Muzzle-loading Rifle Association developed a couple of years later. It has grown by leaps and bounds, and its membership now exceeds 1,200, scattered from Norway to Midway Islands, from Alaska to Cuba. Matches are sponsored annually by the Association, and such great interest has been stimulated that matches have been held from coast to coast. Postal matches have been instituted and have met with remarkable success. Thus has been revived a type of shooting which, outside of the mountains of Tennessee, had become a thing of the past.

It was especially fitting that the first of these matches should be held in the Ohio Valley, on the anniversary of the birth of the Father of Our Country, for on May 26, 1754, Washington gave the command to fire the shot that started the struggle for the Ohio Valley. This shot was fired from a muzzle-loading flintlock rifle at Great Meadows in Pennsylvania; and thus began the French and Indian War, which England won with the aid of her Colonial riflemen. In later years, in the Revolutionary War, it was again necessary for Washington to call for his riflemen. They responded to a man, and with deadly rifles helped to win our independence.

In the struggle for the possession of the Ohio Valley, the battle of Point Pleasant was fought between the Indians and the pioneers, the greatest Indian battle of all history. In fact, the journey of the pioneers into the wilderness of that day was possible only with the

The Revival of the Matches

aid of the long rifles of those early times. Finlay, who first saw and reported the Kentucky country, Boone, Kenton, Harrod, Logan, and other fearless men who followed them, used their long rifles to help settle this great valley.

For that first muzzle-loader revival match in 1931, old family heirlooms were dug up from places long since forgotten and scoured out. Beautiful curly-maple stocks, many of them inlaid with silver and engraved by an artist's hand, emerged from the grease and grime of a century ago. From under the rust of time there appeared the names of gunsmiths well known in the days when the Ohio country was young, and the fierce Wyandots, Shawnees and Mingos were contending in savage warfare for their ancestral homes in the wilderness. Seventy rifles appeared at this first match, the youngest of the lot dating back to 1880, and this youngster was fired in the match by the maker himself. Each rifle was different, and each had its tradition and its story as to how it once performed in the hands of its original owner.

At the second annual muzzle-loading match, held at Portsmouth in February, 1932, there was a noticeable increase in accuracy, as the contestants had become more familiar with the old rifles. Also the gunsmiths of the old days, who still survived, had been persuaded to get out their ancient equipment and call back across the years some measure of their old-time skill; and the rifles were in better shooting condition than they had been on the occasion of the first match. Barrels had been dressed out, locks worked over, new sights fitted and old and needed parts resurrected from their hiding places on top shelves and in dark corners of old hardware and sporting goods houses, where they had lain hidden these many years.

A further increase in skill in the handling of the muzzle-loader was in evidence at the third annual Muzzle-Loading Rifle Match, February 22, 1933, on the range at Portsmouth. While perhaps it may never be possible for riflemen of today to draw from the muzzle-loading rifle the accuracy obtained with it by the famous riflemen of the frontier, it is evident from the climbing scores each year that the small-bore will one day have a worthy competitor.

The Muzzle-Loading Rifle—Then and Now

It was at this time that plans were made for the establishment of a national organization of the muzzle-loading rifle users, for the purpose of promoting muzzle-loading matches throughout the country and stimulating interest in the old rifles of the pioneers.

A special feature of the fourth annual National Muzzle-Loading Rifle Matches, held at Portsmouth February 21-22, was the forty-rod match, which originated many years ago with the riflemen of other days. Its revival was promoted by Mr. Walter Heightshoe, then of Columbus, Ohio, who provided a beautiful trophy for the event.

It had been years since a match of this kind was held, and a number of fine target rifles arose from a long sleep to do it honor. These rifles were of a type made by the early gunsmiths especially for target work, and they set a record for accuracy which has never been surpassed. They were heavy rifles, with false muzzles and bullet starters, and they used conical bullets of a peculiar shape, the so-called picket bullet.

As at all the previous matches, great interest was shown in the old rifles brought to the matches, and they were displayed and talks given on the fine ones. Among those used in the long range match were a 25-pound Reinhardt, made at Loudonville, Ohio; a 24-pound rifle by Ripley (Raible), who worked at Warren, Ohio, about 1850; and an 18-pound Siebert. Siebert was a celebrated rifle-maker of Columbus, Ohio, as early as 1840, and turned out many fine target rifles. All these rifles had false muzzles and bullet starters and used the swaged picket bullet.

Then there was the fine Whitmore rifle of the author, which was the one tested by Dr. Philip Quayle in the laboratory of the Peters Cartridge Company. This rifle and its equipment were in every respect as originally turned out. It weighs 15 pounds, has a 31-inch barrel, and the rifling is cut on a gain twist. C. R. Ripley brought a J. F. Thomas rifle of 18 pounds weight and used in it powder and bullets that had been left by the original owner many years before.

The Revival of the Matches

A rifle belonging to C. J. Kellem, of Joliet, Illinois, was displayed which had been used in the Battle of New Orleans more than a century ago. Another rifle of beautiful workmanship, the property of C. R. Ripley, of Dennison, Ohio, was of English origin and had been made for Sir Henry Halford, Baronet, who was captain of the British team in the International Long Range Matches for the American Centennial Palma Trophy and the Championship of the World, shot at Creedmore, 1877, which match the American team won by a margin of 92 points. F. J. Slyker, of Detroit, exhibited some very fine flintlock rifles.

The Powell Crosley Old-Time Muzzle-Loading Rifle Match was first held in Friendship, Indiana, in 1933. Boss Johnston, originator of the famous R. F. D. program at the WLW Crosley radio station in Cincinnati, remarked over the air that he wondered how many of the long rifles which had helped to settle the Ohio Valley were still preserved, and how many could shoot them and would like to have an opportunity to participate in an old-time match. The response was so great that Mr. Crosley donated a loving cup for the winner, and a match was held with 260 contestants and a great crowd of spectators.

This match, for which almost no preparations were made, was such a success that the next year elaborate plans were made for holding it at Rising Sun, Indiana. The 100-yard match was an added feature this year, and the trophy was known as the Boss Johnston Trophy. The Crosley Championship Match was at the 60-yard range.

Among the interesting highlights of this match was the remarkable accuracy of the flintlock rifles that were used in competition with the percussion locks. Flintlock scores were right up with those of the caplock rifles.

The number of spectators attracted to the match was conservatively estimated at from 2,000 to 2,500. As at all the matches, contestants came from great distances to participate. As a Tennessee rifleman expressed it, "Nine hundred miles to shoot five holes in a piece of paper," but he wanted to go back next year.

The Muzzle-Loading Rifle—Then and Now

It was decided at this meeting to combine the National Muzzle-Loading Matches with the Crosley Match in 1935 and to hold both at Rising Sun. Because of the rapid growth of the national organization larger accommodations were needed than Portsmouth could offer. Since that time the combined matches have been known as the WLW-National Matches.

Two hundred fifty riflemen assembled at the Laughery Club near Rising Sun, Indiana, for the first combined Crosley and National Muzzle-Loading Rifle Matches, September 27-28-29, 1935. Not since the day that George Rogers Clark and his heroic riflemen set out from the Falls of the Ohio for the conquest of the Illinois country has a more colorful band of riflemen assembled on the banks of the Ohio than that which took part in these matches. Not since the Battle of Shiloh, in 1862, has there been such a variation in arms assembled on one field.

I have never seen such innovations and inventions in riflery as appeared on the range at this time. Many had worked out their own ideas in construction of rifles, boring and rifling the barrels and building complete outfits. One rifle that deserves notice was a fifty-three pound one with the barrel made from a piece of line shafting. There were some bolt action muzzle-loaders using the percussion cap. Many types of bullets of original design made their appearance. But in spite of all the modern machinery the rifles of the old masters of several generations ago reigned supreme.

There was an increased number of flintlocks; some that had perhaps seen service with George Rogers Clark at Vincennes and Kaskaskia. There were twenty-five or thirty fine match rifles with false muzzles, whereas the preceding year there were only two. There were several foreign rifles, an English Whitworth, a Gibbs, a double-barreled Jacobs rifle with its winged bullet to fit the grooves. There were round-ball rifles of every description; match rifles using a conical bullet with a circular linen patch; others using two and three paper patches lubricated with every kind of lubricant from sperm oil to skunk oil.

It was the writer's intention to make personal check of all the matches in regard to rifles used, methods of handling, powder charge, pitch of grooves, caliber, sights, etc., and to write his impressions as to just what would lead to improving the accuracy of the muzzle-loading rifle. It was not possible to fully cover all the events but the following is the result of those that came under his observation.

In the Crosley sixty-yard round ball match the winner, C. R. Ramsey, of Portsmouth, Ohio, used a Siebert match rifle which at one time had a false muzzle. Siebert was an exponent of the gain twist and this rifle has a gain twist. The writer, in winning the Class A (for men over sixty years of age), used an old combined hunting and match rifle weighing fourteen pounds. This rifle had originally been a flintlock and was used for years as a hunting rifle in the Cumberland Mountains of Tennessee. It has a forty-eight-inch barrel, with a pitch of grooves of one-half turn in forty-eight inches. The bullet in this slow pitch develops high velocity. Using fifty grains of King's Semi-Smokeless FFG powder, the forty-five caliber bullet was not affected by the wind. The rifle of Joe Lamping of Cincinnati, who won the Class B match (for men under sixty) with a score of 48 x 50 on the fifty-yard small bore target, the writer did not get to examine, but the score speaks for itself, as it was shot with open sights in a high wind. The patching was different for each rifle. The writer used .015 linen. Mr. Ramsey used drilling.

I have searched every available source of information about the material used by the old riflemen for patching, and I find only the following mention. In Kercheval's *"History of the Valley of Virginia"*, written in 1833, I find under a description of an expected attack by the Indians on Doddridges Fort that the following orders were issued in regard to the rifles: "When you run your bullets cut off the neck very close and scrape them, get patches one hundred threads finer than those you are accustomed to use." This evidently refers to linen.

In some of the old ledger accounts back as early as 1774 I find entries of the sale of a cloth called Osnaburgh. This was very similar to our drilling of the present day. As late as the early eighteen fifties it was used by Meredith Wolfe, gunsmith of Tennessee, and one of the best off-hand shots of his day. This cloth came from a town in Germany called Osnaburgh. Bed ticking was also used, for in the days of the muzzle-loader there was always plenty of this material around the home.

In the match of 1935 I saw some of the men using this material and hammering the bullet in the barrel with a short rod and hammer. This has always been productive of inaccurate shooting.

There was more interest this year in the longer range matches. There were many match rifles in the one hundred and the two hundred twenty yard matches. There were rifles by old masters long since passed on: Billinghurst, Lewis, Morgan James, Loomis, Perry, Warner, Whitmore, Rheinhart, Schalk, and Brockway. An English Gibbs and a Whitworth were also used in these matches.

An evidence of the accuracy of these rifles and the success of the present day riflemen in getting them to perform as in the days of old is seen in the Brockway rifle owned and used in winning the 100-yard match by Walter Grote, of Canton, Ohio, a possible with four X. This Brockway rifle deserves more than a passing notice and credit must be given Mr. Grote for his ability in handling it and making it perform with its old-time accuracy.

Mr. Grote's rifle uses the three-strip paper patch. Brockway developed this method and the muzzle for loading both two and three-strip paper patches. The rifle weighs twenty pounds, has a thirty-inch barrel and the bullet measures .380 in diameter at the base and is one and three-sixteenths in length. It takes a pitch of one turn in eighteen inches to handle this bullet. The powder charge is sixty grains of FFG black powder in weighed charges and the bullets are also weighed. Bond paper oiled with sperm oil is used for the patches, the same kind of lubricant that was always used with the paper patches in the match rifles. Sperm oil is not affected by changes in temperature.

Another Brockway rifle also won the 220-yard match with a high score. This rifle was made for C. F. Fletcher of Bellows Falls, Vermont, who was a member of the National Rifle Club organized in 1858. In the years 1894-98 Fletcher won the annual matches with this rifle. These matches were fifty shot affairs, and the results were obtained by measuring from the center of the bullet hole to the cen-

The Revival of the Matches

ter of the target, the shortest string winning the match. For the five matches of 250 shots Fletcher's average was one and one-eighth inches from the center. The matches are recorded in the minutes of the club, and witnessed, so it is no idle tale.

Another interesting rifle was the one used by E. V. Menefee who won second place in the 100-yard match with a score of 99. This rifle weighs twenty-four pounds, has sixteen grooves, with a pitch of one turn in sixteen inches. It is fifty caliber and the bullet is one and one-half inches in length and weighs about 700 grains. It resembles an armour piercing affair with a hard point and soft lead base, a composite bullet. A two-strip paper patch was used in this rifle.

In this match the round ball rifles were right up with the leaders. Clyde Dixon, using a round ball muzzle-loading rifle, was third in the 100-yard match, and that on the small bore target, with a score of 48 x 50. This remarkable accuracy of the muzzle-loading rifle will go a long way to substantiate claims of some of the feats of the muzzle-loading rifle handed down from the days of our ancestors.

Several things developed throughout this match that it may be well to mention so that they can be corrected. One was the leading of the barrels. This is caused by improper lubrication and by not making the bullets right. All three rifles that the writer brought to the match were put out of commission by this leading of the bore. In the last minute rush to get away for the match the bullets were just cast and swaged. The writer knew that this did not make a perfect bullet and that it had been discovered many years ago that it is necessary to hammer the lead after casting and before swaging. A bullet that is cast and swaged will upset or expand with a very rough surface, whereas one that is hammered after casting and then swaged will expand with a smooth surface.

For lubrication, sperm oil is the best for the paper patches and many used this for linen patches, all surplus oil being wiped off. The patches should be oiled fresh just before each match. Relined barrels made their appearance this year, and while there had not been time to fully target them and work out loads and other details, these relined barrels showed fine accuracy. This method is not new, for Brockway relined many match rifles. He always claimed that relined barrels were more accurate than solid barrels. This relining of the barrels of old muzzle-loaders is a splendid way to restore those with a rusted, or too large a bore to be rebored.

The 220-yard match was also won by Mr. Grote with the Brockway rifle with a score of 95 x 100. Second place went to E. M. Farris, of Portsmouth, Ohio, and secretary of the National Muzzle-Loading Rifle Association, who used an English Whitworth, with a score of 90 x 100. This rifle does not have grooves but the bore is cut six-sided (hexagon in shape). The hexagon has one turn in twenty inches. The bullet is cast to fit the bore. Mr. Farris was not able to find a mould for this pitch but did get some bullets for a left-hand pitch of one turn in thirty-six inches. He used this bullet in a right hand pitch cut one turn in twenty inches and scored 90. Maybe some one else can figure this out. It is beyond me. Robert Heightshoe, of Columbus, Ohio, a bright-eyed chap of fourteen years shot a 90 in this match, but was unfortunate in getting one shot on the wrong target. This lad has the makings of one of the very finest rifle shots and we will hear more from him in the future. As in the 100-yard match there was evidence of the bore leading and the bullets tipping. There was not enough powder, or the pitch of the grooves was not steep enough for the length of the bullet.

The Class C Match for women was won by Mrs. Tye Holcomb, of Portsmouth, Ohio, who is nationally known for her skill in the small bore matches.

The John Mench Match at 100 yards was won by Charles Marine with a score of 41 x 50, which was an excellent score for muzzle-loaders with the old open sights, off hand.

The great interest shown in all the matches and the increased number of entries indicated the growing popularity of the muzzle-loading rifle matches throughout the country.

* * * *

Editor's Note: For the concluding portion of this chapter, Mr. E. M. Farris, of Portsmouth, Ohio, Secretary of the National Muzzle-loading Rifle Association, has

The Revival of the Matches

contributed the following account of the Association's activities since its inception to the purchase of a National shooting range in Indiana, which has been appropriately named "The Walter M. Cline Range", honoring the memory of the author of this book.

Competitive muzzle-loading rifle matches have never ceased since their beginning in America, but it is true that this invigorating sport has, in the past, suffered low ebbs at times. But let no one say that at any period there was an end to the era of that fine arm. There was, we all agree, a period of several years which witnessed but few shoots of consequence. But even right through those years there were a few individuals and some groups that kept up the spirit of the frontier marksman, notably at Canal Fulton, Ohio; around Shartlesville, Pennsylvania; in the vicinity of Terre Haute, Indiana; and down in the Kentucky and Tennessee mountain sections. Great credit is due to those who kept their rifles in shooting condition and who remembered how to "fresh out" the bores and who were able to instruct the raw recruits when the real muzzle-loading revival did start in 1931.

Oscar L. Seth, an active small bore shooter of Portsmouth, Ohio, approached the writer late in 1930 and said, "I am tired of hearing these hill born railroad men (we were in the N. & W. Railway Y. M. C. A. at Portsmouth at the time) boasting how their back-in-the-hills uncles and grandpaps always knocked out the eyes of squirrels with the old smoke poles at fifty yards and more." It was just a little remark like that, friends, that started something! Boiling it down, here is what resulted: The "Y" small bore rifle club agreed to spend up to one hundred dollars of its funds to purchase a good trophy to attract shooters of muzzle-loaders. February 22, 1931, was the date set for the initial match and that happened to be a real winter day for Southern Ohio. The day finally arrived and the stage was set. They came and they kept coming until the registration clerk announced that there were sixty-seven entries. Shooters came from the farms and the factories, from the offices and from schoolrooms, from stores and industrial plants,—but not a single hill-rifleman was on hand at this first match. The old legend of hit-'em-in-the-eye-every-time-at-fifty-yards was laid low.

The Muzzle-Loading Rifle—Then and Now

There were re-entry matches and it was in these matches where the boys set their sights and generally learned whether or not the old gun would really shoot. Many old rifles at this match had remained unfired for forty or fifty years or more. A few of them never got warmed up during the entire day. Bullets would not go down or if they did get down they could not be fired for various and sundry reasons. Many locks refused to function. Some rifles would snap a cap and others were so clogged with rust and dirt that it became impossible to ignite the powder. All in all, it was an awful day, Mates! But with all these nonfunctioning rifles being handled by comparatively inexperienced men, who cussed and threatened, still not an accident occurred. This absence of accidents has been the rule right through the years, and the fact bespeaks credit to the good sense of the shooters and the good management of the matches.

Tom Overly, of Omeaga, Ohio, won the trophy the first year. The course was three shots prone and two offhand at sixty yards. The score was 37 x 50, which was not bad considering all conditions under which the shoot was held.

Matches were held each of the next two years (1932 and 1933) on the same range, with fewer entrants but with more guns in shooting condition. An important truth began to dawn on the promoters. They came to a quick realization that they had struck upon an idea which was really captivating the imagination of many shooters from many sections of the country. They recognized the fact that the revival of muzzle-loading shooting could be developed on a national scale. The 40-rod game got its start toward revival in the year 1933 in a full day of practice and record shooting on the day preceding the regularly scheduled short range matches.

About this time, Boss Johnston, of the R. F. D. hour on WLW radio station at Cincinnati, got the idea that the listeners in his radio audience might want to see some of the old-time shooting arms in action. They did! Boss invited them to come together in the schoolyard at Friendship, Indiana, in the winter of 1933, and he had such a turn-out that he was obliged to cut the course to three shots in order to complete the program before dark, but even at that there were so many entries that some scores were never fired. "Bull" Ramsey, a

The Revival of the Matches

Portsmouth shooter, attended this Indiana WLW shoot and his contact with Boss soon resulted in a plan for both groups working together—that is, the WLW shooters and the group with headquarters in Portsmouth.

In 1934 everyone was invited to a much-expanded shoot in the alfalfa field adjoining Laughery Park at Rising Sun, Indiana. The radio publicity had done its work most effectively. So had Pete Menefee and his Rising Sun assistants. The short range, mid-range, and long range events got a great run and the scores were all well above the previous tabulations at Portsmouth. It was on this occasion that Boss invited Walter M. Cline, President of the National Muzzle-Loading Rifle Association, together with the writer, Secretary of the Association (N. M. L. R. A. had been formed at Portsmouth during the 1933 shoot), to join with the Hoosier folks and hold the next National in connection with the WLW shoot on these same grounds. This invitation was accepted and all of the annual shoots have been held in Southern Indiana right up to and including 1941.

In the meantime, our bulletin service had contacted groups at Shartlesville, Pennsylvania; Detroit; Cincinnati; Dayton; Canal Fulton, Ohio; Huntington, West Virginia; Marion, Indiana; Marietta, Ohio; Pikeville, Kentucky; Croyden, Indiana; Pine Bluff, Arkansas; Chicago; Lexington, Kentucky; Chattanooga, Tennessee; Cos Cob, Connecticut; Fort Ticonderoga, New York; Santa Ana and San Diego, California; Seaside, Oregon; Lewistown, Montana; Kansas City, Missouri; Wichita, Kansas; Brownsville, Texas; Salem, Ohio; Lockport, New York; and many other communities. Many of the groups in these centers flourished, while others were only feebly successful for a time. Canada began to take notice of the old game and we have had the pleasure of receiving many members from above the border. Frantz Rosenberg, a great sportsman and grand gentleman of Littlehammer, Norway, early enlisted as a life member of the Association and it was our pleasure to maintain constant contact with him until this connection was broken during the vicissitudes and uncertainties of the great World War No. Two. Our membership covers the entire United States and some of our members receive their mail in Manila, Midway Island, Hawaii, Mexico, Cuba and England. The war has made it difficult to keep alive our contact with these shooters in foreign lands.

With the movement well on its way toward permanence, there were two important factors of major consequence which have accelerated our growth tremendously,—first, the establishment of *"Muzzle Blasts"* magazine and second, the purchase of a National range, which has been named "The Walter M. Cline Range", honoring the author of this volume. *"Muzzle Blasts"* was founded in an effort to give the members of the association an improved news service. The long-established mimeographed bulletins were limited in length, style, make-up, and appeal. The first four-page printed sheet in September, 1939, was a modest effort, but at least it found response and created a demand for its continuance. Soon we realized some income from advertising and we noted that members in the Association would renew more readily by virtue of the little magazine which they received at no extra cost. Up until the time of writing this article, sixteen pages has been the maximum size of *"Muzzle Blasts"* and this was for a special WLW edition and also for the issue of March, 1942, when we had such a wealth of good material that we found it could not be contained in the usual twelve-page magazine. *"Muzzle Blasts* has up to this writing served for a consecutive run of thirty-four monthly issues, outliving several other good gun publications that had enjoyed a somewhat limited clientele. If it continues to live and expand the fans will have proven their loyalty and sportsmanship, and the editor will be deeply appreciative.

About the beginning of 1942 it became apparent that moving from range to range and shooting in miscellaneous clover, alfalfa, or stubble was not conducive for the permanency of the Association. Walter M. Cline had passed on to the Eternal Happy Hunting Ground in April, 1941. With no little audacity, the widow and children of Mr. Cline were approached by officers of the Association with the proposition that they might wish to memorialize the husband and father by having a range named for him. Their enthusiastic response was immediate, and they generously made a substantial contribution to head the subscription list for a National range

The Revival of the Matches

and expressed the hope that land and facilities best suited to the Association's activities could be secured. The meadow and hill tract at Friendship, Indiana, where the 1940 and 1941 matches had been held, was investigated. A meeting of both directors and members of the Association was called to be held at the Dillsboro, Indiana, health resort on February 8 for consideration of an offer from Mr. Wilkie Lemon, owner of this farm. Briefly, the fifty-three and one-half acres were purchased for three thousand dollars. An option of three months was taken and the campaign to raise funds was on. All of this is of such recent history that one is tempted to write of non-essential details, for we are at present still in the midst of this program. When the three months had expired we paid Mr. Wilkie two thousand dollars on the property and gave him a mortgage for the remaining one-third of the purchase price; and coincident with the publication of this book, the Association is privileged to announce its ownership of as fine a range as could be found in all of the United States, needing only the usual improvements that will be added from time to time.

The response to the range fund appeal has proven the popularity of the Association. The designation of the tract as "The Walter M. Cline Rifle Range" has been enthusiastically endorsed as fitting and timely. The muzzle-loading shooting here in future years will, without doubt, re-establish this great American recreative pastime, which has maintained its hold upon the hearts of shooters for these many years. Deep thanks are due to the efforts of the late Walter M. Cline and his companions of the early days of the revival. I feel safe in hazarding the unqualified prophecy that muzzle-loading matches will never again go into an eclipse in America.—E. M. F.

APPENDIX

Editor's Note: In this appendix is included certain interesting matter from the Author's files which does not seem to lend itself particularly to any of the classifications in the regular text. Emphasis in the appendix will be especially upon random excerpts from the voluminous correspondence files of Mr. Cline. Mr. Cline enjoyed writing to and hearing from shooters and students of arms throughout the country for a great many years, and while it would not be possible to include in this book all of the informative correspondence he bequeathed, yet we have tried to include herewith a small representative group of excerpts from a few letters in his files.

* * * * *

From:
Hon. William de V. Foulke,
Divide P. O.,
Fayette County, West Virginia.

March 1, 1925.

I fear you are investing the riflemakers of "Auld Lang Syne" with more credit than they deserve. Up to the time of Tom Cherrington, Sr., of Pennsylvania, none of the makers, except by accident, attempted a "choke".

Cherrington reamed his barrel, a cylinder, clear through, then took a light cut up to about ten inches of the muzzle. Capt. Dillin gave me a fine specimen of a flint rifle made by Cherrington, Sr., which was cut off to thirty-six inches, reamed with a choke, and rifled with a *gain twist*. The muzzle was turned for a starter, and the starter, and swage were turned for a true "picket" ball. The alterations were made by T. Cherrington, Jr. You have seen enough of the work done, and the tools used by the early makers to agree with me on second thought.

I have in my small collection a noted rifle. It is, I believe, the last of the *Precision Rifles* made prior to advent of the breech-loading target rifles. It was made for my friend J. D. Kelly, of Williamsport, Pennsylvania, by the famous rifleman, Horace Warner. Kelly boarded Warner for six months while he built the rifle and paid him one hundred fifty dollars ($150.00). It weighs close to 30 pounds. Barrel 29 inches long. Bore .52. Hammer is on under side of barrel, and the trigger guard is the mainspring. Has false muzzle and starter. The ball weighs 716 grains and is composite, the base of soft lead, the upper half babbit metal and these are swaged together. Kelly was a noted rifleman, among the old-timers, to which I belong. With this gun he fired a ten-shot string at 100 yards, from machine rest, and every shot cut the point of the first shot.

Another reason for this letter is my real love for a fine shooting rifle, and the great regret I have felt on unbreeching some fine specimen to find a straight even bore up to where the rod wear has funneled the muzzle and thus ruined its accuracy. It is to save you from soon spoiling the "Kentucky" you have just recut (as I have

Appendix

a number, too) that I make you a suggestion, to-wit: Make a protector for your muzzle. Turn in the lathe, and drill and ream without removing from chuck, a cylinder of tool steel, outside diameter a loose "running fit" over "lands" when finally polished. 1½ inches is long enough and 1/50 inch is thick enough for its walls. Now bore and ream a hole in a piece of flat machine steel or brass plate in which the steel cylinder is a snug fit, place it on middle of cylinder and sweat fast with tin. Now cut your piece of plate either oval or octagon about 1/16 inch larger than end of the barrel of your rifle. Make your rod a loose fit in the cylinder. Now on one end of the rod, fit a piece of horn and glue it and pin it to dowel on end of the rod. On other end of rod (after passing the protector on it) put either a brass, or horn jag, to hold wiping patches. Glue or pin, or both. Your protector is then always at hand on your rod and as you start the ball, or a wiping patch, the protector slides into the bore. No funneled muzzle will occur to worry you.

The two-inch group you made at 100 yards (if over five shots) is phenomenal for a round ball.

Few men living have had wider experience in rifle shooting than myself,—a rifleman for more than fifty years and still shooting at sixty-seven years. In fact, I think an impersonal account of those fifty years would interest the youngsters. I have some of the manuscript already in shape.

(Editor's Note: Mr. de V. Foulke unfortunately never lived to publish his manuscript).

March 22, 1925.

Yours of March 13th at hand. I thank you much for the photographs. It is regretted you quite misunderstood the meaning of my ill-expressed "Ipse Dixit" as to the taper boring. What I should have said was this:

If the barrel was tapered it occurred as a natural result of reaming (your "Long Bit") a long barrel of iron, full of greys, with a reamer and wooden pad; not as result of design. The taper bore is no doubt one of the secrets of close grouping. My finest shooting rifles, both breech and muzzle-loading (except my Pope) were made so by my use of a long lap and emery to *taper* the bore either part or all of the barrel length. The *apparent* equal depth of grooves could also be ascribed to use of rifling "saws" set in hickory, as was the general practice, aided by "saw" teeth with either no "rake", or negative back rake.

I had years of great fun corresponding with my friend (alas! now dead), Dr. F. W. Mann, of Milford, Massachusetts, author of *"The Bullet's Flight"*, and whose book you should get. Dr. Mann is truly an authority on ballistics, whose life of research will be appreciated more fifty years from today than it is now. He is that much ahead of his time.

In the thousands of ten-shot groups shot by me with round ball at 100 yards I have never equaled your group, the original of which J. D. sent me to look over, but I have not used a scope. I will now mount scopes on some of my round ball rifles and try to equal it.

The Muzzle-Loading Rifle—Then and Now

As to true round balls: I never had but two factory-made moulds with an error less than .0002 inch. The best one I ever made casts a ball with an average error of .0005 inch,—the error being due to *shrink* and varying in position on the ball as was the zenith of the mould at time of *setting* of the cast. A round ball mould to cast a ball for consistent accuracy must have a "cutoff"; it must be "vented", and the casting should be done with a nozzled dipper which gives a heavy sink head, and the lead kept at a uniform high heat. The sprew hole should be the smallest you can make the shank of a cherry to stand. The quickest way to make the cherry round is to make a circular scraper; the hole in this should be about ¼ inch less diameter than the cherry, reamed or bored true, then further trued by lapping in the lathe after chilling. It is used the last thing after turning the blank up to a template. The expansion of the cherry on chilling must be allowed for. The flutes should be diagonal, unequally spaced, and the cutting edges made by simply removing the arc of the sphere. The major part of the cavity in mould should be cut with drill, and a round nose flat drill. This method makes it easier to equally harbour the ball in the mould. And the cherry must be helped as the cutting goes on. Now having made your mould and cast 100 or more bullets, go over them and select fifty of the most perfect to the eye. Run these over your powder scales and sort them into lots, heavy, medium, and light. Splitting open the lightest, you will find shrink holes varying from 1/10 grain to 3 grains, and all varying in position. All such on leaving the muzzle go off at a tangent. It is wise also to orient, or place every ball on the muzzle in same relative position to its mould position.

I also believe (may I say *I know*) that a "starter" (if muzzle be turned for it) will obviate error due to crowding the patch harder on one side than the other when entering the ball in the muzzle. I go into these details because you are young enough to make the record round ball groups,—and I hope you do so.

I never made but one rifling leader. I wanted a gain twist starting at zero and ending 1 to 30. I made the scale drawing on paper, wrapped it round a two-inch beech cylinder and cut a groove by the lines of the drawing. It worked well. Later it warped and was thrown away. Wish I had kept it.

What a match we can have some day. Flintlocks, mountain percussion rifles, and precision rifles—Oh! I shall think of that as a pipe dream, hoping it might come true some day before I get too blind to take a hand in it.

That curly maple stock is sure a peach. I have had some experience with curly maples as I have made (for the fun of it) two cellos, two violas, and sixty-one violins. Do you or any of your kiddies happen to play the violin?

I cut 1½ inches from muzzles of a 36-inch Winchester S. S. doweled it back for a false muzzle, made mould and starter, and with it have made some fifty shot groups at 100 yards from rest less than one inch. Tried to get Pope and several others to do it but they said it could not be done successfully. Pope was surprised when he saw it. Have made many mounts for my scopes. Made and used the first ever put on a Krag in 1900.

Appendix

April 22, 1925.

Yours of April 12th at hand. Sorry indeed to hear of the flash powder accident. What a mercy your eyes escaped. This is No. 1 of our Rifle Talks,—and the subject is *The Barrel*. And as we are threshing over our first love, the "Kentucky", I will confine all matter in this series to it. This is really matter from my little book I hope to publish in *talk form*.

The material seen by me is in every case iron, and in most cases rotten coarse iron full of "greys" and sand cracks. Have seen them butt welded, skelp welded, and of coarse twist. Have seen a very few barrels of perfectly refined charcoal iron free from all "greys" and flaws, drilled and reamed from the solid (and such are by all means the best for accuracy) as it is impossible to drill others true, ream them round in bore, and cut even depth grooving in them.

It is mechanically impossible to drill straight, ream round, (or even lap round) a welded barrel, or one not homogenous in texture. The heaviest barrel seen by me was a 60-pound "Wall Piece" fired from swivel; the lightest a little gem I just restored for our friend Dillin, barrel 36 inches long, bore 100 to pound, weight 3½ pounds. The longest barrel known to me was 73 inches long. The shortest, one of 18 inches, is owned by an uncle, who on his hunting trips to Maine about cleaned up the bully marksmen of those woods with it. He used peep and aperture sights on it.

The chronograph has told us that after 110 calibers in length no gain in velocity was noticed (black powder, of course).

The question of "whip" hardly needs consideration where the relative weight of ball to mass of rifle had the average ratio of the Kentucky. It is surprising though how much "jump" there is from muzzle rest. Have never seen a "Kentucky" with barrel much tapered from breech to muzzle. Have seen some with barrels which had barrel thickest at muzzle, supposed to give the same weight steadiness to the "hold" as a heavier barrel, but making a lighter gun to carry.

The Bore

The largest known to me are the two-ounce ball rifles made on General Washington's request, for long range sniping. A letter of Washington's is in existence in which he says of those rifles, "My best marksmen at 80 rods had no trouble in hitting a sheet of note paper as often as three in five shots." A sheet of note paper then averaged about eight by ten inches.

The smallest bore I have ever seen was 100 to the pound.

It is agreed that with a round ball a rifle's range and accuracy are inversely proportional to its bore. (Editorial Note: length or diameter?)

The Rifling

Since, when in 1548, at Nuremburg, Germany, old Gaspard Zoller first used real rifling in a firearm, no form of rifling, or pitch of grooving has been left untried which thought could approve, or reckless ignorance suggest. There are in museums abroad ancient Arquebuses rifled with even twists, with gain twists slowest at breech, with gain twist reversed, and with slow at breech, gaining to middle of barrel, and decreasing thence to muzzle.

Experience shows that for a round ball the slowest practical pitch is best. My experiments show that a round ball fired from a quick twist has marked groove drift; it acts like a curve-pitched baseball, and increasing powder charges will cut a line, rising and toward the groove direction of that barrel, to right if right-hand pitch, and vice versa. The "Kentuckys" were grooved in the main too deep. Least number of grooves noted, 2, up to 8, and for some reason 7 was very common in early American rifles.

The deepest grooving known to me was in "Old Killdeer", i. e., .022 inches, but as she was funneled .035 inches and had the usual power bed at breech and numerous pits, I freshed her out. Not wishing to destroy the original appearance of her, I left the grooves .0185 inches. Now when grooves are so deep that the patch cannot dam the powder gases, gas escape is certain, and the hot gases char, and carry ahead of the ball up the barrel all of the patch which lay in the grooves, and the ball if tight may not jump, but it is very likely to do so. For instance see that target sent you of "Killdeer" as typical deep groove devilment.

Have never seen original grooving shallow in a "Kentucky".

The "starring" or deepening of the grooves at muzzle, next comes to mind. No doubt, this came into use as an aid to entering the ball. I have ideas though as to its influence on accuracy. As it would take a number of barrels, or several niches off one barrel to prove or disprove I have not yet threshed them out enough to speak with positive knowledge. My yet unproven theory is that the escaping funnel of powder blast tends to lessen the angular error of an unbalanced ball, as centrifugal force throws it from line of fire or axis of bore.

Not many "Kentuckies" in original bore condition exist today. We can only theorize, basing theory on the results ensuing from the mechanical operations used by their makers, as to whether they aimed at a cylinder, taper, or choke bore. If you think it would interest you enough to take time to mail them back to me, I will send you some really good, and some freak targets, made with modern rifles which I have here.

May 22, 1925.

Yours of May 9th received today. Your letters are very interesting. Those grooves wider at one end of barrel came to pass thus: The leader by accident or intent was of shorter pitch at muzzle end. Long saws were set by a "scoibe" made at short pitch end of leader. Have never seen a rifle barrel counter bored as you describe. Have seen a pair of duelling pistols so treated. In that case it was done to use rifling in defiance of prohibition, to gain an unfair advantage. Your instance must be the only one or we would heard or seen more of it.

Appendix

That rifling system you speak of would be far better with lands in corners of octagon instead of grooves. Henry, of England; G. Schalk, of Pottsville, Pennsylvania, and Harry Pope used the octagonal with lands in corners. Schalk made many famous barrels. H. M. Pope has cut, I believe, the best barrels of history, and is still cutting them.

We must not expect, except by accident, to cut barrels by our crude methods which will equal those cut by proper rifling heads used in proper leaders. When a youngster I wanted a gain twist leader. The curves were laid down on paper, the paper rolled on a glue-coated 2½ Beech roller, the India ink lines on the paper being the guide for one side of the groove, and a template was used to pare the other side by. The index plate revolved, and I had the stop pin holes bored in a B. and S. Miller, so registration was very good. Dillin loaned me old Gumph's leader; it is here now. This is not a good one; it is warped. The two guide ribs are not equidistant, and it has been bruised. In spite of all, it must cut several barrels before I return it.

In freshing a barrel, I use a cast of hard No. 1 Babbit to set the saws in. For the first cuts about four inches long; for finish work, five to ten inches long. It takes about three casts, with three saws before I get through a barrel. Yes, it's much work, but seems more sure than using hickory and lead. Set screws are under saw recess for feed, and you can use just as little or as much cut as suits your fancy.

Does not cutting lands and grooves at the same time make you trouble by reason of the cutters skidding?

You ask what I know of "Whitworth Rifles". In the early 80's one was loaned me and I shot perhaps 1,000 shots from it at ranges from 200 to 1,000 yards. I remember no possibles made with it past 800 yards, but then I was a beginner at long range work. I used my Sharps 45/550 gr. M. P. bullet, and various naked, lubricated balls, such as U. S. 45/500 grooved, 45/405, 45/340, etc. Powder charges ran from 70 grs. FFG to 150 grs. FG, Hazard, black. The rifle was very accurate. It was of the Match Military type. Stock of walnut. Barrel 32 inches round, same diameter through its length. Bore .451 inches, grooves (6) hexagonal, with rounded corners. Pitch one—twenty inches, L. H. The hammer was musket, and the tube for a musket cap. Fly in lock and 6-pound pull (then the rule). Elevating leaf military sight on barrel, but on tang it had a finely made Vernier peep with elevation for 2,230 yards. The front sight was Globe with a wind gauge, the graduations were 1/50 inch, and cut in a silver inlay. Weight 8½ pounds. I mean to try to trace it and secure it. The barrel was of the then new and famous Whitworth Fluid compressed steel. The tensile strength 110,000 pounds. Whitworth was said to bore his barrels to a guage limit of .0001. That one loaded like velvet. I have read about the battery of Whitworth field guns with Armstrong breeches which the South had. The bores of these were pure hexagon and the shells for them milled to size and form.

I had Dillin's Leman rifle here for two months. Lapped it out, and it shot finely till the rust burnt out of some bad places, when it began cutting patches and scattering the balls. It was rifled very narrow and deep, .017 depth of grooves.

The Muzzle-Loading Rifle—Then and Now

August 1, 1925.

Friend Cline:

Yours of July 27th last at hand. I am glad to have definite information, so far as it went, of the Confederate Whitworth. I had always understood they were .45 caliber, same as the one loaned me. You do not cover sort, and number of grooves, or twist which to me are vital points of interest; nor the shape, weight, length, etc., of ball, and the sort of patch used. I had always read Whitworth used the "hex" form of rifling, and sometimes a naked lubricated ball.

Glad to hear your precision rifle is gilt edged in accuracy. I have stated, and still believe, those old precision rifles to be yet the most accurate arms on earth. Next winter when I hope to get mine down here we can have a "correspondence match," write up our rifles and methods, and send them with photographs of rifles and tools to the *Sporting Press*. Many will be glad to read it.

Congratulations on your invention of the round ball seater.

I have always set sprue up (in spite of the irregular surface opposed to air in flight), but know that a slight gain is had by your new method. It was not possible otherwise to seat sprue down with any certainty.

I have no information as to the maker "Farris", who made your big gun. Many fine makers turned out but few rifles, and hence their field of fame was narrow.

You ask "why the double cone barrel shoots so well?" Beyond doubt it is due to the "choke" principle. Yesterday I set my five-power 'scope on the 110-to-pound rifle and made a try at your record group. I send you herein a target, and the paper back of another fired at 50 yards; muzzle and elbow rest. I mean to target each of fifteen barrels I have here at 50 and 100 yards and will send you the targets and notes on the rifles, etc. My cross-hairs are too coarse, as they cancel out one-fourth inch at 50 yards. I will replace them with dyed spider web as soon as I can find a proper spider to weave them!

I have used Ferro-grained, Ferri-cyanide, and pure cyanide of potassium for case-hardening, but have never used it in tempering steel because it enlarges the grain, and because of that decreases the strength of steel. I use P. S. Stubb's, or William Jessop's English tool steel for cutters, etc. Harry Pope uses the Austrian "Poldi" steel. He stated it would hold its edge for more feet duty than any other. He showed me a .22 caliber barrel drill with which he had just bored a perfectly straight barrel. The edges of this drill were yet near razor edge. He stated the tool had cut about one and a quarter miles of chip' (at his rate of feed) and had not been sharpened since made. He uses a cutting lubricant of oil and sal soda, and it is fed by gravity to the cutting edges.

Do not ever abandon the attempt to perfect, as near as you can, everything connected with your rifles. While I must admit it is possible for a round ball to upset, such upset (unless using a very fine grained violent powder) can hardly be enough to so squat the ball as to make its mass balanced. My friend, the late Dr. Mann, made many experiments on upset of the ball. He used fine hardwood sawdust saturated

Appendix

with light machine oil to catch the bullets and it caught over 90% without the least mutilation. I have so far never noted any signs of upset on the round balls examined after firing, but none of those were caught in oiled sawdust.

I am sending you in this same mail some bullets. The round ball is that of the last rifle I cut for a friend. It is the best round ball I ever made from a hand filed cherry. With a good lathe I can make both a cherry and mould to within .0005 inch, but hand work is not easy. The large, much-abused ball is one of those for my precision rifle. It has been run through the bore with a tissue paper patch. I have two adjustable moulds for lubricated bullets which range from 650 to 1,200 grains. The composite ball sent is a good thing to keep for your collection. The .45 ball is one for my .45/70 which I converted to a "Pope System". The .32 caliber ball is that of my Pope .32/40. I cut the .45 mould. H. Warner, the maker of "Old Betsy", was a crank on tight fitting bullets. For my part I pin my faith (if a ball be over 2 calibers long) to a ball just fitting tight enough to hold its place by friction, knowing that upset will care for the spin. If over 2½ calibers long the trouble is to control the upset by proper alloying; and that, too, depends on other factors such as patch used, grains, and amount of powder, etc.

I have always preferred coarse powder, using a grain in proportion to bore, but even in small bores, if the barrel be over 75 calibers long, my best groups are with coarse powder. I learned to use it from the old bunch of precision rifle users whom I used to "buck" when a mere kid.

I have so much in my old head that is interesting to a real rifle crank that I fear you begin to think that I think I know it all. Please do not abase me by such an opinion. You have shown me in your last letter a new thing, and you doubtless have more wrinkles in store for me.

August 28, 1925.

Thanks for the photograph of the Whitworth. The "scope" as mounted sets me thinking. At first I thought it merely a "finder" glass, but the means provided for elevation indicate the presence of colleniation X lines, and its use in aiming. How a man could use it, however, is a mystery. Its position would make it almost impossible to get the eye to the eye-piece with the piece in any conceivable position for firing.

Reverting to the process of recutting grooves, I find for the finish cuts, at least, a single tooth cuts cleanest. Mine are made thus, and castor oil or tallow applied at each passage of the rod, chips being cleaned off by a tooth brush. I also find it necessary to guard against too fast travel of the cutter. About 35 feet per minute, you know, is close to the cutting speed limit when the mass of the cutter is so small.

Too fast travel either welds the chips to edge of cutter and tears, or it burns the temper from the small piece of steel. Also, as new casts are made each is better made longer. Where my finish cutter is carried by a six-inch or eight-inch number 1 babbit cast, I am sure a "line" will throw no shadows, and the bore is practically straight.

The Muzzle-Loading Rifle—Then and Now

Like yourself, I have seen occasionally, such work as you speak of at 40 and 60 yards. My shooting experience covers some territory from Canada to Mexico, and west to Colorado. I like the romance of the "old times", but, except precision rifle work, (and some of that was ragged) most of the best work done by round ball was, of necessity, only on occasions fine. When you remember the geometric patterns of the balls used, when you remember that weighing powder was not practiced, and that the necessary "kinks" needed to keep elevation even from a muzzle rest were known to but few, you will admit that it was on rare occasions that "Lady Luck" kept ten balls together.

In making your fine target all the refinements known as to load were employed but one,—that is, the use of a starter fitted to a turned cylinder on the muzzle, the use of which obviates the chance of driving the ball more or less against the side of the bore, which would unbalance it surely to a greater or less extent. When you have fitted accurate centers to that barrel and turned a seat for a starter at the muzzle, and made an accurate starter, I will bet my violin against a Jews harp no man ever made such work with round ball in the past, or will excell now, or in the future, the work you will do with it in still air or, if you jam wind well, under any conditions.

The pressure of the ball on the powder influences elevation strongly. I have thought of rigging a simple dynamometer to my loading rod to stabilize that factor. The increase of velocity surely increases "derivation" or the groove drift, so we must conclude that both the vertical and horizontal errors are present.

Have you read *"The Bullets Flight"*, by F. W. Mann? If not, I will send you my copy. There is much in it of use to a rifleman. We were corresponding friends till his death. He was a fine fellow, far ahead of his time. His book should live forever.

I have the last rifle I restored at work now. So far have had no still day. A ball 145 to the pound is a feather in the wind. I shot a few shots at 100 yards with her using 48 grains powder behind a 48 grain ball. Seven would have hit a silver dollar, but the other eight made a "group" (wind drift) which at times was eight inches. Drop from 50 yards point blank aim was 2½ inches.

October 11, 1925.

Bullets received and examined. That fired with 50 grains weighs 209 grains and shows no visible evidence of upset. The two fired with 100 grains FFG, weigh 205 and 203 grains, either losing some lead by attrition or were not necked alike. Both show upset. Patches sent are .007; both show gas leakage; hence, the upset was not enough to fill grooves. Those grooves must be over .02 deep. Hawken, Grove, and others, building rifles for the Mountain Men, bored them for half-ounce, or larger; and many a big grizzly has fallen to such. Queer how far back a bear's heart lies and also how hard it is to make a round ball stick in his wedge-shaped skull when fired directly from in front.

Appendix

Now speaking of the 30-pound rifle,—if you have not already done so, put master lines on your swedges and on your plunger (if it forms base of ball) with a prick punch. Orient your marks when giving last blow with mallet, or at least squeeze with Arbor press, whichever you use, so ball will be every time alike, and oriented at loading. Now put like master lines on your starter, and orient ball in that, and orient starter on muzzle. Shoot 10 shots with balls swedged without regard to master lines, and loaded without either orienting ball or starter. Now shoot 10 which are swedged and loaded as advised above. Please send me the targets for examination. I always use the above method even with my "Pope". You may get some wonderful targets. It is so much work using an old-time precision rifle that it pays to use every kink known to get adequate results.

Had snow and ice yesterday; day before, green beans, roasting ears and watermelon for dinner. Weather here is in a class to itself. It is as temperamental as some of the old guns we handle.

November 19, 1932.

Yours of the 17th last at hand. Your letter was surely much appreciated and enjoyed. Have barked squirrels with balls from 32 to 90 to the pound. The principle is concussion. The smaller the ball the faster you must drive it, and the closer to the animal it must hit. The number of your rifles surprised me. How good it must make you feel. But like in all other possessions. a plentitude usually produces surfeit, more or less; but am glad to see that you (like myself) still have the enthusiasm of a boy and its accompanying enjoyment.

We have turkeys here but now we are in a two-year closed season. Two hens hatched on the little farm where I board.

Now for some more talk on "Precision Rifles"! A picket ball is, even if perfect in itself, very difficult to load, so its virtues are questioned. After having proved the right powder load, which must be adapted to it so there is not too much "upset", the problem is to seat it axially true on the powder. I have found but one way to be sure, i. e., make a special loading rod as follows: Turn a cylinder of hardwood (dogwood, well dried) to a close sliding fit in the bore, six inches long. Then fit one end to a limber hickory rod; at the other fit a ferrule (horn is best, but copper or soft brass will do) in a true chuck counter bore and ream with a cherry to fit exactly the nose of the ball. To prove your work before removing from chuck, stick a ball in the cherried counter-sink with a little thin shellac or hot wax and spin it to prove it exactly true. That rod will insure a perfectly seated ball. To clean, I use seven patches, three wet, two dry, then one barely greasy, no more, with sperm, or hard oil, then dry patch. I use tallow for the ball patch, or beeswax one-third, sperm oil two-thirds, rubbed over one side.

To load the powder, you can either use a loading tube or a loading spoon. I make the spoon of horn on end of a rod. The powder is put in by the spoon while the rifle lies on the bench. Then when the piece is stood up the spoon is withdrawn, the idea being to leave no powder scattered along the bore to soak grease and affect elevations. I like the tube best though, because the powder falling through it packs just alike every time in the chamber and is dense so a little variation in pressing the ball home has no effect.

As we are after precision results, no factor may be ignored. To tell the truth, I am looking for you to make a world's record with "Mons Meg". That barrel sure seems well nigh perfect. The old way of scraping the ball slugs to even weight before swedging is error. Sort the blanks over the scales, the number 1's being those exact, the 2's those being not over one-third grain less in weight; keep these separate, and put back in the melting pot all over one-third grain less than number 1. Then swedge.

Now for one more suggestion: Wind. Make three flags of bunting three times as long as wide. Set one at firing point (in front, where you can see it), one at 50 yards, and one at target. The poles should be just long enough for flags to swing clear of ground, for it is the air in line of flight we want to observe. Choose a day when wind is at three or nine o'clock, and get some data on the drift of your ball. As soon as the shot leaves, run your eye from flag to flag and set down on your note book the rise of the flags and the drift of the ball at target. It will not be long before you are able to run eye along down the flags and hold off for a perfect center. Under the supposition you have not paid much attention to the wind, I send you as a loan the last of a booklet I got up (which is a proof copy and with errors) for teaching our regiment. The Krag was replaced by the Springfield Model 1903 then, and my work nearly wasted. From it you can get the idea of diverging, elevating, and depressing winds. Light does not seem to count with a scope, but barometer and thermometer do. The levelling of the rifle, a heavy gun, is best done either by a "buggy" on the barrel, or a block screwed to toe of stock. To use these, a firm smooth plank is needed on the table rest, and it must be fastened to keep it in place with nails or screws. My rifle has a "buggy" and V-block at the front. A V-block is screwed to the plank, and the piece is shoved home in it before aiming. As the line of sight is far above the bore, a small error in levelling is needed to put the ball to right or left and low at target.

By the way, if your Picket has a flat base, it is most accurate. Have seen some with bases almost semi-spherical. The point is best when flat, about one-fifth ball diameter.

I learn new things every day in spite of my sixty-eight years. You may find some wrinkle heretofore unknown, or untried, set forth in my preaching. I find much that is new and interesting in your letters and I respect your judgment highly. Capt. Dillin sent me a fine old F. L. to play with, by "Scho'b", circa 1780. It has been bored smooth. Will rebore, straighten and re-rifle it, and will send you some targets when done. I wish you a happy Thanksgiving.

Editor's Note: The lapse in the file of letters of the year and one-half is not accounted for; but it is known that Mr. Foulke visited Mr. Cline in 1926 and that he was very ill in the first half of 1927.—E.

Appendix

June 2, 1927.

Have been plenty sick, kidney and bladder trouble, but now am so much better that I am wanting to shoot again.

My big precision rifle is now the subject of my inquisition. How few of our pets will stand close analysis. The bore measures .505 inches. Choke is three inches long and is .0005 inches less than bore. Major groove diameter .524 inches. The false muzzle is .0005 inches smaller than choke; hence, a ball will run down barrel readily after seating. The cylindrical part of bore is straight and even, eight grooves, depth .008 inches; lands and grooves same width. Pitch is R. H. one in twenty inches. This is too fast for 50 caliber; it restricts ball speeds, and as Dr. Mann proved, increases both X and Y errors. The starter is mechanically correct. The arrangement for mounting a scope on the grip is all wrong in execution. The swedge is too big, forms a ball which is full major groove diameter, no room for the patch. Warner used thin tissue paper soaked in shellac, but how he ever got a ball down with a perfect patch is a mystery. The moulds for grooved balls are too small and .0025 out of round.

I wrote Belding and Mull requesting a price on a mould for her. They asked $22.00—fierce!

I will make a cherry by hand and ream out old moulds. I have a 1¼-inch tube telescope 36 inches long, which I may use on her. Oh, Boy! How I look forward to getting her tuned up. I hardly expect she will beat my Pope .32/40, which has a gilt-edge barrel, or my .45 M. L. Winchester single shot.

Hope you can run up for a visit later in the summer and here you will stay until we have an old-time shoot. That shoot may be the "Swan Song" for this old boy, for after seventy good shooting is an accident. Found a box of .22 long Klean-bore cartridges in the country store, and enclosed find a string made with them, which is good for any .22 with any cartridge. The barrel used was a Winchester which I chambered and fitted to a Maynard action.

Don't want to wish my complaints on others, but I fear I am nearing the end of the "Long Trail". But I shall be deeply interested in the old shooting irons to the very last breath I draw.

WILLIAM DE V. FOULKE.

To:
Dr. Thomas B. Hall,
Kansas City,
Missouri.

July 3, 1936.

My Dear Dr. Hall:

I am very glad indeed to observe from your letters that you are deeply interested in the muzzle-loading rifle, and I shall attempt to answer some of the questions which you have asked me in our recent correspondence.

I have found that I can see the sights better on the long barrelled rifles as the rear sight is farther from the eye. The long barrel rifle with caliber around .45 is usually in the money if the rifle is in good condition. My flintlock rifle that I use in the

The Muzzle-Loading Rifle—Then and Now

matches weighs eleven pounds, 43-inch barrel and .46 caliber. I have shot possibles with it at sixty yards. Usually I shoot around 45 to 47 and this with the open sights. The percussion rifle I use is one of the mountain match rifles, weighs twenty pounds, has a 54-inch barrel, caliber .45 with a pitch of one-half turn in the length of the barrel. This rifle is very accurate up to one hundred yards.

The pitch of the grooves of the flintlock is one turn in 49 inches. I had it rebored and rerifled by Wyatt Atkinson, Hidalgo, Kentucky. He is the best of the old-time gunsmiths that I know of. If you should have a rifle the bore of which is too large to rebore, D. C. Addicks, of Rome, Georgia, can reline it. By the way, one of the most accurate round barrel rifles that I know of is one that he relined. It is a fifty-inch barrel, caliber .45, one turn in 42 inches.

In order to more intelligently answer some of the other questions which you have raised, I shall take the liberty of repeating your question herewith, which will be followed by the answer.

Question (in regard to sights): What type of open sight do you consider the best? How do the old-fashioned blade and buckhorn sights compare with the modern open sights? Are the peep sights a big advantage, although I understand they are barred in the 60-yard matches? In the match rifles, which shoot a conical bullet, is a long barrel advantageous when using peep sights?

Answer: The type of open sight which I consider the best is an open sight very similar to the Partridge revolver sight. Blade sight is not good for match shooting. Peep sights are better and I can usually shoot two or three points higher with them than I can with open sights. They are barred in 60-yard matches but allowed in the 100-yard. Answering your last question above, a barrel of about 30 inches would be better than a long barrel where conical bullet is used.

Question (in regard to patches): I note that you advise "coat linen" as being desirable. The stores do not seem to know what is meant by this. Are not many cloths which are sold as linen really not linen or else a linen mixture? Do the spit patches give a greater accuracy than the greased patches? I thought of the possibility of lubricating the patches with some hydroscopic grease as anhydrous lanolin or aquaphor, incorporating in the same, sputum or water up to 50 per cent.

Answer: This coat linen is what women use in making coats. All stores have it. The spit patch is best, as it cleans the bore and keeps the powder residue moist. I have never gotten as accurate results with lubricated patches.

Question (in regard to size of bullet): I infer from your articles that you advocate a bullet of land diameter—one that just approximates the land surface when it slides through the barrel with the weight of the ramrod. This being the case, would there not necessarily be some crimping of the soft lead bullet? A lateral displacement of the bullet with its patch into the grooves? In reading Dillin's book, I found the statement that the bullets found in the Indian skeletons in Tennessee plainly show the markings of the lands and were, therefore, shot bare. Is it not true that any well-fitting bullet will show the markings of the lands when patched?

Appendix

Answer: Yes, a bullet of bore diameter seems to be the best, and it is a rule that has come down with the muzzle-loading rifle. Yes, the patch is forced into the bullet but this prevents it striping. If the bullets mentioned in Dillin's book had been shot with a patch, the imprint of the cloth patch would have been shown. As it was, the lands were sharp and clear cut.

Question: Is it an advantage to have the rifles cut out at the breech for a formed chamber? If so, what length should this formed chamber be?

Answer: It is of no advantage to have a chamber made for the powder.

Question: What tools are necessary for making a breech pin and rebreeching the bore, also for cutting the cylinder and nipple threads? I have been told that special dies were used, which are at present unobtainable.

Answer: There were no special tools for cutting the cylinder and nipple threats. They were all sizes of dies and taps.

Question: Can you recommend anyone who is good at repairing and completing the missing parts of flintlocks?

Answer: Mr. Farris has someone who is good at restoring flintlocks. You might write him.

Question: Are the nipples for the rifles different from shotgun and musket rifles?

Answer: The nipples are the same for rifles and shotguns but not for musket, as this is a much larger size.

In conclusion, I would make the observation that the Indians, as a general rule, might have been pretty fair shots; but ordinarily I do not think that their shooting was very exceptional, because of their lack of care of their rifles.

I am sending you photographs of the so-called "plains rifle". Incidentally, "plains rifle" is a term that I believe was coined by Sawyer. This photograph I am sending you is of an exceptionally fine specimen and true type. There is no name on the barrel but the name Griffith is on the lock. Griffith was working in Cincinnati as early as 1839.

The narrow land is fine for round ball. I have had Mr. Addicks cut several on this principle, and I got fine results. He now has two barrels of mine and they are both being cut on that principle. Do not use Kings Semi-Smokeless in a round ball rifle. I have tested it thoroughly and have not been able to get results with it. A good black powder of FFG granulation is by far the best for a round ball gun.

In regard to the patching, I use linen altogether and as thin as it will stand. No thick heavy patching when the bore is perfect. If you will just think of the heavy folds that occur when using a heavy grade of material for patches, you can see what variations occur. A round ball must be loaded just as tight as you can load it to get the best results.

I wish you could have been at the matches at Dillsboro. It was a very colorful affair and, as the *Saturday Evening Post* sent special feature writer and their photographer, it will get world-wide publicity.

WALTER M. CLINE.

The Muzzle-Loading Rifle—Then and Now

208 Osborne Terrace,
East Springfield,
Massachusetts.

May 28, 1934.

My Dear Mr. Cline:

I am very sorry to have been so slow in answering your letter of April 30th. Will try to answer the questions you ask in your letter. Brockway says that he doesn't remember of any of the members of the National Rifle Club serving in the Civil War, either in sharpshooter organizations or regular army ranks. Most of the members were older men who had businesses of their own, so they were not called into the Civil War.

He doesn't know just how long it took him to complete a rifle. He just worked on a rifle without any thought as to time. Most of the complete rifles he made were done in between smaller jobs, such a rerifling a barrel, restocking, making a new lockworks, etc. He said he would bore a barrel in about three or four hours. Rifling could be done in a little less time. As to the time required to straighten, make a stock and lock works, he does not have much idea except that he just did it.

A barrel drilled on a lathe, as Brockway did, showed ring bores; so to smooth these out he passed a reamer through the barrel 20 or 30 times or until smooth. After every two or three times through the barrel with a reamer, he would straighten the barrel. After reamer was passed through barrel four or five times with one setting, a shim of paper was inserted under it to make it cut larger. The reamer was eight or nine inches long and square. The diagonally opposite corners were honed off. Under one side was inserted a soft pine shim. Paper was inserted between this shim and the reamer proper to make a large cut.

Brockway did not do what I should think would be termed taper boring. The only taper in his bore was so small it could hardly be detected. It was obtained as follows: after the gun was all rifled, he then lead lapped,—he always put the emery and oil on at the breech, which would tend to make the breech a little larger; and then when the inside of the barrel looked perfect, he lapped a little while longer, letting his plug go only within two inches of the muzzle, thus enlarging the rest of the barrel. He always has claimed that the shooting qualities of a gun comes within two inches from the muzzle.

Brockway says he developed the paper patch for all he can find out. When he brought it into the Club nobody would use the idea and did not for quite a number of years. He knew Edward Wesson well enough to speak with. He used to see him when he worked at the Smith & Wesson factory. Frank Wesson came to the factory quite often to see his brother. Some of the gunsmiths he remembers are: Durkee, Sebanon, N. H., target and sporting guns; Dennison, Haverhill, Massachusetts; Perry, Jamestown, New York; Hilliard, Cornish, N. H., made good sporting guns; Frank Wesson, Worcester, Massachusetts. (I can't keep the two names straight,—is it Frank or Edward Wesson who started Smith & Wesson? The Wesson who worked in Worcester later moved to Hartford, Connecticut). Brockway says at the last of

Appendix

his shooting days Harry Pope, of Hartford, Connecticut, made guns. Artamus Leonard & Son, Saxons River, Vermont, tried to make a target gun but were not successful. They made a good sporting gun. Another son of Leonard had a shop in Keene, New Hampshire. W. W. Whitmore worked for Durkee, then had a shop of his own in Springfield, Mass. Tarrington worked for Durkee then in Springfield, and in gun shops all around; was never at one place long. Lewis was a noted gun maker of Troy, New York. Edwin Phillips, New York City, was quite well known in this section of the country and the oldest gunsmith in New York. Brockway saw some nice rifles made by a man in Scranton, Pennsylvania, but cannot remember his name.

To make a swedge, Brockway made a tool the same shape as his bullet; then he cut it in half and used it to ream the hole in the swedge, which had previously been drilled to as near size as possible. He then fitted a plug to start the bullet out. The swedges were made of cast steel and then I believe they were hardened. He determined the powder charge by the shoot. He used the charge which put all the shots nearest center. The amount of powder required for best results depends on the hardness of lead bullets used. He always shot all the powder that would burn or whatever lesser quantity that gave best results.

I spent nearly three months this spring in the same house with Brockway. I used to have a talk with him nearly every day. He is an accomplished surveyor and still has a very fine transit. He used to make his own telescope lenses. He told me all about grinding of lenses. Brockway says some gunsmiths used to have a favorite gun,— but he would sell his own gun any day, as he always felt he could make another as good. In fact, that was the way he sold the most of his guns. When he made a good score, some shooter would buy the gun.

I mentioned before that his pressed bullets when flattened out in a parallel jaw vise came out a perfect circle where a cast and swedged bullet would not. Some other shooters arrived at the same results a different way without a press. S. Amadon was one who used the following method: the bullet was cast, then hit on the butt with a hammer on an anvil, then it was peened back round until it would go into a swedge and then swedged. A bullet like this would swedge into a perfect circle in a vise. Brockway has a lot of different bullets he has squeezed out flat in a vise.

As I told you on a previous occasion, Brockway has shot two woodchucks with one shot several times, and he feels that before his purpose on earth is fulfilled he ought to kill three chucks with one shot!

Wish you could come up and see Brockway. He is very keen and witty. I will be honored truly to make you comfortable at my home in West Brookfield during your stay.

WILLIS E. WOOSTER.

The Muzzle-Loading Rifle—Then and Now

Mr. Walter M. Cline,
Chattanooga, Tennessee.

June 30, 1934.

Dear Walter:

You know, Walter, I blame you for getting inoculated with the muzzle-loading rifle germ. My interest in guns runneth back to early boyhood when I owned a Quackenbush (is that word spelled correctly?) and then a Flobert (another question about that word). But the trouble all started one day in your studio when you showed me some of your beautiful old Kentuckies. I fairly itched to look down the barrels of them and ease off the trigger. That itching was gratified on December 10th, 1927, when you took me to the match at Jim Barker Kelley's farm and initiated me by letting me shoot Long Tom. With your coaching, I was successful in winning two choices of fresh pork and returned home that night pretty tired but a confirmed long rifle shooter. So confirmed in fact that I returned with you the following Saturday to shoot another match, with the same rifle, and again win some of the meat. There is a fascination about shooting these old rifles that is difficult to describe,—one has to experience the sport before he can even faintly realize just what I mean. Once the technique of loading and aiming them is acquired, there comes a satisfaction in shooting that cannot be compared with firing a modern piece. As keen as my interest had become after attending several of the matches, it was not until I became the proud owner of one of these old rifles that I really qualified and was eligible to be classed as a "long rifle devotee". The first one I got through your kindness. You will remember the stock was broken and we got old Uncle Bob Freeman to make a new one, and what a beauty it was, all inlaid with beautiful brass carvings, and a patch box. Later I acquired three or four others, including one given to me by Mr. Wm. Parks at Lynchburg, Tenn. This one weighs 14½ pounds, has a 48-inch barrel, full-length curly maple stock and shoots a .52 caliber ball. The only mark on the rifle is "1804" stamped on the breech, which is evidently the year it was made. I well remember the condition of it when I got it, and how you dressed out the barrel, cleaned up the stock, put on target sights to replace the hunting sights, and cleaned up the lock so that it would work. And well do I remember also the surprise and satisfaction both of us got the first time we tried it out. You said it would give a good account of itself in a match and it surely did, not frequently, but in every match where it was shot. On two occasions, yes, three, friends of mine who had never before shot a long rifle, won second and third places with it, which proves that it will shoot just as accurately for a greenhorn as it will for the more experienced shooter. While I have made some remarkable groups with this rifle, I have never been able to put five shots in the same hole as I did with Long Tom the day I won the short, heavy rifle from Gilbert.

Aside from the sheer sport of shooting these old rifles that played a most important role in conquering the untamed country of a century and more ago, I feel that the gentlemen whom I have met at the matches are just about the truest sportsmen I have ever known. Oftentimes when the scores were measured at the close of the match, I have seen some of them so close that no two men could agree which was

Appendix

the best, but the decision of the scorer was never once questioned. His word was accepted as final and the loser came back to the next match determined to win.

I started out by saying that I blame you for getting me into the game, but I want to add that I am deeply indebted to you for doing it. I have never participated in any other sport that has furnished as much real pleasure and where I have made as warm friends as I have at the old-fashioned rifle matches.

CHARLES J. KELLEM.

Mr. Walter M. Cline,
Chattanooga, Tennessee.

Dear Sir:

I read in the *Bangor Daily News* your letter to the Chamber of Commerce inquiring about the Ramsdell Rifle. I can give you quite a lot of information in regard to the maker, Charles Ramsdell, as I have seen the man and know several who were acquainted with him.

He had a shop on Harlow Street in Bangor and was in company with a man named John Neal, the firm name being Ramsdell and Neal. This must have been soon after the Civil War, as John Neal, whom I knew quite well, told me they started business about that time. They made guns and ran a sort of sporting goods store. After a time, I can't say what date, they dissolved partnership and each ran his own shop. Mr. Neal had a shop on the corner of Harlow and State Streets and Mr. Ramsdell's was up State Street. Some time later Mr. Ramsdell sold out. I think this must have been about fifty years ago, as that was about the time I saw him last. He sold the shop to James Holt, a gunsmith for whom I afterward worked.

For some time after he sold out he used to come into the shop every few days to pass the time of day, loaf around awhile and then go home. One morning he came in and called Mr. Holt over to the showcase where the revolvers were displayed. "Holt," he said, "if you were going to shoot a man, which revolver would you use?" Holt said, "I guess I would use a .38 caliber." "Well," the old man said, "I guess I would too." Holt said the next morning Mr. Ramsdell came in, sat down and talked for a few minutes, then walked out back of the shop and shot himself with a .38 caliber revolver.

Mr. Ramsdell made some fine target rifles. Those that I have seen were around .40 caliber and were quite heavy, as they were made only for target shooting. He also made over old army rifles into breechloaders. The action he used was almost the same as the British Snider. Mr. Ramsdell has one or two grandsons here in Maine but they are not gunsmiths.

I have been working on guns for twenty-five years, learning my trade from James Holt in the old Ramsdell shop. These facts about Charles Ramsdell are as complete and correct as I can give.

Very truly yours,
ERNEST W. WENTWORTH, <i>Gunsmith,</i>
500 French Street, Bangor, Maine.

PIONEERS
Barton Rees Pogue

Their livelihood;
The good women at their spinning wheels
And looms, at storing food, at meals,
Bore mightily their part,
Gathering things so dear and near to human heart.

They were individualists, rugged and staunch,
Not the baggy eye and sagging paunch
Of indolence that asks
Easy cash for petty tasks;
They carried high a sacred light
And asked for naught but chance to shape and fight.
In honor of their strength and fortitude,
With highest praise and gratitude
To those who wrought for us this land
We raise our heart and hand.
Each time you hear an old gun shoot
The intonation is salute
Powder and ball and patchin'
And everyone catchin'
The spirit of the pioneer ways,
Of the olden days,
When men wrought a new land
And fashioned, by hand,
The long barreled rifles they used,
When the Indians refused
These rugged men abode.
Today we patch and load
And fire in the pioneer way,
Just as they did in the day
When families were proficient
And might nigh self sufficient.
The men, in the woods and field,
Made the land to yield
And solemn pledge that America shall be
Ever strong and ever free!

Appendix

Mr. George D. Winchester,
West Gloucester, Massachusetts. September 9, 1936.
Dear Mr. Winchester:

I have your letter in regard to relining your rifle barrel. This is the only way to restore these fine old rifles. If I wanted to use the rifle that you write about and get the best results—the most accurate—I would have Mr. Addicks, of Rome, Georgia, reline your barrel to .35 caliber; have a new false muzzle for the two strip paper patch and a new starter. Then you can get accurate results. I would use black powder. It would be necessary to work out a load.

I have five barrels that Mr. Addicks relined and all give good results. Can get two-inch groups at two hundred yards.

These old rifles are worth keeping and restoring to their original accuracy or better. I will be pleased to help you in any way I can as I have always been very much interested in the muzzle-loading rifle, and am always glad to be of service to a muzzle-loader shooter. Yours very truly,

WALTER M. CLINE.

Hubbardsville, New York.

February 25, 1936.
Dear Mr. Cline:

Your welcome letter at hand and hope you can visit me this summer. E. Loomis (or Earl Lummis, as the old Yanks around here called him) was still living in the 70's, an old man who walked very much bent, well over six feet tall in his younger days. He repaired guns for my father, who was born in 1860. He had a son, Alonzo, who learned the trade and I knew him in 1900. He was seventy-six then—died some years later. Also had another son, George, whom I knew before he died. Nearly every hunter around here in the 50's, 60's and 70's had from one to three Loomis guns. Nearly all were decorated with German silver. The average number of decorations was seven to thirteen or fourteen pieces. They were mostly round bullet rifles of medium caliber. He came from New England at a very early date; must have learned the trade in the flintlock days, probably in Connecticut. Do not know the H. Loomis or Horace Loomis you speak of. E. Loomis' address in the early days was E. Loomis, Colchester, N. Y., now East Hamilton, N. Y.

Morgan James probably came to Utica in the late 30's or early 40's from Litchfield, Connecticut. Was at one time in business with George H. Ferris. Have seen a rifle marked James and Ferris, Utica, N. Y. He was an old man in 1858, learned his trade in flintlock days; he was mentioned by Chapman as one of the three leading rifle makers in the United States. He was in Utica when Chapman wrote his book on the early rifle.

R. R. (Rause) Moore first made guns at Cinnatus, afterwards at Cortland, N. Y. I once asked Old Man Hollenbeck, of Syracuse (Hollenbeck of three-barrel gun fame), where he learned his trade. He said, "God, I learned it of Rause Moore."

The Muzzle-Loading Rifle—Then and Now

George Ferris died in the late 70's or 80's; he made guns of the muzzle-loading Creedmoor type. I have one of them, Creedmoor stock and all. James never gave up the idea of the true picket bullet as against longer muzzle used by Ferris, Perry, etc.

I had a relative, Hiram Risley, born 1806, who made flint and percussion rifles. Have seen a Kentucky flint by him marked on barrel in script and two percussion rifles stamped. He worked for E. Remington, master mechanic.

M. S. RISLEY.

Pontiac, Michigan.
Route 7.

Dear Friend Cline:

November 15, 1940, found me in the woods near Red Oak, Michigan, where I have hunted for the past six or seven years—a country I know well. At daybreak I was all set, the old flintlock was loaded with 70 grains of 3 FG black powder; for hunting I prefer 3 FG because it gives faster ignition and also simplifies loading, having only one kind of powder to carry. The rifle shot a ball weighing 34 to the pound, about .50 caliber. This rifle has a forty-two inch barrel made by J. Snevely, of Pennsylvania.

I started out along the edge of a swamp and after an hour or more I saw two deer coming through a clump of birch. After watching them for a while I saw that neither had horns. I had a lot of fun with these two, as they stopped about ninety or a hundred yards away and I sneaked up to within twenty paces of them. Just at this time, three more came into view about a hundred and fifty yards further over, and they were really carrying the mail. One flashed through, no horns. The next one, just a flash of horns and he was gone—no chance for a shot. The third one went through the bush and I couldn't see whether it had any or not.

About two hours later, while examining some tracks in a runway, I heard twigs crackling in a popple thicket on my left. Looking up, I saw two deer coming toward me at a lope. The first one burst out of the thicket and stopped in the edge of the pines in which I knelt. She was a doe. The other stopped behind and to the left of her with its head concealed by a low hanging jack pine bough. They evidently had my scent for they became very nervous, the doe stamping her forefeet and fidgeting around. Finally the other lowered his head and I saw nice curved spikes standing up between the ears. The old rifle came up slowly and the silver bead came to rest on the white patch on his throat, my finger began to squeeze the trigger. Suddenly the sight hung on empty air, he was gone, running behind some jack pines with the doe leading. I saw they would go through an open space about forty yards to my left and jumped to my feet holding the old gun pointed toward the opening. The doe went bounding through, the buck close behind running smoothly, not all the way out as though he didn't know just whether to trust the doe's judgment or not. I took a quick aim at his head and touched her off. As the smoke blotted out the view momentarily, the picture imprinted on my mind was the buck's ear standing above the silver bead. The

Appendix

ignition was as fast as I have ever seen with a flintlock, the flash of the pan and the report coming as one. At the crack of the rifle the buck folded up like an umbrella and dropped dead as a dodo. The distance of the shot was just 46 paces. I have never seen anything quite as sudden as the way that buck hit the ground. Upon reaching him, I found that the ball had taken effect about six inches behind the ear. The blood welled up from the hole in a good stream, thereby making it unnecessary to stick him, a job well done. Turning him over to see where the ball came out I was surprised to find no hole, so exploring along the neck opposite the hole where the ball entered my fingers encountered a lump just under the skin. I drew my knife and split the skin; there was the ball in plain view. Digging it out, I found it to be flattened out to about the size of a twenty-five cent piece. The ball had connected with the neck bone, pulverizing one vertebrae and causing instant cessation of all action.

A good many people have asked me why I shoot for the neck when the deer's body makes a much better target; some have even intimated it might be accidental, but if it is accidental, then four out of the five I have been fortunate enough to bag have been accidents. I have helped men trail deer for miles that were shot too far back behind the shoulder, only to lose them. I have never had to trail one shot in the neck. I may miss one some day, but I will have the satisfaction of knowing that he will not drag himself off to suffer and die with a ball through his belly. And then, too, a man that hunts with a flintlock in this day and age must be just a little bit "touched" anyway. Have heard hunters whom I have met in the woods walk away muttering something to that effect. Hunters in buckskin with flintlock rifles are not as common as they used to be at one time.

My two companions both got their bucks the same day, one using a .35 Remington automatic and the other using a .30-30. The one with the Remington got his just behind the shoulder, a broadside shot. I helped him skin his buck out when we got home and strange as it seems we found his bullet embedded between the meat and the skin just as mine was. You couldn't have told them apart only for the metal on the back of it.

Les C. FitzGerald.

Macedonia, Ill.
March 18, 1941.

Mr. Walter M. Cline,
Chattanooga, Tennessee.

Dear Old Timer:

Yours of the 15th just received. Sorry to hear that you are needing some real hot sunshine and a chance to exercise your muscles working a prone rifle. Am in same fix myself. Have been working pretty steady since last October and have not had much time for relaxation at my favorite pastime.

Did get out Sunday and fired the Wesle 18 shots off hand. Did pretty good and had one exceptional five-shot group. Used bullets from the last swage you sent me. The rifle loads much easier than before, but still just a suspicion of fouling causes quite a job to load. Think will have Mr. Prince or Mr. Winchell make a new ram for swage, as I firmly believe the swaged bullets are unbalanced before loading and the weight varies as much as seven grains after trimming off the heavy fin from base of bullet. Think a perfectly flat base ram of slightly increased diameter will swage them full weight as cast without fin or base.

GUY BURCH.

Columbus, Ohio.
November 25, 1934.

Dear Mr. Cline:

I enjoyed my visit with you last month, although I should like to have talked longer.

I have not done very much towards the rifle business this year for a number of reasons, but I have managed to keep all that I have and have not lost my intense interest in them,—and never shall.

A friend from Flint, Michigan, stopped off at my place last week with a big 40 rod rifle; it is a 24-pound rifle made by William Wingert, Detroit, about .42 caliber, six grooves, left hand gain twist, false muzzle, starter, swage, and full-length telescope sight,—but the sight is somewhat on the bum. Otherwise, the rifle looked about eighty per cent good as new. Inside was perfect. He said Dr. Lamb of Detroit wanted it. You will remember Dr. Lamb from the Portsmouth meet in 1934. I presume that next year we will see this rifle at Portsmouth, as he intends to shoot it there in the 40-rod event. It might offer serious competition for somebody. It is a rather plain rifle, but thoroughly well made and has been built for business. One curious thing about it is that the picket bullet, which is sharp pointed, is almost a copy of old Siebert's type pickets, with the flared-out petticoat base.

I have been interrupted by a pleasant surprise visit by "Bull" Ramsey of Portsmouth. I had not seen him since last spring. He had two fine heavy rifles he had bought from Van Renssalaer at Williamsburg, Virginia. You, no doubt, saw them in the Jamestown-Williamsburg Museum. One is a 20-pound rifle, elegantly made by C. V. and J. W. Ramsdell, Bangor, Maine; .50 caliber, 4 grooves, left hand gain twist, circular patch, side-lock, 1/30 ct barrel.

The other is an H. Warner, Philadelphia, Pennsylvania, 29-pound rifle, under hammer type, .48 caliber uniform twist, which is very quick. No chance to measure it, but to my eye it looked like about 15-inch spiral. It has a combination false muzzle for the use of either circular or cross patches. Rifling is 16 grooves, right hand twist. Obviously it has been an 8-grooved rifle using circular patches. When the "second story" was added to the false muzzle to use cross patches, the eight lands of the rifling were split or recut to make sixteen grooves. Originally, the grooves and lands were of equal width. Have you ever seen anything like it? I never have, nor do I know anyone else who ever did. It may be long on theory; but how it works in practice, I do

Appendix

not know. The proof of the pudding will be next May and I imagine there will be some very keen competition then. Do you know, nothing would tickle me any more than if "Old Man Angel" could cop that cup again! I hope it can be arranged that he is able to come next year.

WALTER HEIGHTSHOE.

Guy Burch,
Macedonia, Ill.

April 12, 1938.

Dear Guy:

Was glad to get your letter and learn that you had acquired a flintlock. It evidently was a match flintlock. The stock should be repaired at the wrist with sheet steel and then browned to match the wood. I just had one finished that way and it is the best and strongest that I have seen. Just rebuilt three flintlocks. Tried Steelite for refacing the frizzen but could not get a spark. Had a heck of a time grinding it off. There is nothing but the old-time steel, water hardened, that will give the proper sparks. We used the steel spring out of a door stop; annealed it so we could work it and then brazed it on the frizzen and ground it to shape; hardened after the brazing in water.

The touch hole should be rebushed, made cone shape with the small end towards the pan. This speeds up the ignition. If the bore is in too bad shape and it is not too large already, it could be rebored and rerifled. If the bore is not too much worn, it could be dressed out by some one who knows his business. Wyatt Atkinson, Hidalgo, Kentucky, is one of the best, either for reboring or dressing out. I could have the lock taken care of here, as I have a friend who knows how to rebuild them. He does all my work. He could fix the stock also. Kirkman and Ellis were lock makers in Nashville, Tennessee. The rifle was made, no doubt, by John Horn, a Cumberland mountain gunsmith. Kirkman Brothers were in Nashville from 1835 until 1857. A. C. Cross has almost a duplicate of your rifle except it weighs twenty pounds and has a fifty-inch barrel. If I can help you in getting it fixed up, let me know.

Just got a new relined job in from Addicks. Tried it out yesterday. Got an inch and three-eights group the first five shots. Have made a composite bullet for it. I believe it is going to be good. Addicks is making barrels now, both for muzzle-loaders' round ball and the long bullet with false muzzles, etc. He is surely good, certainly one of the best.

Glad to hear that you are going places with the Wesle Schuetzen. I looked up my notes that I made when I had Addicks reline that barrel. We copied as nearly as possible the fine Whitmore that I have. The barrel is as near like it as it was possible to make it. It does open up near the breech but that seems to be an advantage to the accuracy. I have some targets that I made when I got the gun home from Addicks. The smallest one is an inch and three-sixteenths center to center, five shots. Two others under two inches. It has been over two years since it has been shot.

The Muzzle-Loading Rifle—Then and Now

I am sending you by today's mail under separate cover some bullets for you to try out, also some patches of different thicknesses, and the template for cutting the patches. In regard to cutting the end of the paper patches, it is possible that the end of the false muzzle is not beveled enough or that the patches are too long. I do not have a .35 caliber mould such as you mention.

The liner in the Wesle is high carbon steel and will outlast you. The nipple is a special one and I do not remember the size. You can send it to me and I can send it to Mr. Addicks and have a couple made. I can have a swedge made for a bullet tapered more so it will load easier if you think it is necessary.

This Wesle rifle, regardless of the little difficulties that we are having with it, is a fine accurate rifle with any bullet up to two hundred and fifty grains weight. In fact, it will shoot with any of them, at least it will when we finish our analysis.

Sincerely,
WALTER M. CLINE.

Ironton, Ohio.
June 11, 1934.

Mr. Walter Cline,
Chattanooga, Tenn.

Dear Mr. Cline:

Here is some information on my method of cutting-out and rerifling muzzle-loading rifles which you requested.

In making the groove saw, I think it is best to use the same radius as the groove diameter. The angle of the teeth in the saw depends upon whether the barrel is right hand, left hand, gain, or regular twist. The number of teeth depends upon the twist, the greater the twist the less the number of teeth to the inch. In a hard barrel it is best to use about twenty-five to thirty teeth to the inch when set in lead slugs or one tooth filed on a piece of tool steel about $5/8$ inches long running a 30 degree angle across from one corner to another. The teeth should not have a hook on them but should be scraping tools as this takes all the hard places out evenly.

The saws should be inlaid between two lead slugs on a hickory stick of bore diameter. This will turn out an accurate job if cutting tools are fine knife-edged and great pains are taken. Teeth on land saw should be filed at from 30 to 40 degrees of angle to the bore, depending upon quickness of twist. The best job can probably be done by using a steel rifling rod with cutters inlaid in lead or babbit metal. When finishing up the barrel use new saws and run the lead around the saws to prevent uneven cut or wobbling. Barrel should be cut from both ends using lard oil or groundhog oil as lubricant. A cut should never be forced as the saws may dig in. The saw should be run through at a constant speed without stopping.

The radius of the circle of the land saw depends on the steel, the width of the grooves and the width of the lands. Never use a land saw with radius much shorter than that of bore on a porous steel barrel or one with small flaws. On a perfect barrel

Appendix

with lands and grooves of the same width the finished land should have a radius which will allow one to see a little light when a naked ball is fitted—that is see a little light at center of land. When the surface of the ball just fits the curve of the land, the groove must be made deeper, a bad practice, in my opinion. I think this type of land prevents rapid wear on the edges caused by the patch in firing and promotes accuracy. I think a groove depth of between seven and nine thousandths, depending on twist, caliber, and width of grooves, works the best. Deep grooves, which are necessary when the groove is narrow, allow gas leakage around the patch.

When the teeth on a rifling saw have been filed correctly (using a slitting file with four-inch cut) the cuttings should be in the form of small hair-like strings. The teeth should be filed so that the saw as it cuts will unload its cuttings along the edge of the saw. Saw should not be cleaned except when cuttings pile up enough to get on the lead guides. If cutting tooth becomes dull it will jump over hard places and cause tight spots in the barrel.

In fitting the ball, I always like a bore diameter bullet with patch made of eight-ounce duck for all over .40 caliber, and six-ounce duck for under .40 caliber. Above .48 caliber it is better to use a ten-ounce duck.

When starting the ball, use starter to seat one-half the diameter, seam of ball to be lined up with sights. Patch should be cut off even and pushed down good but never tamped.

I use several methods in cutting because I have found it impossible to use the same in all cases. In some barrels one cannot use a single saw successfully except where diameter of the bore is perfect. For 5, 6, 8, 10, and 16 groove rifles I have found that it is best to use two groove saws and one land saw at once in the same cutting head. One land saw and one groove saw placed opposite does well in a seven-groove barrel. Saws should only be shimmed up when they cut free. When finishing both saws should be about one or two thousands above leads—in other words, one should not be crowded to make the other cut. Land should be cut until it is well finished by raising land saw and then only groove saw should be raised to finish. After the barrel is finished I sometimes get fine results by using very thin paper shim under groove saw and relieve the bore from the breech to within six inches of the muzzle. Before doing this the saws are worked back and forth fast on the portion within six inches of the muzzle to improve the bell as most bells are not true.

You will note that on the land and groove saw which I sent you that alternate teeth are filed in different directions. This is used in a babbit slug and worked back and forth in barrel to even up hard places. A better method is to have slots for saws milled out in a steel rod in a machine shop.

I use the old-time method of finishing stocks. First I sand wood perfectly smooth. Then I put on warm water to draw grain, and sand again when dry. Put several spike nails in nitric acid and allow to stand for five minutes. Make swab of felt and apply this solution to stock. If any light places show up give them another coat. When dry, sand with 00 sandpaper. Apply linseed oil, let set an hour, then rub

The Muzzle-Loading Rifle—Then and Now

with an oiled piece of sandpaper. Apply more oil and rub with an old woolen cloth. Rub a lot and repeat oiling and rubbing for two weeks. This will give a mirror-like finish.

I have adapted my methods from many old-time gunsmiths of this section of the country. I have owned many rifles and have worked on many more. I have visited several old shops in this vicinity and used some tools procured from them as well as ideas I got from inspecting them. Dr. C. C. Carpenter, of Huntington, W. Va., (now of Lexington, Ky.), and I recently visited the shop of a prolific riflemaker named Wickline of Cadmus, Ohio, who died thirty-five years ago. His tools were nearly all intact and much evidence of his work was found.

I have hurriedly written this but hope it is what you want.

Very truly yours,

WILLIAM LARGE.
Route 1, Ironton, Ohio.

SOME OLD MUZZLE-LOADER SUPERSTITIONS

"Bull" Ramsey, of Portsmouth, Ohio, relays the following muzzle-loading superstitions through E. M. Farris:

Never count your bullets before going to a shoot.

Never sleep the night before the shoot.

Never cross a bridge on the way to a shoot.

Never shoot across any water in a match.

Always walk to a shoot.

Farris insists that nothing is said about "hooty owls and hants".

The following are the "choices" distributed as prizes at any regulation muzzle-loading Beef Match:

First and second—a hind quarter.

Third and fourth—a front quarter.

Fifth—hide and tallow.

Sixth—lead that can be picked out of the backstop.

Boss Johnston,
Aurora, Ind.

December 7, 1934.

Dear Boss:

When your voice came across the open spaces Saturday night in your R. F. D. program from Radio Station WLW with the announcement of the results of the match at Rising Sun, it seemed that I was back on the firing line and I could smell the powder smoke and hear the reports of the old muzzle-loaders and their echo back from the purple hills of old Kentucky. I had a hard day Saturday, one of those trouble-

Appendix

some days with business worries that make you feel "O H-ll what's the use anyway." But after hearing your program and living over the matches again, I decided that maybe things could be worse. So when I got up Sunday morning the old world seemed brighter and life worth living. You know it is a fine thing to be of service to someone and be able to make the dark spots seem brighter for others.

I do not think I ever had a finer time than I had at your match at Rising Sun. It was a great vacation for me and you may know how much satisfaction I derived from having won the Boss Johnston Trophy. It means so much more than just the winning of match. It means winning the friendship of a man that I respect because this man is rendering a service to the public and giving pleasure to the millions in his radio audience.

With cordial good wishes,
WALTER M. CLINE.

Charles J. Kellem,
Joliet, Illinois.

March 15, 1941.

Dear Charlie:

Would have answered your letter before this, but I have not been well and have had almost a nervous breakdown. I am not sure whether I will get over it or not.

Lucia Jane (Mrs. Kellem) was in to see us, and we were so pleased to see her.

I ran across two pictures the other day that brought back memories. I am sending them to you. One of them was taken at the match at Rudolph Holt's, when you were introduced to peach and apple brandy. I am sure you will remember it. The other picture is just one of the old matches.

I sold Long Tom to the movie company that is producing the Alvin York picture. You must be sure to see it. There are four long rifles in it. I am disposing of all my collection, as I will not be able to use it very much and I would like to have some one have the rifles that will use them—and I have some very nice ones.

The world is not going like it once did, and none of us are sure just what will happen. I hope you are well and getting along nicely. I often think of you and hope I will be able to get up to see you, but am not sure of it. How about coming down this summer?

Yours sincerely,
WALTER M. CLINE.

Walter M. Cline

March 10, 1941.

Dear Chief:

Now listen, you—book or no book, photos or no photos—I am writing in the name of the Association to command that you take care of yourself! You will regard this as orders from the whole capoole of the Muzzle-Loading Fraternity. See that you do it.

No kidding,—we are insisting that you watch the corners and keep yourself fit. We don't want any nervous breakdown to make a casualty out of one of the finest members we have in the National Muzzle-Loading Association. I am no doctor, but I am giving you this prescription just the same: DO TAKE CARE OF YOURSELF and listen to your regular doctors and forget about the manuscript for that book, which seems to be bearing heavily on your mind.

Best wishes—we are all with you.

Cordially,

E. M. FARRIS.

Williamsburg, Virginia.
March 25, 1941.

E. M. Farris,
Secretary N. M. L. A.,
Portsmouth, Ohio.

Dear Farris:

I arrived in Williamsburg yesterday to visit my daughter and shall leave here shortly for Chattanooga. I have not been feeling very well since I got here. The automobile trip from Chattanooga to Portsmouth and from Portsmouth over here was apparently almost too much for me. I am now hoping that I can get well enough to get back home.

I want to thank you for the many things you did for me in Portsmouth and for the friendship which you have always shown. I hope I can live to repay you.

WALTER M. CLINE.

THE CAST OF THE COMING SHADOW

Editor's Note: Doubtless some of the readers of this volume believe that dreams sometime serve the purpose of premonitions and forewarn us of coming events. Without entering into argument for or against the efficacy of such premonitions, we are publishing the following letter from Gilbert Angel, Pikeville, Tennessee, gunsmith, who was a faithful friend and constant shooting companion of the author of this book. Mr. Angel addressed this brief statement to Mrs. Cline shortly after Walter's death:

Dear Mrs. Cline:

You may not believe in dreams, but I want to tell you sincerely about a dream that I had just a few nights before Walter's death, in April 1941. I dreamed that Walter and I were hunting together in the forest above Cane Falls and that we talked of match shooting as we walked along. I can remember vividly our conversation as we climbed the hills.

He told me that he had nearly completed the manuscript for his book and said that he had hoped it would be received well by the muzzle-loading people all over the

Appendix

country. While he was still talking to me, he apparently walked away and presently I turned to speak to him and I vividly saw Walter some distance from me, walking away and fading out into a distant part of the forest. He completely disappeared from my view and I dreamed of making a frantic search for him without any success.

I spoke of this dream the next morning and told some of the folks how plainly it had fixed itself on my mind. It was just a few days after this that I learned that Walter had died and that in reality he had actually left these earthly shooting grounds and gone to a better range.

I truthfully report to you the experiences of my dream, and at the same time I express to you the great love and esteem which we all had for Walter.

GILBERT ANGEL.
Pikeville, Tennessee.

THE END OF THE TRAIL

Editor's Note: We publish in the following paragraphs the news story announcing the passing of Mr. Cline, who died on April 12, 1941. This news story is taken from the April 13, 1941 issue of "The Chattanooga Times":

Walter M. Cline, prominent Chattanooga photographer and collector of old-style firearms, was accidentally shot and killed almost instantly at his home yesterday morning about 8:15 o'clock when a .44 caliber, muzzle-loading rifle which he was preparing to take on a shooting match discharged and struck him in the region of the heart.

Although no one was with him at the time, it was surmised that he was tamping a load into the rifle without realizing that a cap had already been placed in the chamber. Mr. Cline had planned a shooting match with C. W. Shackleford and he was preparing his guns for the match at his home, 2000 Vance avenue, when the accident occurred.

Funeral services will be held tomorrow morning at 10:30 o'clock at the Second Presbyterian church, with the Revs. R. M. Stimson and P. L. Cobb officiating. Interment will be in the Forest Hills cemetery.

Minnie Reed, colored maid, was the only other person in the Cline home when the accident occurred. She reported that Mr. Cline called faintly for help after the gun discharged. A physician was called immediately, but the photographer died before Dr. E. E. Reisman, Jr., could reach the home.

Collection of muzzle-loading pistols and rifles and other types of old firearms was a hobby with Mr. Cline, and at one time he had over 100 rifles. One of his prize possessions was a flintlock pistol said to have been used at the battles of New Orleans and King's Mountain. He also had a collection of about 5,000 bullets fired in the War Between the States and picked up by Mr. Cline on the battlefields of Donelson, Shiloh, Murfreesboro and Franklin.

The Muzzle-Loading Rifle—Then and Now

Organized Rifle Club

Mr. Cline was one of the organizers of the National Muzzle-Loading Rifle Association and served as president of the organization for five or six years. He had written many articles for *National Rifleman* and other magazines devoted to guns. He and Mr. Shackleford had planned a shooting match yesterday at the cabin of Fred McKinney in the valley near Daisy.

Mr. Cline was a commercial photographer and he specialized in landscape and scenic photography. He photographed the mountains of East Tennessee and his pictures of Moccasin Bend and Chattanooga, taken from Point Park, were well known in Chattanooga. His pictures have appeared in almost every national photographic magazine and he has traveled across the country many times, seeking new objects to photograph. His pictures can be found at most every tourist shop in scenic regions.

When the community advertising campaign was in full swing here almost 3,000 of his pictures were used. He took scenic moving pictures for Paramount, Pathe, Universal and Bray companies and it has been estimated that he took more than 75,000 pictures of the scenery around Chattanooga. He maintained two photographic shops here, one located at 923 Market Street, and the other at 115 East Eighth Street.

He was a member of the Second Presbyterian Church, the Rotary Club, the Chattanooga Chamber of Commerce and the Chattanooga Automobile Club. He served as a director of the automobile club for many years.

Mr. Cline was born on a farm in Guernsey county, Ohio, on April 28, 1873, the son of Isaac and Sara Matson Cline. He received his early education at Cambridge and started his photographic career at the age of seventeen while still in high school. He earned his first camera by teaching a worker in an iron mill to read and write.

Photographer since Eighteen

At the age of eighteen he went to work in a portrait studio at Cambridge, but after a few months he went to another studio at Pittsburgh and stayed there about two years before going to Birmingham. After six years at Birmingham he came to Chattanooga in 1904 and has been a resident of this city since that time.

During his first years in Chattanooga he was associated with the late E. L. Mudge, A. W. Judd, and Albin Hajos. Some time later he opened his own shop at 815½ Market Street and subsequently he opened the shop at 115 East Eighth Street. In 1914, he married Miss Lucy Haley, of Chattanooga.

Mr. Cline is survived by his wife; son, Walter M. Cline, Jr.; daughter, Mrs. Robert James Caldwell, of Williamsburg, Va.; a grandson; nephew, Walter White, of Hillsboro, N. J.; niece, Mrs. Paul White, of Canada.

Funeral services will be in charge of Page-Hancock.